THE LIFE AN
MARTIN LUTHER

Dave Keir

01702 333767

Also available in the Spiritual Lives series

The Life of St Augustine

THE LIFE AND LETTERS OF
MARTIN LUTHER

Preserved Smith, PhD

Edited by Robert Backhouse

Hodder & Stoughton
LONDON SYDNEY AUCKLAND

British Library Cataloguing in Publication Data.
A catalogue record for this book is available from the British Library.

ISBN 0–340–57772–X

Published by Hodder and Stoughton, a division of Hodder and Stoughton Ltd, Mill Road, Dunton Green, Sevenoaks, Kent TN13 2YA. Editorial Office: 47 Bedford Square, London WC1B 3DP.

Typeset by Watermark, Norfolk House, Hamilton Road, Cromer, Norfolk.

Printed in Great Britain by Cox & Wyman Ltd, Reading, Berks.

Contents

Editor's Introduction

Preserved Smith's *The Life and Letters of Martin Luther* was first published in 1911 by John Murray of Albemarle Street. This abridged edition omits the illustrations, the bibliography, the index, and many of the footnotes. Only occasionally has it been necessary to update some of the vocabulary.

The great strength of this classic biography of Luther comes from Preserved Smith's ability to combine the fruits of his original researches into Luther's writings with his grasp of Reformation theology, while keeping Luther's spiritual state of mind in full view. Many of Luther's own letters are interspersed throughout the book, allowing him to speak for himself and giving the reader insight into every aspect of his life.

Before Oliver Cromwell allowed his portrait to be painted, he is reputed to have said to the artist, 'Mr Lely, I desire you would use all your skill to paint my picture truly like me, and not flatter me at all; but remark all these roughnesses, pimples, warts, and everything as you see me, otherwise I will never pay a farthing for it.' Martin Luther had many 'roughnesses, pimples and warts' in his character, and these have been faithfully portrayed by Preserved Smith. He reveals that this 'Champion of the Protestant faith' had feet of clay. Some of Luther's actions,

conversations and letters were far from honouring to the
Lord whom he served with such devotion and vigour. His
close friend Melanchthon touched on the downside to
Luther's character at Luther's funeral oration when he
said that in 'a violent age God had given a violent physician'.

Nevertheless, Preserved Smith's portrait of Luther
reveals a man of monumental stature. In the pages of this
book we meet a theologian, scholar and pastor; we meet a
humble Christian who put his trust in the One he experienced as his own 'Mighty fortress'; we see a sinner who discovered for himself the overwhelming forgiveness of God
and as a result changed the course of history.

Robert Backhouse
Crostwight Hall, 1992

Preface

It can hardly be denied that the men who have most changed history have been the great religious leaders. 'Priest, Teacher,' says Carlyle, 'whatsoever we can fancy to reside in man, embodies itself here, to command over us, to furnish us with constant practical teaching, to tell us for the day and hour what we are to do.' Among the great prophets, and, with the possible exception of Calvin, the last of world-wide importance, Martin Luther has taken his place. His career marks the beginning of the present epoch, for it is safe to say that every man in Western Europe and in America is leading a different life today from what he would have led, and is another person altogether from what he would have been, had Martin Luther not lived. For the most important fact in modern history is undoubtedly the great schism of which he was the author, the consequences of which are still unfolding and will continue to unfold for many a century to come. In saying this we do not attribute to him the sole responsibility for the revolt from Rome. The study of history, as of evolution in other forms, has shown that there are no abrupt changes—appearances to the contrary—and that one epoch follows another as naturally and with as gradual a development as one season follows another in the year. In a sense the Protestant revolt, and the larger movement of which it was but the chief symptom, the expansion of the human mind, was inevitable. In another sense, equally true, it was the courage and genius of a great man which made it possible. If some such crisis was inevitable, he at least determined its time and to a large extent its direction. Granting, as axiomatic, that essential factors of the movement are to be found in the social, political, and cultural conditions of the age, and in the work of predecessors and followers, in short, in the environment which alone made Luther's lifework possible, there must still remain a very large element due directly and solely to his personality.

The present work aims to explain that personality; to show him in the setting of his age; to indicate what part of his work is to be attributed to his inheritance and to the events of the time, but especially to reveal that part of the man which seems, at least, to be explicable by neither heredity nor environment, and to be more important than either, the character, or individuality.

A new biography of Luther, however, requires more apology than is to be found merely in the intrinsic interest of the subject. A glance at the catalogue of almost any great library—that of the British Museum for instance— will show that more has been written about Luther than about any man, save one, who ever lived. Why bring another coal to this Newcastle?

One main reason is to be found in the extraordinarily rapid advance of recent research, which, within the last ten, and still more, of course, within the last twenty years, has greatly changed our knowledge of the man. For example, the publication, in 1908, of the long-lost *Commentary on the Epistle to the Romans* has revolutionised our conception of the Reformer's early development; the opening of the Vatican Archives by the late Pope, by which many important documents were first (1904) brought to light, has at last revealed the true history of the legal process taken against the heretic by the Curia; the researches of Dr Kroker have but lately (1906) enabled us to speak with precision of the early life of Catherine von Bora; those of Dr Rockwell (1904) have performed a similar service for an important incident in Luther's life. Again, the great edition of Luther's Works published at Weimar, and of the letters by Dr Enders and Professor Kawerau, both of which are still in progress, have now made possible a more scientific study of his most important works. A few random instances, however, can give no adequate idea of the number of details, not to mention larger matters, which have first been revealed within the last decade. I have aimed to gather up, correlate, and present the results of recent research now scattered through a host of monographs. This has seemed to me the most pressing need of the present, and I have, therefore, only to a limited extent used unpublished material. In several points, however, my own studies have led me to different conclusions from those commonly held, and I venture to hope that this feature of the book will not be without value to specialists.

In another respect the present work undertakes to present Luther to English readers from a standpoint different to that from which he is usually approached. I have endeavoured to reveal him as a great character rather than as a great theologian. In order to do this I have given copious extracts from his table-talk and letters, those pregnant documents in which he unlocks his heart. No such self-revelation as is found in them exists elsewhere. Neither Pepys, nor Cellini, nor Rousseau has told us as much about his real self as has Luther about himself. Every trait of character is revealed: the indomitable will, 'and courage never to submit or yield', the loyalty to conscience, the warm heart, the overflowing humour, the wonderful gift of seeing the essence of things and of expressing what he saw, and also the vehement temper and occasional coarseness of a rugged peasant nature. In the tremulous tone of the first epistles is reflected the anguish of a soul tortured by doubt and despair; later the writer tells with graphic force of the momentous debate at Leipzig; again, in the same hour in which he stood before the Emperor and Diet at Worms, asked to recant and expecting death if he did not, he writes to a friend that he will never take back one jot or tittle. The letters from the Wartburg and Feste Coburg breathe the author's fresh, almost idyllic communion with nature; in the table-talk it is now the warm family affection which charms, now the irrepressible, rollicking joviality which bursts forth. The man's faults, too, stand in his unconscious autobiography, neither dissembled nor attenuated. Two blunders, his incitement to bloody reprisals against the rebellious peasants and his acquiescence in the bigamy of Philip of Hesse, blunders which his enemies called crimes, are frankly told in all the hideousness of their conception and consequences. It is, moreover, plain to the reader of the letters and table-talk that Luther was often in language and sometimes in thought the child of a coarse age. But of him it is especially true that to understand all is to pardon all. Through all his mistakes, and worse, he emerges a good and conscientious as well as a very great man: a son of thunder calling down fire from heaven; a Titan hurling Pelion upon Ossa against the hostile gods.

It is a pleasure to acknowledge the help I have received from many quarters. Professor Adolph Harnack has personally assisted my researches in the Berlin Royal Library. To Dr Cowley and Professor Reginald Lane Poole I am indebted for special facilities in the use of the Bodleian Library at Oxford. Dr Ernest Kroker, of Leipzig, has given me several valuable suggestions. Principal J. Estline Carpenter, of Manchester College, Oxford, has kindly placed at my disposal the excellent collection of Lutherana made by the late Dr Beard, whose *History of the Reformation to the Diet of Worms,* unfortunately left unfinished at his death (1888), is a well-known contribution to the subject. Mr friend Dr David Saville Muzzy, of New York, has kindly revised the chapter on the Peasants' Revolt; Professor

R. L. Poole, and Mr Percy S. Allen, Fellow of Merton College, Oxford, have done the same for the chapter on Luther and Henry VIII as it originally appeared in the *English Historical Review*. My friend, Professor Herbert P. Gallinger, of Amherst, has read the proofs. I feel under especial obligations to Professor Gustav Kawerau, of Berlin, who, during my long stay at the Prussian capital, with the greatest possible kindness placed at my disposal his rare books and manuscripts and his more valuable time. To all these gentlemen I tender my warmest thanks. Last, but not least in love, I must acknowledge the help received in my own family. My father, the Rev. Dr Henry Preserved Smith, has read the whole manuscript, and thus given me the benefit of his lifelong studies in divinity and experience as a writer. My sister, Miss Winifred Smith, and my wife have also aided me with criticism and suggestion.

Preserved Smith
Paris, May 16, 1910

List of Libraries and Archives
used in the preparation of this work

1

Childhood and Student Life, 1483–1505

The hills and forests of Thuringia, in the very heart of Germany, unite great natural loveliness with the romantic attractions of ancient historical association. If the traveller stopping at Eisenach, the tiny metropolis of this favoured region, will walk south for about fifteen miles through the fairy forest, he may visit the hamlet of Möhra, famous as the home of the Luther family, still flourishing here in several branches. Here lived Martin Luther's great-grandfather and grandfather as peasants—for it is with them that the family pedigree begins. Attempts to connect the name with that of the Emperor Lothaire, as well as with other noble though less remote people, have failed.

In the old days when Columbus was contemplating his momentous voyage, and Richard III was about to murder his nephews in the Tower, Hans Luther married Margaret Ziegler of Eisenach. Following the ancient peasant custom, by which the older sons were sent out into the world to make their way, while the youngest inherited the farm, Hans was forced to take his wife away from home. He was attracted to the county of Mansfeld, about sixty miles northeast of Eisenach, then as now a mining district.

The first stop of the young couple was at Eisleben, and here, on November 10, 1483, their oldest son was born, and the next day baptised by the parish priest, Bartholomew

Rennebrecher, with the name Martin, after the saint whose day it was. The little room under the tower of the church of St Peter and St Paul where the baptism took place is shown, with part of the antique font, exactly as it was then; the house exhibited as the birthplace is not, on the other hand, well authenticated.

While Martin was still a wee baby, the Luthers moved to the town of Mansfeld near by, where they were to spend the rest of their days. It is a pretty little village in the midst of its hills, on one of which stands the red sandstone castle of the Counts of Mansfeld.

The boy's life here was one of grinding, squalid poverty. The comely little cottage going by the name of the Luther house was bought or built by his father long after Martin had left home.

Hans Luther was a sturdy, frugal, hardworking man; that admirable type of character who, having small natural gifts and no advantages, by sheer industry and will-power makes his way in the world. Starting as a stranger and a common miner, he gradually won a place of honour among his fellow-citizens, who eventually elected him to the highest office in the town. A man of natural shrewdness, his pointed and pithy sayings more than once made a lasting impression upon his son. He was ambitious to give this promising child the education he himself had lacked, and but for the wisdom and self-sacrifice with which he pursued this aim, Martin's career would have been impossible.

The mother, Margaret, was a quiet woman, bowed a little by poverty and toil. The son remembered seeing her carry on her back wood gathered from the forest. Both parents were strict, and even harsh. 'My father', Luther said many years later, 'once whipped me so severely that I fled from him, and it was hard for him to win me back. . . . My mother once beat me until the blood flowed, for having stolen a miserable nut. It was this strict discipline which finally forced me into the monastery, although they meant heartily well by it.'

Martin had at least one brother and three sisters. He rarely saw them and never wrote to them after he left home, at the age of thirteen. Late in life his relations with them were disturbed by a quarrel about the division of his father's estate; but this was smoothed over, and the Reformer did his duty by the family in nobly caring for several of his orphan nephews and nieces.

The natural question, What were the first religious influences experienced by Martin Luther? can be briefly answered. He was taught a few simple prayers and hymns at his mother's knee. God the Father and Jesus were represented to him as stern, even cruel judges, to appease whose just wrath the intercession of the saints must be secured. No doubt was entertained by the humble peasants concerning the effectiveness of the ministrations of the church; the ecclesiastical hierarchy, and especially the Pope, were regarded with reverent awe.

One prominent element of the popular religion of the time was superstition. The gloomy old northern mythology, full of witches, good spirits and evil spirits, survived from heathen times. It is hard to imagine now how vivid was the belief in the supernatural in Hans Luther's house. Martin never freed himself from it, and many are his reminiscences of the witches who plagued his mother. Even his bare-legged rambles through the hills were haunted by the dread of surrounding demons. 'In my native country,' he once said, 'there is a high hill called the Pubelsberg, on top of which is a lake; if one throws a stone into the water a great tempest will arise over the whole region, for it is the habitation of captive devils. Prussia is full of them and Lapland full of witches.'

The boy's education began very early in the village school, which may still be seen by the traveller. Latin was the principal subject taught; the boys were required to speak as well as read it. Martin's recollections of the ignorance and brutality of his first teachers were very unhappy indeed. He was flogged repeatedly on the same morning for faltering in a declension. 'Ah!' he exclaims, 'what a time we had with the *lupus* and Donatus!' (The *lupus*, or wolf, was the monitor who punished the pupils for speaking German; Donatus was the Latin grammar then and long after in use—Luther once said it was the best.) 'My teachers made us parse everything, and made obscene jokes. The examination was like a trial for murder.'

When Luther was only thirteen years old, he was sent to the school of a religious brotherhood—the 'Nullbrüder'—at Magdeburg. Here he began to contribute to his own support by begging, in those days one of the recognised means by which a poor lad might get an education. No more stigma attached to it than attaches to the acceptance of a scholarship by a student nowadays. One of the few things known about this year is that the miserable life brought on a fever, which might have proved fatal had not the patient drunk some water in disobedience to the doctor's orders.

It may have been at Magdeburg that Martin's thoughts first turned in the direction of the monastic life. Erasmus, who attended one of the schools of the same order, relates graphically how hard the brothers tried to guide their pupils into the cloister. One incident, at any rate, made so deep an impression on Luther's mind, that thifty-five years later he wrote:

> When, in my fourteenth year, I went to school at Magdeburg, I saw with my own eyes a prince of Anhalt . . . who went in a friar's cowl on the highways to beg bread, and carried a sack like a donkey, so heavy that he bent under it, but his companion walked by him without a burden; this prince alone might serve as an example of the grisly, shorn holiness of the world. They had so stunned him that he did all the works of the cloister like any other brother, and he had so fasted, watched, and mortified his flesh that he looked like a death's head, mere skin and bones; indeed he soon after died, for he could not

long bear such a severe life. In short, whoever looked at him had to gasp for pity and must needs be ashamed of his own worldly position.

After one year at Magdeburg, Martin was transferred to Eisenach to attend the school of St George the dragon-killer. His mother had, in this her native town, a relative named Conrad Hutter on whose help she counted for her son. Hutter was sexton of St Nicholas' church, and it may have been through him that Luther came to know and love the parish priest, John Braun. It was not with his kinsman that he lodged, however, but with a certain family identified by most biographers with the Cottas. Luther sometimes speaks in later years of 'his hostess of Eisenach', but never by name, assuming her to have been well known to his audience. She took him in, according to tradition, 'for his hearty singing', and under her charitable and pious roof the boy for the first time tasted modest comfort. Frau Cotta was by birth a Schalbe; this wealthy family had founded a little Franciscan monastery at the foot of the Wartburg, with whose inmates young Luther, serious and pious beyond his years, became friendly. So priestly indeed was his circle of friends that he heard with astonishment from his hostess a little verse to the effect that nothing was dearer on earth than the love of women to him who could win it.

The promise of the industrious, bright boy induced his father, whose circumstances, though not easy, were improving, to continue his liberal education. Accordingly, at the beginning of the summer term (about May 1501) 'Martinus Luther ex Mansfeld' matriculated at the old and famous University of Erfurt. It was the custom of students who did not board with one of the professors to live at a 'Burse', a combination of dormitory and eating-club. Luther lived at the 'Burse' of St George, which once stood on Lehmann's bridge, but is now no longer in existence.

The course of studies began with logic, dialectic, grammar,

and rhetoric, followed by arithmetic, various natural sciences, ethics, and metaphysics. All the studies were set in the shadow of scholasticism. Mediaeval thought had progressed little, if at all, beyond Aristotle, who was regarded as an inerrant authority, but it had elaborated his rules of argumentation into fantastic extremes, at once dry and ridiculous. The two most celebrated professors at Erfurt in the early sixteenth century, Trutvetter and Usingen, were entirely under the sway of the Stagirite, and one may well believe Melanchthon's testimony 'that a particularly thorny kind of dialectic' prevailed there. The natural sciences were studied absolutely without experiment or original research, in perfect reliance on Aristotle's ancient works. The philosophy, too, was founded on his essays, though in this case some changes in his system had been made by the great thinkers of the Middle Ages in their endeavours to harmonise it with Christianity. The great question which agitated mediaeval thought was whether the individual or the class was the reality; e.g., in the word 'horse', is the essential thing each particular horse, or the abstract of all the qualities which make up the conception? The realists, who decided in favour of the latter, flourished in the heyday of scholasticism, but the nominalists, who maintained the former, had now supplanted them, and Erfurt philosophy was therefore of this school.

The universities in the sixteenth century were undergoing a change somewhat similar to that which they are experiencing in the twentieth. The old mediaeval course, which has just been sketched, no longer prevailed without opposition. Some rays of the 'new learning', the glorious rebirth of classical antiquity, had penetrated Erfurt. Indeed there were several courses in the classics, and a circle of students devoted to the humanities. The inclinations of the miner's son, however, did not lead him that way. His serious, religious mind preferred the rough road of scholasticism to the primrose path of poetry and oratory. He later regretted that he had read no more history and poems, and added that the study of scholastic philosophy prevented his reading any verse except Baptista Mantuan, Ovid's *Heroides,* and Virgil.

Of the student's life little is known. That it was pure and godly may be inferred from the fact that his enemies never found any reproach in it and because of the absence of self-accusation. He sometimes suffered from ill-health and depression. One day he found a Bible in the library, and began to read the passage about Hannah and Samuel, but a lecture called him away, and he apparently did not pursue his reading farther at this time.

After taking, with high rank, the degrees of bachelor of arts in 1502 and of master in 1505, Luther began to study law. This was in accordance with the wishes of his ambitious father, who bought him an expensive Corpus Juris. He had worked in law only two months, however, when he abruptly decided to enter the monastery.

2

The Monk, 1505–1512

Various reasons have been assigned for the sudden decision of Luther to become a monk. The real cause lay in a torturing sense of sin and a longing for reconciliation with God, experienced by many deeply spiritual Christians at one time or another in their lives. The cloister had been the refuge of such persons for a thousand years; to it the Saxon student naturally turned to find rest for his soul. After all, the seemingly abrupt vow is only the natural culmination of previous experiences. The strict discipline of a stern and pious home, the terrible vision of the begging prince, the priestly circle of friends at Eisenach, had all pointed the boy to the career then regarded as the perfection of Christianity.

The influences in the same direction at Erfurt were also very strong. This flourishing but by no means large town boasted twenty cloisters, twenty-three churches, thirty-six chapels, and in all more than one hundred buildings devoted to religious uses. Among the numerous orders represented by chapters at 'little Rome', as the devout city was called, the strongest were those of the begging friars, the Franciscans, Dominicans, and Augustinians.

This last order could not claim, like the others, a great saint as founder, for Augustine had not written their rule. Since their first incorporation by Innocent IV in 1243, confirmed by Alexander IV in 1256, the Augustinian Hermits, as they were officially called, flourished mightily. By the middle of the fifteenth century, there were two thousand chapters, and the order, like most of the older ones, had begun to show some signs of degeneracy. A reform had been carried through many of the chapters by Proles, for the last quarter of the fifteenth century Vicar of the German province. Erfurt had joined 'the congregation of the observants', as the reform movement was called, in 1475. What made Luther choose this monastery cannot be certainly told; perhaps some personal ties and the good fame of the Hermits attracted him.

The spring and early summer of 1505 was a terrible time at Erfurt. The plague broke out, some of the students died of it, and most of the others left town in a panic. It is at such times that men's thoughts turn to the other world, and Luther, who had already been asking himself the question, 'When will you be righteous and do enough to win a gracious God?' seriously considered abandoning a worldly for a spiritual calling. The faculty of law began lecturing on May 19, but the young student had hardly attended their courses for a month before he became thoroughly disgusted with a profession which, to his mind, had no relish of salvation in it. Towards the end of June he returned to his father's house, perhaps to get permission to drop his legal studies.

As he was coming back to the university, on July 2, he was overtaken at Stotterheim, near Erfurt, by a terrible thunderstorm, and, in a fright, vowed to St Anna to be a monk. If it may seem strange that a young man of twenty-two should be panic-stricken by a clap of thunder, it must be remembered that the miner's son regarded such phenomena as frequently occasioned by the direct inter-position of the devil. Moreover, it has been shown that he probably had the more than half-formed intention already in his mind. He later speaks of being warned to enter the cloister by a heavenly vision. What this was, whether connected with the storm or not, is entirely unknown.

Old Hans Luther was bitterly opposed to his son's step, which he believed destroyed all chance of a successful career. Martin also cast some longing, lingering looks behind, but dared not turn back, and hastened the day of his entrance to shorten this temptation. On July 16 he invited some friends, including 'honourable matrons and maidens', to a farewell supper. The evening was spent in music and good cheer; the next day he entered the monastery.

The reception of a would-be brother was a solemn occasion. The young man fell down before the feet of the prior and was asked what he wanted, to which he replied, 'God's mercy and yours.' The superior instructed him in the hardships, the duties, the sacrifices, and also in the blessedness of the life he had chosen. He was then put under the care of an older brother, and obliged to fulfil a year of probation. During this period he not only learned the rules of the order—such as the prayers five times a day—but he was instructed in the higher spiritual life. At the same time he was obliged to do the humblest menial service, such as sweeping and cleaning. Luther's novitiate ended in September 1506, when he took the irrevocable vows of poverty, chastity, and obedience, through which he was supposed to die to the world and be 'rebaptised' to a higher life.

Brother Martin was ordained a priest in February 1507. The celebration of the first mass was a great occasion, to which he invited his father, his kinsman Conrad Hutter of Eisenach, and the parish priest of that town, whom he had learned to love while at school. Luther's first extant letter is the invitation to this friend to attend the mass:

TO JOHN BRAUN AT EISENACH
Erfurt, April 22, 1507
. . . God, glorious and holy in all his works, has deigned to exalt me, wretched and unworthy sinner, and to call

me into his sublime ministry only for his mercy's sake. I ought to be thankful for the glory of such divine goodness (as much as dust may be) and to fulfil the duty laid upon me.

Wherefore the fathers have set aside Sunday, May 2, for my first mass, God willing. That day I shall officiate before God for the first time, the day being chosen for the convenience of my father. . . . Dearest father, as you are in age and care for me, master in merit and brother in religion, if private business will permit you, deign to come and help me with your gracious presence and prayers, that my sacrifice may be acceptable in God's sight. . . .

Whether Braun accepted the invitation is not known. Luther's father, who seems to have been partially reconciled, came, bringing a number of friends, and gave his son a handsome present. The two had an earnest talk, the son urging that he was warned to become a monk by a terrible heavenly vision, to which his father replied that he hoped it was not an apparition of the devil. Again, when Martin tried to justify himself, and gently reproached his father for his anger, the old man replied, 'Have you never heard that a man should honour his parents?'

Luther's studies were not long interrupted by his vow. On the contrary, he continued philosophy and took up divinity, a nearly allied science. He applied himself with such zeal and success that about eighteen months after his first mass he was called to the recently founded University of Wittenberg to teach Aristotle's *Ethics*. He spent a year in this position, at the same time continuing his own studies. He took his first theological degree (*baccalaureus ad biblica*) on March 9, 1509, and at about the same time wrote his second extant letter to Braun, apologising for leaving Erfurt without bidding him farewell. The letter, which is hastily written, and somewhat faltering, has one extremely interesting passage:

Now I am in Wittenberg, by God's command or permission. If you wish to know my condition I am well, thank God, but my studies are very severe, especially philosophy, which from the first I would willingly have changed for theology. I mean that theology which searches out the meat of the nut, the kernel of the grain and the marrow of the bones. But God is God; man is often, if not always, at fault in his judgement. He is our God, he will sweetly govern us for ever.

In the autumn of 1509 Luther was sent back to Erfurt 'because he had not satisfied the Wittenberg faculty'. This sentence in the Dean's book, with Luther's own later addition, 'because he had no means:—Erfurt must pay', is usually taken to mean that he had not the money to pay the academic fees. It is also probable that there was some trouble about the lectures he was to give; he wishing to discontinue philosophy and take up the Bible. It was the academic rule that before lecturing on the scriptures a young professor should devote three terms to expounding Peter Lombard's *Sentences,* the common textbook in theology. This Luther did at Erfurt, where he remained for about twenty-one months, until he was called back to a permanent position at Wittenberg in the summer of 1511. This stay at Erfurt was interrupted by the journey to Rome.

Such is the bare history of the outward events of the seven years in the cloister. Far more interesting, though more difficult to trace, is the record of his inward life during the same time. What did the young monk experience which fitted him for the great duties which lay before him? What, in short, was his development?

Instead of finding peace within the monastic cell, at first doubt and despair only increased. His table-talk, taken down late in life, is full of statements about the utter depth of the sufferings of the doubter concerning his own salvation. God appeared to him as a cruel judge; he felt that he could never do enough to win his favour and deserve free pardon. Though there is some reason to believe that in looking back he painted his past even darker than it really was, there can be no doubt that he went through agonies before he attained strength and peace of mind. His course of thought can be followed by studying the books he read, with his own notes on them.

The theologians he read belonged to what was then called 'the modern' school—'the modernists' of the sixteenth century. Thomas Aquinas, perhaps the greatest of the schoolmen, was not much regarded; he belonged to the old-fashioned, superseded faction. The philosopher most studied was William Occam; next to him Gabriel Biel, the Parisian doctors Ailly and Gerson, Bernard of Clairvaux, Bonaventura, John Mauburn, and Gerhard of Zütphen. The fundamental thesis of the Occamists was that man can do anything he will—fulfil the Ten Commandments to the letter or persuade his reason that white is black. The cloister adopted this view and held that by a man's own acts, asceticism, prayer, and meditation, he could prepare his soul for union with God. Biel especially emphasised the possibility and duty of a man hating his own sins—fear, said he, is not enough to make repentance acceptable to God.

Luther took all this in and tried to act accordingly. He fulfilled all the monastic duties with punctuality; he buffeted his body with zeal to keep it under; he froze in his unheated cell, he starved himself until he was a skeleton 'so that one could almost count his bones', he underwent such austerities that he was found fainting by his brothers. But all this did not bring him peace. After each time of devotion came a fresh time of despair.

A second doctrine that Luther imbibed from the theologians was that God is pure, arbitrary will. He had created the world solely for his own pleasure; his will made right and wrong; and finally his arbitrary choice alone conditioned man's salvation. But in this latter particular, having promised to consider certain actions as meritorious, he has put in each man's power to obtain his favour by performing these acts, and his acceptance of man is sealed by the sacraments of the church. The young monk could not bring himself to love a God like that; he feared, he even hated him. 'When I looked for Christ,' he said, 'it seemed to me as if I saw the devil.'

Luther's development is largely a history of his liberation from the Occamist theology. But even after he had freed himself from the oppressive doctrines he bore lasting marks of the apprenticeship in Occam's school. In 1515 we find him calling these scholastics the 'hog-doctors', but throughout his life he carried certain of their teachings with him. Occam—the 'modernist'—was the sharpest critic of the mediaeval church, and especially of the hierarchy. He said flatly that popes and councils could err, and remembering this doubtless made the break with Rome easier for Luther.

But taken as a whole the reading of scholastic philosophy only deepened his perplexity and anguish of soul. Several of his fellow monks helped him with counsel and comfort, especially his spiritual director who sought to combat his doubts by giving him orthodox literature. Of this man Luther speaks long afterwards:

> I remember with what ardour and pleasure I read Athanasius' dialogue on the Trinity during my first year in the cloister when my monastic pedagogue at Erfurt, an excellent man and a true Christian under the cursed cowl, gave me a copy of it made by himself.

This same wise old man pointed out to him that God was not angry with him, but he with God, and emphasised the *duty* of believing in the forgiveness of sins. This was the first comfort he received.

Most of all he was helped by John Staupitz, since 1503 the Vicar of the German province of Augustinians, and dean of the faculty of theology at Wittenberg. With statesmanlike breadth combining energy and tact, he constantly sought to purify, consolidate, and enlarge his order, but while prosecuting these comprehensive plans never forgot small chapters and young brothers in need of help. His relations with Luther were so special that some have proposed to regard his influence as the decisive factor in the Reformer's development, but this view is hardly justified by the known facts. With many expressions of gratitude from the young man to the elder we have his own sorrowful statement that even Staupitz did not rightly understand him. His superior, a mystic in doctrine, helped him not so much by teaching as by loving him. The vicar was a man who understood men, and it was due to his recommendation that Luther received the call to Wittenberg.

The young monk was chiefly illumined by the perusal of the Bible. The book was a very common one, there having been no less than one hundred editions of the Latin Vulgate published before 1500, as well as a number of German translations. The rule of the Augustinians prescribed diligent reading of the scriptures, and Luther obeyed this regulation with joyous zeal, in spite of the astonishment of Staupitz and discouragement on the part of Dr Usingen.

Next to the Bible, St Augustine was the most helpful of all the writers read by Luther. He began to know him at the latest in 1508; a recent find has given us the very copy of Augustine's works that he used, with the margins crammed full of notes. According to these indications, what impressed him most was the saint's mysticism—his philosophy of God, the world, the soul, the worthlessness of earthly life and the blessedness of the life hid with God. These thoughts so cheered him that at times he felt as if he was 'among choirs of angels'.

Yet, with all the helps that he received, it was years before he found even the key of his solution. The letter to Braun of 1507 witnesses the downcast, trembling posture of his soul. At the first mass he experienced torturing doubts: 'When I came to the words "thee, most merciful

Father",' he says, 'the thought that I had to speak to God without mediator almost made me flee like another Judas.'

It was one day at Wittenberg in 1508 or 1509, as he was sitting in his cell in a little tower, that his life-message came to him, and with it the first assurance of permanent comfort and peace. He was reading Paul's Epistle to the Romans, and came to the verse, 'The righteous will live by faith' (1:17). Pondering this, it came to him that it was not, as he had been taught, by man's own works that he was redeemed, but by faith in God and the Saviour. Justification by faith has been rightly selected as the cardinal doctrine of the Lutheran theology; he himself recognised in it the corner-stone of his whole life.

Of course Luther's development was not completed at once. Even after the master-key had been found, the long struggle continued, and other factors entered in to modify and enrich his character. He entered the monastery to save his soul, and the struggle took twelve long years before the monk was ripe for the great deeds he was called on to perform. No one can get even an idea of what the struggle must have cost him save by reading after him the folios and quartos he perused, and trying to follow him in all that tangled labyrinth. And yet his development was perfectly normal and even. That his health suffered somewhat from asceticism is undoubtedly true, but there were no morbid symptoms in his conversion. Comparing it to that of other famous Christians, there were no visions such as Loyola saw, and no moral breakdown such as that of Augustine. In those years of hardship, meditation, study, and thought, he laid the foundations of that adamantine character which stood unshaken amidst a tempest that rocked Europe to its base.

3

The Journey to Rome, 1510–1511

Work at Erfurt was interrupted by one of the most important and interesting events in Luther's early career, the journey to Rome. The cause of the trip is connected with the history of the Augustinian order. As previously stated, when Proles carried through his reform of 1473–1475 all the cloisters did not adhere to the movement. Staupitz was anxious to complete the work of his predecessor by uniting all the chapters again, and some years after he was elected vicar of the Augustinian Observants in 1503, the opportunity arrived. Securing the interest of the general of the order at Rome, and of the Curia, on June 26, 1510, he was appointed provincial of the whole Saxon province, with authority to force the non-observant cloisters into the reformed congregation. Several of these chapters, who felt themselves aggrieved, decided to appeal to Rome, and their motion was supported by some of the cloisters under Staupitz's jurisdiction, including Erfurt. The disaffected chose as their agent John von Mecheln of Nuremberg, and with him went Martin Luther.

It is probable that the latter had little or nothing to do with the business in hand. At any rate he never mentions it. Moreover, his warm relations with Staupitz make it unlikely that he would be willing to take a decided part against him. The laws of the order required that the brothers should always travel two and two, and he was simply the travelling companion of John von Mecheln. He grasped eagerly at the opportunity to visit the Eternal City; indeed, he once stated that the purpose of his going was to make a general confession of all his sins and to receive absolution.

The brothers set out in October, not cheerfully talking side by side, but walking silently in single file. The journey took the brothers through Florence, rich then as now with the art treasures which are the delight and wonder of the world. It is characteristic of Luther, who says very little about the painting and sculpture he saw, that he should have carefully visited the hospitals. The principal one was the Spedale di Santa Maria Nuova, just behind the cathedral, founded by Portinari, the father of Dante's Beatrice. Not far from it is the foundling hospital, the Spedale degli Innocenti, founded in the fifteenth century and richly decorated with medallions by Andrea della Robbia. The pilgrim related his experiences thus:

> The hospitals of the Italians are built like the palaces, supplied with the best food and drink, and tended by diligent servants and skilful physicians. The painted bedsteads are covered with clean linen. When a patient is brought in, his clothes are taken off and given to a notary to keep honestly. Then they put a white bed-gown on him and lay him between the clean sheets of the beautifully painted bed, and two physicians are brought at once. Servants fetch food and drink in clean glass vessels, and do not touch the food even with a finger, but offer it to the patient on a tray. Honourable matrons, veiled, serve the poor all day long without making their names known, and at evening return home. These carefully tended hospitals I saw at Florence. They also have foundling asylums, where children are well sheltered and nourished and taught; they are all dressed in uniform and most paternally provided for.

Continuing the trip south, the brothers finally caught sight of Rome. The emotions of the young man were overpowering; he fell on his face and cried: 'Hail, holy Rome!'

The month of December was spent here. While his companion did the business of the order, Luther spent the time seeing the sights. There was then a guidebook, the so-called *Mirabilia Romae*, which had been published as a block-book before the days of movable type. That Luther used it is probable from parallels found in the table-talk, and Professor Hausrath has constructed his whole visit from this hint, just as one might imagine what a modern tourist saw by consulting Baedeker. What impressed him most of all the sights were the remains of classical antiquity, the Coliseum, the baths, the Pantheon. He also speaks of the catacombs of Calixtus and of some of the churches.

'I was a foolish pilgrim,' says he, 'and believed all that I was told.' He visited all the shrines to take advantage of the indulgences granted to pious worshippers, and even went so far as to wish that his parents were dead, that he might get their souls out of purgatory, for which charitable work so many opportunities offered. One of the most celebrated shrines of the Holy City is the chapel Sancta Sanctorum at the eastern end of the Piazza di San Giovanni, in which was, and still is, the flight of twenty-eight steps, taken, as the Romans fabled, from the judgement hall of Pilate in Jerusalem. Leo IV had granted an indulgence of nine years for every step climbed by the pilgrim on his knees while saying the appointed prayers. If one may trust the story which Luther's son Paul remembered hearing his father tell, he started climbing these stairs and praying, but suddenly remembered the verse in Romans, 'The righteous will live by faith,' arose and descended.

Luther could not fail to be shocked by many things he saw. At the time they did not shake his faith in the church, nor his allegiance to the Pope, but when the breach came in after years his heart was hardened by the remembrance

of the visit. He could never have attacked Rome so vigorously and successfully in 1520 had it not been for what he
saw in 1510. He often refers to it in words like these:

> Rome is a harlot. I would not take a thousand gulden
> not to have seen it, for I never would have believed the
> true state of affairs from what other people told me, had
> I not seen it myself. The Italians mocked us for being
> pious monks, for they hold Christians fools. They say six
> or seven masses in the time it takes me to say one, for
> they take money for it and I do not. The only crime in
> Italy is poverty. They still punish homicide and theft a
> little, for they have to, but no other sin is too gross for
> them. . . .
>
> So great and bold is Roman impiety that neither God
> nor man, neither sin nor shame, is feared. All good men
> who have seen Rome bear witness to this; all bad ones
> come back worse than before.

The return journey took about seven weeks. Passing
through Milan, Luther was surprised to find priests who
claimed not to acknowledge the supremacy of the Pope,
for they followed St Ambrose. His eyes were open to the
beauty and fertility of the Lombard plains. He arrived at
Erfurt in February.

It is not without interest to note another trip, though
one of infinitely less importance than the Italian journey,
taken by Luther in his monastic days. This was to Cologne,
where he saw the relics of the three kings. He never forgot
the wine he drank in this city, which he said was the best he
ever tasted.

4

The Professor, 1512–1517

Wittenberg is situated on the banks of the Elbe, about half-way between Leipzig and Berlin. The broad and winding river is not at this point navigable. The country is flat, the soil sandy and poor. Towards the end of the fifteenth century Wittenberg was a mere hamlet, containing about three hundred and fifty low, ugly wooden houses, with an old church and a town hall. To explain its rise to prominence as a university town and military post a short digression on contemporary history is necessary—an explanation which will also serve to clear up the matter of the two Saxonys, a standing puzzle to foreigners who read German history.

The treaty of Leipzig, in August 1485, divided the lands of the house of Wettin for ever into two parts. The so-called 'Electoral District' (*Kurkreis*) of which Wittenberg was the centre, together with some territory to the south-ward including Eisenach, Weimar, and Coburg, was given to the elder brother, Ernest, with the title of Elector of Saxony. The younger, Albert, who was called Duke of Saxony, obtained the smaller but better portion of the land, including the two cities of Leipzig and Dresden, with the surrounding country.

Frederick, surnamed the Wise, who became Elector of Saxony in 1486, at once started to replenish his diminished

resources. He chose Wittenberg as a sort of capital of his
northern territory—usually himself residing at Altenberg
in the south. He began immediately to ornament the town
with public buildings, including a castle and a church, for
the decoration of which he employed Albrecht Dürer, the
Nuremberg painter. In 1502 he founded a university, in
order that his subjects might not have to go to Leipzig,
belonging to his cousin, or to Erfurt, under the jurisdiction
of the Elector of Mainz. He appointed Staupitz first dean
of the faculty of theology, intending that most of the professors should be monks of the Augustinian order, which
had a chapter at Wittenberg. Staupitz entered into the
work with zeal; he rebuilt and enlarged the Black Cloister
(as the monastery was called, from the popular name of
the Augustinians as Black Monks), began to lecture on the
Bible, and gathered around him some young men whom
he intended to train to fill positions as teachers.

The one in whom he had most confidence was Martin
Luther. It was at his recommendation that the young
brother had been made instructor in philosophy during the
year 1508–1509, and it was also at his recommendation that
Martin was again called in the summer of 1511 to be professor of divinity. The vicar was anxious to retire, and wished
the younger man to take his own place. In order to do this a
degree of doctor was considered necessary, to which, at
first, Luther was averse. Many years later he told the following story, so characteristic of the vicar's gentle humour:

> Dr Staupitz said to me one day as we were sitting under
> the pear-tree still standing in the court, 'You should take
> the degree of doctor so as to have something to do.' . . . I
> objected that my strength was already used up, and that I
> could not long survive the duties imposed on me by a pro-
> fessorship. He answered: 'Do you not know that the Lord
> has a great deal of business to attend to, in which he needs
> the assistance of clever people? If you should die, you
> might be his counsellor.'

Such argument could not be withstood, and accordingly October 18, 1512, was set aside for Luther to take the highest degree in theology, that of doctor of divinity. His invitation to his brothers at Erfurt to attend the ceremony is interesting, both because of the matter it contains, and because of its perfect self-possession in contrast to the previous letters.

TO THE PRIOR ANDREW LOHR AND THE CONVENT OF AUGUSTINIANS AT ERFURT
Wittenberg, September 22, 1512

Greetings in the Lord! Reverend, venerable and dear Fathers! Behold the day of St Luke is at hand, on which, in obedience to you and to our reverend Vicar Staupitz, I shall take my examination in theology in the hall of the university. . . . I do not now accuse myself of unworthiness, lest I should seem to seek praise and honour by my humility; God and my conscience know how worthy and how grateful I am for this public honour. . . . I beg that you will deign to come and be present at the celebration, if convenient, for the glory and honour of religion and especially of our chapter. . . .

After taking the degree, to which he seems to have been thoroughly reconciled, Luther began to lecture on the Bible, a practice which he kept up all his life. Glancing first at the more external qualities, these lectures and notes show extreme thoroughness—not a bad quality in a professor, and one for which German professors have ever been justly famous. He not only turned the pages of his books, he read, marked, learned, and inwardly digested them. He criticised his authors and with such acumen that two works attributed to Augustine, the genuineness of which he first disputed, have been proved by modern criticism to be spurious. He sought diligently for the best authorities and the most recent books. In his *Commentary on the Psalms* he used the edition of the French humanist Lefèvre d'Étaples, published in 1509. This author, 'a little Luther' as Michelet called him, is a chief guide in the exegesis of the text. Next to him, or perhaps one should say, ahead of him, the influence of Augustine, and through him of the neo-Platonic school, is the most important element. Comparing these lectures with the notes on Lombard (1509–1510), a considerable advance in freedom and power is noticeable. The early work is stiff, formal, and timid; in the later, though the text and authorities are still followed fairly closely, there is more freedom of treatment and more of the subjective element. The new religious ideas, especially that of justification by faith, can be plainly made out, and several opinions which could find no room in the Catholic church come forward. In fact, as far as we can judge, it was in these lectures, his first on the Bible, that Luther began to formulate his peculiar theology.

In the summer term of 1515, about May, Luther began to lecture on Romans, continuing the course for about three terms. His principal guide, at first, was again the humanist Lefèvre, whose text of St Paul's epistles had appeared in 1512. While Luther was still lecturing, in March 1516, Erasmus' edition of the New Testament with a new Latin translation and notes came out, and was immediately procured by the Wittenberg professor. From this time on, beginning, namely, with the ninth chapter of Romans, Erasmus took the lead as an exegetical authority. Not that the lecturer follows him slavishly; he balances authorities, and occasionally disagrees with all of them. Nevertheless we can hardly overestimate the importance of the Greek Testament on the Reformer's thought; from this time on almost all of his important theological work is founded on it, and of course on the material supplied by its editor.

The *Commentary on Romans* is a great human document, priceless for its biographical interest. So important is it in the history of the author's thought that Father Denifle, who first called attention to it, was inclined to date the commencement of the Reformation from it. Though we cannot agree with him in this, for, according to our reading of the sources, Luther had attained his fundamental convictions in previous years, we must assign immense importance to these lectures for the development and perfection of these ideas. The care with which he prepared the lectures is plain; he laboriously annotated almost every word of the text, and then wrote out, in a fair, legible copy, the whole discourse. There is still some remnant of mediaevalism in the manner in which he explains the text in two or three different ways, but through the old dress the modern spirit shines forth. Luther was one of the first to show what Paul really felt, thought, and taught, though some others, like Lefèvre and Colet, had preceded him by a few years in applying the new learning to the elucidation of scripture. These commentaries were and are valuable contributions to exegesis.

But they are far more; they are living epistles from Brother Martin's heart. His lofty ideas are taking shape, and what an insight into his deep ponderings do such sentences as these give: 'We are partly sinners and partly just, but nothing if not penitent, for repentance is the mean between sin and righteousness'; and again, 'We are not called to ease but to labour against our passions.' Throughout the whole, the theological, practical, and moral interest is the dominant one. The lecturer is even more interested in his own day than in Paul's. With what solemn words does he arraign the princes and prelates who oppress the poor and live only for luxury and pride! How often does he refer to the events of the day, the Reuchlin trial, the wars of Pope Julius, or of Duke George, or of the Bishop of Brandenburg! Again, in words which have a double meaning for us who know their sequel, he blames the sellers of indulgences who deceive the poor people, and 'are cruel beyond all cruelty, not freeing souls for charity, though they do for money'.

In this commentary can first be seen how far Luther is from the doctrine taught him by his professors Trutvetter and Usingen, the old philosophy of Aristotle and the schoolmen. Of them he says:

Wherefore it is mere madness for them to say that a man of his own powers is able to love God above all things and to do the works of the law in substance, if not literally, without grace. Fools! Theologians for swine! According to them grace would not be necessary save for a new requirement above the law. For if the law is fulfilled by our own powers, as they say, then grace would not be necessary for the fulfilment of the law, but only for a new exaction beyond the law. Who can bear these sacrilegious opinions?

It is from this high opinion of the function of grace that Luther deduced the doctrine of determinism, which he carried to the utmost lengths of logic.

These lectures also give a vivid idea of the author's reading at the time. The humanists, especially Erasmus, are his favourites. He often quotes, however, from the Fathers, either directly or as he had learned to know them through textbooks and compendiums. Moreover, he is interesting. Similes, illustrations, examples from current events, apt translation into German, with careful summaries at the end of each subject, made the lectures a wide departure from the ordinary. The students flocked to them with enthusiasm.

Luther's work at the university was so successful that within a few years he was able to carry through a complete reform of the whole curriculum. The bondage of the old-fashioned professors to Aristotle has already been described in connection with Martin's education at Erfurt. The humanists, eager for the cultivation of the classics, rebelled against the reign of the Stagirite, and had been partly successful in dethroning him. Luther was in thorough sympathy with them, but his motive was different; he objected to the study of that 'cursed heathen' (*verdammter Heide*), because his ethics were not Christian and his philosophy not Pauline. This dislike, noticeable as early as 1510, grew until, on September 4, 1517, Luther published ninety-seven theses calling into question the value of Aristotle's works as textbooks. Everyone is familiar with the *Ninety-five Theses* against indulgences published the following month, but only specialists know of this Disputation against scholastic theology. And yet Luther, who did not think the theses on indulgences worth publishing, printed this protest against Aristotle and his followers, and sent it around to numerous friends for opinions. Among the theses, the forty-first calls Aristotle's *Ethics* bad and inimical to grace, the fifty-first expresses the well-founded suspicion that the Latin translations used in the university do not give his exact sense, and the fifty-second states that it would be a good thing if he who first started the question of nominalism and realism had never been born. Luther was especially anxious to have his opinions known to his old professors at Erfurt, who were strong adherents of the Greek philosopher, and accordingly sent the theses with this letter.

TO JOHN LANG AT ERFURT
Wittenberg, February 8, 1517

Greetings. I enclose a letter, dear Father, for the excellent Trutvetter, containing propositions directed against logic, philosophy, and theology, i.e. slander and malediction of Aristotle, Porphyry, the *Sentences*, the wretched studies of our age. The men who interpret them are bound to keep silence, not for five years, as did the Pythagoreans, but for ever and ever, like the dead; they must believe all, obey always; nor may they ever, even for practice in argument, skirmish with their master, nor mutter a syllable against him. What will they not believe who have credited that ridiculous and injurious blasphemer Aristotle? His propositions are so absurd that an ass or a stone would cry out at them. . . . My soul longs for nothing so ardently as to expose and publicly shame that Greek buffoon, who like a spectre has befooled the church. . . . If Aristotle had not lived in the flesh I should not hesitate to call him a devil. The greatest part of my cross is to be forced to see brothers with brilliant minds, born for useful studies, compelled to spend their lives and waste their labour in these follies. The universities do not cease to condemn good books and publish bad ones, or rather talk in their sleep about those already published. . . .

Brother Martin Luther, Augustinian

The professor's efforts to rid his own university of Aristotle were completely successful, as on May 18, 1517, he wrote to Lang:

Our theology and St Augustine prosper and reign here, by God's help. Aristotle is gradually tottering to a fall from which he will hardly rise again, and the lectures on the *Sentences* are wonderfully disrelished. No professor can hope for students unless he offer courses in the new theology, that is on the Bible or St Augustine or some other ecclesiastical authority.

While teaching, Luther continued his own studies. Hebrew he had already begun to learn at Erfurt, with the help of Reuchlin's new grammar-dictionary. There were no courses in Greek at either Erfurt or Wittenberg, but he began to study it under the private tuition of his friend Lang, who taught at Wittenberg for three years from 1513 to 1516. Besides these linguistic pursuits he continued his reading in mediaeval theologians—Bernard of Clairvaux, Bonaventura, Gerson, and Gerhard Zerbolt of Zütphen.

Towards the end of 1515 or early in 1516 he became acquainted with a school of German mystics which had an important influence on his development. The leader of this movement had been Tauler, whose sermons, in an edition of 1508, Luther bought and annotated in his own careful way. He was still more impressed by a manuscript of one of this school known as 'the Frankfürter', a work to which the young professor gave the name of 'A German Theology', when he edited it in an incomplete form in 1516 (his first publication) and fully in 1518. In the preface he says that there is no better book, after the Bible and Augustine, and none in which one may better learn the nature of 'God, Christ, man, and all things'. He warns the reader not to be repelled by the archaic German, and the influence of this rough, but pure old speech, has been noted on his own style.

What attracted Luther to the mystics was their doctrine of the necessity of a spiritual rebirth of anguish and despair before a man could approach the felicity of union with God. Just as Christ had gone through pain to blessedness, so, they taught, man must experience woe before he can appreciate happiness. A person who seeks God with all his heart is left by him for a time in doubt and distraction, that God may thereby teach him his absolute dependence on him. This was balm to the soul of one who had been at a loss to explan the long period of suffering through which he had just come; now he felt sure that he had not gone astray, but that even in the depths God had loved and watched over him.

The young professor's work was not confined to the classroom. Soon after his transfer to Wittenberg he began to preach, at first to the brothers in the convent, and then in the tiny, barn-like chapel at that time standing near the cloister. He was at first very timid about it, but gradually developed a wonderful homiletic gift. Even his earliest addresses are full of fresh earnestness and have some touches of uncommon power. The first extant sermon, probably preached on Whitsunday, 1514, takes the text from the golden rule, 'In everything, do to others what you would have them do to you, for this sums up the Law and the Prophets' (Matthew 7:12). The preacher begins by classifying goods as wholly external—such as money, houses, and wives; partly external and partly internal—health and beauty; and wholly internal—wisdom, virtue, charity, and faith. He then shows how a man may help or hurt his neighbour in any of these goods. He asks if it is enough to abstain from hurting our fellow men, and answers by inquiring if we should be satisfied if all that they ever did for us was to let us alone. We must give to others, teach them, incite them, and help them to do right even as we want them to do unto us. Christ judged the wicked servant, not for wasting his talent, but for letting it lie idle; he condemned the persons at his tribunal, not for despoiling him, but because when he was hungry they gave him no meat. Thus it will be with us if we do not help each other to the utmost of our ability.

So I might go on with other sermons, and show how simple, direct, interesting, moral, and saintly they are. They reveal the heart of young Luther striving with all his might to be the best and do the best that was in him. What flashes of revelation there are now and then, as in the comment on John 3:16 ('God so loved the world that he gave his one and only Son')—'There is a wonderful emphasis and propriety in these words, as is the wont of the Holy Spirit!'

In both sermons and lectures many a trenchant word against spiritual wickedness in high places reminds one that the monk was already a reformer. Many of the abuses he later attacked are scored or glanced at in these early years. He says, for example, that the Canon Law needs a thorough cleansing; he speaks against fasts, ceremonies, and pilgrimages. He criticises the hardness and tyranny of the princes, the coarseness of the priests, the arrogance of the monks, the ignorance of indulgence-preachers, the superstition of religious foundations, the laziness of workmen, and the irreligion and greed of lawyers. Sometimes he rebukes by name or clearly indicates persons in high stations, among them the late Pope Julius II, the Bishop of Strasbourg, Duke George of Albertine Saxony, and his own sovereign, the Elector.

Of more than common interest, as showing Luther's general attitude towards the church, is his opinion on a *cause célèbre* of that day, the trial for heresy of John Reuchlin. This learned man's refusal to participate in the scheme of a converted Jew to burn all Hebrew books except the Old Testament was made the ground of action against him by the Dominicans of Cologne, among whom the most conspicuous was Hochstratten, aided by the humanist Ortuin Gratius. The trial, which lasted from 1510 to 1516, excited the interest of the whole of Europe. The monks and obscurantists sided with the inquisitors, the humanists, all but Ortuin, with Reuchlin. The contest was carried on by a hundred pens, and gave rise to a great satire—the *Epistles of Obscure Men*. This work, most of which was written by Crotus Rubenaus, in the form of a series of letters addressed to Ortuin Gratius by poor monks, ridicules the bad Latin, ignorance, gullibility, and superstition of the theologians.

Luther, though a monk, sided with the progressive party against the inquisitors. His letters on the subject are written to a man who was, throughout life, one of his best friends, George Burkhardt of Spalt. Spalatin, as he was always called, was of the same age as his friend, whom he probably came to know first in 1512, when he was tutor to some young princes at Wittenberg. About 1514 he was appointed chaplain and private secretary to Frederick the Wise, after which he was rarely at Wittenberg. Of the voluminous correspondence of the two friends about four hundred and fifty of Luther's letters to him have survived. Among the first of these are two on the Reuchlin trial:

TO GEORGE SPALATIN AT ALTENBERG
Wittenberg, February, 1514

Peace be with you, reverend Spalatin! Brother John Lang has asked me what I think of the innocent and learned Reuchlin and whether he is, as his prosecutors of Cologne allege, in danger of heresy. You know that I greatly esteem and like the man, and perhaps my judgement will therefore be suspected, but my opinion is that in all his writings there is absolutely nothing dangerous.

I greatly wonder at the men of Cologne ferreting out such an obscure point, worse tangled than the Gordian knot, though the case is really as plain as the day. . . . What shall I say? That they are trying to cast out Beelzebub but not by the finger of God. I often regret and deplore that we Christians are wise abroad and fools at home. A hundred times worse blasphemies than this exist in the very streets of Jerusalem, and the high places are filled with spiritual idols. We ought to show our superabundant zeal in removing these offences, which are our real, close enemies, instead of abandoning all that is really urgent and turning to foreign matters, under the inspiration of the devil, who intends that we shall neglect our own business without helping others. . . .

Your brother,
Martin Luther

TO GEORGE SPALATIN AT ALTENBERG
Wittenberg, August 5, 1514

Greetings. Hitherto, most learned Spalatin, I considered that poetaster of Cologne, Ortuin Gratius, simply an ass. But you see he has turned out a dog, or rather a ravening wolf in sheep's clothing, if not indeed a crocodile, as you quite properly suggest. I really believe he has felt his own asininity (if you allow the word) since our Reuchlin has pointed it out, but that he thinks he can shake it off and put on the lion's majesty. The change is too much for him; presto! he remains a wolf or crocodile, for to turn into a lion is beyond his power.

Good Heavens! How can I express my feelings? From the example of this fellow alone we may form the truest, sanest, and justest estimate possible of all who have ever written or now write, or will write from envy. The most insane of all passions is that envy which ardently desires to hurt but has not the power. . . .

This little Ortuin gets together a lot of ridiculous, contradictory, painful, pitiful propositions, twisting the words and meaning of innocent Reuchlin, only to increase the penalty of his own blindness and obstinacy of heart. . . .

In addition to preaching and teaching, Luther had numerous duties connected with his order, in which he was rapidly rising to a leading position. In May 1515, he was elected vicar of the district, a responsible position involving the superintendence of eleven cloisters. How seriously he took his duties is shown by his letters to priors of monasteries under his charge. Two of them especially reveal the writer's deep spiritual life at the time when he was most under the influence of the mystics. The first is conceived in the spirit of Paul's epistle to Philemon.

TO JOHN BERCKEN,
AUGUSTINIAN PRIOR AT MAINZ
Dresden, May 1, 1516

Greetings in the Lord! Reverend and excellent Father Prior!—I am grieved to learn that there is with your Reverence one of my brothers, a certain George Baumgartner, of our convent at Dresden, and that, alas! he sought refuge with you in a shameful manner, and for a shameful case. I thank your faith and duty for receiving him and thus bringing his shame to an end. That lost sheep is mine, he belongs to me; it is mine to seek him, and, if it please the Lord Jesus, to bring him back. Wherefore I pray your Reverence, by our common faith in Christ and by our common Augustinian vow, to send him to me in dutiful charity either at Dresden or at Wittenberg, or rather to persuade him lovingly and gently to come of his own accord. I shall receive him with open arms; only let him come; he has no cause to fear my displeasure.

I know, I know that scandals must arise. It is no miracle that a man should fall, but it is a miracle that he should rise and stand. Peter fell, that he might know that he was a man; today the cedars of Lebanon, touching the sky with their tops fall down. Wonder of wonders, even an angel fell from heaven and man in paradise! What wonder is it, then, that a reed be shaken by the wind and a smoking flax be quenched? May the Lord Jesus teach you and use you and perfect you in every good work. Amen. Farewell.

Brother Martin Luther
Professor of theology and Augustinian Vicar of the
district of Meissen and Thuringia

TO MICHAEL DRESSEL,
AUGUSTINIAN PRIOR AT NEUSTADT
Wittenberg, June 22, 1516

. . . You seek peace and ensure it, but in the wrong way, for you look to what the world gives, not to what Christ gives. Know you not, dear Father, that God is so wonderful among his people that he has placed his peace in the midst of no peace, that is, in the midst of all trial, as he says: Rule thou in the midst of thine enemies? It is not *that* man, therefore, whom no one disturbs, who has peace—which is, indeed, the peace of the world—but he whom all men and all things harass and who yet bears all quietly with joy. You say with Israel: 'Peace, peace,' and there is no peace; say rather with Christ, 'Cross, cross,' and there is no cross. For the cross ceases to be a cross as soon as you say joyfully: 'Blessed cross, there is no tree like you.' . . .

Seek peace and you will find it, but seek only to bear trials with joy as if they were holy relics. . . .

It may be imagined that such varied occupations kept Luther busy. Of his work he gives a lively account in a letter to his recent colleague and instructor in Greek:

TO JOHN LANG AT ERFURT
Wittenberg, October 26, 1516

Greetings. I need a couple of amanuenses or secretaries, as I do almost nothing the livelong day but write letters. I do not know whether on that account I am always repeating myself, but you can judge. I am convent preacher, the reader at meals, am asked to deliver a sermon daily in the parish church, am district vicar (that is eleven times prior), business manager of our fish-farm at Litzkau, attorney in our case versus the Herzbergers now pending at Torgau, lecturer on St Paul, assistant lecturer on the Psalter, besides having my correspondence, which, as I said, occupies most of my time. I seldom have leisure to discharge the canonical services, to say nothing of attending to my own temptations with the world, the flesh and the devil. You see how idle I am!

I think you must already have my answer about Brother John Metzel, but I will see what I can do. How in the world do you think I can get places for your epicures and sybarites? If you have brought them up in this pernicious way of life you ought to support them in the same pernicious style. I have enough useless brothers on all sides—if, indeed, any can be called useless to a patient soul. I have persuaded myself that the useless are the most useful of all—so you can have them a while longer. . . .

You write to me that yesterday you began to lecture on the second book of *Sentences*. I begin tomorrow on Galatians, though I fear the plague will not allow me to finish the course. The plague takes off two or at most three in one day, and that not every day. A son of the smith who lives opposite was well yesterday and is buried today, and another son lies ill. The epidemic began rather severely and suddenly in the latter part of the summer. You would persuade Bernhardi and me to flee to you, but shall I flee? I hope the world will not come to an end when Brother Martin does. I shall send the brothers away if the plague gets worse; I am stationed here and may not flee because of my vow of obedience, until the same authority which now commands me to stay shall command me to go. Not that I do not fear the plague (for I am not the Apostle Paul, but only a lecturer on him), but I hope the Lord will deliver me from my fear.

How great is the contrast between this letter and that written ten years before! The shy boy has become a man of unusual power, universally respected and trusted. Indeed, he had already attracted the notice of his sovereign, the

Elector Frederick. This prince, who enjoyed a great and deserved reputation for wisdom, was a pious man according to mediaeval standards. He had made a pilgrimage to the Holy Land, and brought back a large collection of relics to which he kept adding from time to time. He built the Castle church at Wittenberg, 1493–1499, to keep these sacred objects of which by 1505 he had accumulated 5005, graced with enormous indulgences, reckoned, according to the scale of measurement adopted, as equivalent to 1443 years of purgatory. In addition to this provision for his future life, Frederick had ten thousand masses said yearly in Saxon churches for the benefit of his soul.

Luther had now come to regard such things as superfluous and wrong, and consequently judged his sovereign severely for superstition, as is shown in the next letter written to answer Spalatin's request for his advice about the proposed appointment of Staupitz to a bishopric:

TO GEORGE SPALATIN AT ALTENBERG
Wittenberg, June 8, 1516

. . . I by no means wish that the reverend father should receive the appointment simply because it pleases the Elector to give it him. Many things please your elector, and appear glorious in his eyes, which displease God and are base. I do not deny that the Prince is of all most wise in worldly matters, but in those which pertain to God and salvation I think he is seven times blind, as is your friend Pfeffinger. I do not say this privily as a slanderer, nor do I wish that you should in any way conceal it; when the opportunity comes I am ready to say it to both of them.

Dear Spalatin, these are not such happy times that it is blessed, or even not most miserable to be a bishop—that is to carouse and practise the vices of Sodom and Rome. You will clearly understand this if you compare the bishops of our age with those of ancient times. The best of modern prelates wage foreign wars with all the power of artillery, or build up their private fortunes, a hell of avarice. And although Staupitz is most averse from such wickedness, yet would you, with your confidence in him, force him to become involved in the whirlpools and racking tempests of episcopal cares, when chance, or rather fate, urges him on any way? . . .

Staupitz did not get the appointment, and about a year later fell into such disfavour with his sovereign that Luther had to intercede for him. The letter in which he does so has an uncommon interest as indicating how free the Wittenberg professor felt to remonstrate with his prince on matters of state:

TO THE ELECTOR FREDERICK OF SAXONY
AT ALTENBERG
Wittenberg, November, 1517

Most gracious Lord and Prince! As your Grace promised me a gown some time ago, I beg to remind your Grace of the same. Please let Pfeffinger settle it with a deed and not with promises—he can spin mighty good yarns but no cloth comes from them.

I have learned that your Grace is offended at Dr Staupitz, our dear and worthy father, for some reason or other. When he was here on the way to see your Grace at Torgau, I talked with him and showed him that I was sorry your Grace should take umbrage, and after a long conversation could only find that he held your Grace in his heart. . . . Wherefore, most gracious Lord, I beg you, as he several times asked me to do, that you would consider all the love and loyalty you have so often found in him.

My gracious Lord, let me now show my devotion to you and deserve my new gown. I have heard that at the expiration of the present impost your Grace intends to collect another and perhaps a heavier one. If you will not despise the prayer of a poor beggar, I ask you for God's sake not to do this. For it heartily distresses me and many who love you, that this tax has of late robbed you of much good fame and favour. God has blessed you with high intelligence in these matters, to see further than I or perhaps any of your subjects, but it may well be that God ordains it so that at times a great mind may be directed by a lesser one, so that no one may trust himself but only God our Lord. May he keep your Grace in health to govern us well, and afterwards may he grant your soul salvation. Amen.

Your Grace's obedient chaplain,

Dr Martin Luther

5

The Indulgence Controversy, 1517–1519

Notwithstanding Luther's severe criticism of the Elector for venerating relics, and notwithstanding his despondent estimate of spiritual wickedness in high places, he was, as yet, a true son of the church. In attacking a flagrant ecclesiastical abuse, the indulgence trade, he did not intend to raise the standard of revolt, nor did he do so until forced, gradually if rapidly, by the authorities of the church herself, into irreconcilable opposition. In order to understand his protest against indulgences, it is necessary to glance at the history of this institution.

According to the theory of the Roman Catholic church, forgiveness is imparted to sinners in absolution after confession, by which the penitent is freed from guilt and eternal punishment in hell, but still remains liable to a milder punishment to be undergone in this life as penance, or in purgatory. The practice had arisen in the early church of commuting this penance (not the pains of purgatory) in consideration of a good work such as a pilgrimage or a contribution to a pious purpose. This was the seed of the indulgence which would never have grown to its later enormous proportions had it not been for the Crusades. Muhammad promised his followers paradise if they fell in battle against unbelievers, but Christian warriors were at first without this comforting assurance. Their faith was not

long left in doubt, however, for as early as 855 Leo IV
promised heaven to the Franks who died fighting the Mus-
lims. A quarter of a century later John VIII proclaimed
absolution for all sins and remission of all penalties to soldiers in the holy war, and from this time on the 'Crusade
indulgence' became a regular means of recruiting, used,
for example, by Leo IX in 1052 and by Urban II in 1095.
By this time the practice had grown up of regarding an
indulgence as a remission not only of penance but of the
pains of purgatory. The means which had proved successful in getting soldiers for the Crusades were first used in
1145 or 1146 to get money for the same end—pardon
being assured to those who gave enough to equip one soldier on the same terms as if they had gone themselves.

When the Crusades ceased, in the thirteenth century,
indulgences did not fall into disuse. At the jubilee of Pope
Boniface VIII in 1300 a plenary indulgence was granted to
all who made a pilgrimage to Rome. The Pope reaped
such an enormous harvest from the gifts of these pilgrims
that he saw fit to employ similar means at frequent inter-
vals, and soon extended the same privileges to all who contributed for some pious purpose at home. Agents were
sent out to sell these pardons, and were given power to
confess and absolve, so that by 1393 Boniface IX was able
to announce complete remission of both guilt and penalty
to the purchasers of his letters.

Having assumed the right to free living men from
future punishment, it was but a step for the popes to proclaim that they had the power to deliver the souls of the
dead from purgatory. The existence of this power was an
open question until decided by Calixtus III in 1457, but
full use of the faculty was not made until twenty years
later, after which it became of all branches of the
indulgence trade the most profitable.

The practice of the church had become well established
before a theory was framed to justify it. This was done
most successfully by Alexander of Hales in the thirteenth

century, who discovered the treasury of the church consisting of the merits of Christ and the saints which the Pope, as head of the church, could apply as a sort of credit to anyone he chose. This doctrine, so far as it applied to living men, received the sanction of Clement VI in 1343 and became a part of the Canon Law, but the popes usually claimed to free the souls of the dead from purgatory simply by prayer. The mere dictum of the Supreme Pontiff did not at that time absolutely establish a dogma. A powerful party in the church held that a council was the supreme authority in matters of faith, and it will be remembered that the infallibility of the Pope was not made a dogma until 1870. Luther was therefore not accused of heresy for his assertions regarding indulgences for the dead.

It was not so much the doctrine of the church that excited his indignation as it was the practices of some of her agents. They encouraged the common man to believe that the purchase of a papal pardon would assure him impunity without any real repentance on his part. Moreover, whatever the theoretical worth of indulgences, the motive of their sale was notoriously the greed of unscrupulous ecclesiastics. The 'holy trade' as it was called had become so thoroughly commercialised by 1500 that a banking house, the Fuggers of Augsburg, were the direct agents of the Curia in Germany. In return for their services in forwarding the Pope's bulls, and in hiring sellers of pardons, this wealthy house made a secret agreement in 1507 by which it received one third of the total profits of the trade, and in 1514 formally took over the whole management of the business in return for the modest commission of one half the net receipts. Naturally not a word was said by the preachers to the people as to the destination of so large a portion of their money, but enough was known to make many men regard indulgences as an open scandal.

The history of the particular trade attacked by Luther is one of special infamy. Albert of Brandenburg, a prince of the enterprising house of Hohenzollern, was groomed for the church and rapidly rose through political influence to the highest ecclesiastical position in Germany. In 1513 he was elected, at the age of twenty-three, Archbishop of Magdeburg and administrator of the bishopric of Halberstadt—an uncanonical accumulation of sees confirmed by the Pope in return for a large payment. Hardly had Albert paid this before he was elected Archbishop and Elector of Mainz and Primate of Germany (March 9, 1514). As he was not yet of canonical age to possess even one bishopric, not to mention three of the greatest in the empire, the Pope refused to confirm his nomination except for an enormous sum. The Curia at first demanded twelve thousand ducats for the twelve apostles, Albert offered seven for the seven deadly sins. The average between apostles and sins was struck at ten thousand ducats, or fifty thousand dollars, a sum equal in purchasing power to near a million today. Albert borrowed this, too, from the Fuggers, and was accordingly confirmed on August 15, 1514.

In order to allow the new prelate to recoup himself, Leo obligingly declared an indulgence for the benefit of St Peter's Church, to run eight years from March 31, 1515. By this transaction, one of the most disgraceful in the history of the papacy, as well as in that of the house of Brandenburg, the Curia made a vast sum. Albert did not come off so well. First, a number of princes, including the rulers of both Saxonys, forbade the trade in their dominions, and the profits of what remained were deeply cut by the unexpected attack of a young monk.

Albert did his best to put his holy wares in the most attractive light. A short quotation from his public advertisement will substantiate what has just been said about the popular representation of the indulgences as an easy road to atonement:

> The first grace is a plenary remission of all sins: one might say no grace could be greater than this, because a sinner

THE INDULGENCE CONTROVERSY

deprived of grace through it achieves perfect remission of sin and the grace of God anew. By which grace . . . the pains of purgatory are completely wiped out. The second grace for sale is a confessional letter allowing the penitent to choose his own confessor; the third is the participation in the merits of the saints. The fourth grace is for the souls in purgatory, a plenary remission of all sins. . . . Nor is it necessary for those who contribute to the fund for this purpose to be contrite or to confess.

Albert's principal agent was a certain Dominican named Tetzel, a bold, popular preacher already expert in the business. He did all in his power to impress the people with the value of his commodities. When he entered a town, there was a solemn procession, bells were rung, and everything possible done to attract attention. Some of his sermons have survived, painting in the most lively colours the agonies of purgatory and the ease with which anyone might free himself or his dead relatives from the torturing flames by the simple payment of a gulden.

Though forbidden to enter Saxony, Tetzel approached sufficiently near her borders to attract a number of her people. In January 1517, he was at Eisleben, and in the spring came to Jüerborg, so near Wittenberg that Luther could see the bad effects of indulgence in his own parish. After preaching against the abuse several times in 1516 and 1517, the earnest monk finally decided to bring matters to a head by holding a debate on the subject. He announced his intention in a rather dramatic way. On the Feast of All Saints (November 1), the Elector's relics kept in the Castle church were solemnly displayed and the special grace attached to them publicly announced. This festival drew crowds to Wittenberg, both from curiosity and from desire to participate in the spiritual benefits then obtainable. It was to give notice to these people that on October 31, 1517, Martin Luther posted up on the door of the church an announcement of his intention to hold a debate on the value of indulgences, 'for the love and zeal for elucidating the truth', ninety-five theses or heads for debate being proposed.

The *Theses* are a good specimen of much of Luther's work. Their chief defect is lack of perfectly logical order. They evince a tolerably deep acquaintance with mediaeval theology, but their main interest is not theoretical but practical. Each proposition is a blow at some popular error or some flagrant abuse. Though occasionally qualifying, they deal trenchantly with the nature of repentance, the power of the Pope to release souls from purgatory, the virtue of indulgences for living sinners, the outrageous practices of the preachers of pardons, the treasury of the church, and other matters.

The first thesis cannot be understood without a slight knowledge of Latin. This language has but one word (*penitentia*) for the two very distinct ideas of penance and penitence. Consequently the words of Christ translated in the Vulgate '*Penitentiam agite*' might equally well mean, 'Repent ye,' or 'Do penance.' They were taken in the latter sense by the average priest, but Erasmus in his *Paraphrases* to the New Testament had seen the real signficance of the words, and so had some other doctors known to Luther. Accordingly, in the first two theses he says:

1. Our Lord and master Jesus Christ in saying '*Penitentiam agite*' meant that the whole life of the faithful should be repentance.

2. And these words cannot refer to penance—that is confession and satisfaction.

Among the other propositions the following are the most important:

5. The Pope does not wish, nor is he able, to remit any penalty except what he or the Canon Law has imposed.

6. The Pope is not able to remit guilt except by declaring it forgiven by God—or in cases reserved to himself. . . .

11. The erroneous opinion that canonical penance and punishment in purgatory are the same assuredly seemed to be a tare sown while the bishops were asleep.

21. Therefore those preachers of indulgence err who say that a papal pardon frees a man from all penalty and assures his salvation.

22. The greater part of the people will be deceived by this indiscriminate and pretentious promise of pardon which cannot be fulfilled.

26. The Pope does well to say that he frees souls from purgatory not by the power of the keys (for he has no such power) but by the method of prayer.

28. It is certain that avarice is fostered by the money chinking in the chest, but to answer the prayers of the church is in the power of God alone.

29. Who knows whether all the souls in purgatory want to be freed? . . .

30. None is sure of the sincerity of his contrition, much less of his full pardon.

31. They who believe themselves made sure of salvation by papal letters will be eternally damned along with their teachers.

33. One should be aware of them who say that those pardons are an inestimable gift of the Pope by which man is reconciled to God.

36. Every Christian truly repentant has full remission of guilt and penalty even without letter of pardon.

37. Every true Christian, alive or dead, participates in all the goods of Christ and the church without letter of pardon. . . .

38. Nevertheless papal pardons are not to be despised.

40. True contrition seeks and loves punishment, and makes relaxations of it hateful, at least at times.

43. Christians are to be taught that he who gives to the poor or lends to one in need does better than he who buys indulgences.

50. Christians are to be taught that if the Pope knew

the exactions of the preachers of indulgences he would rather have St Peter's church in ashes than have it built with the flesh and bones of his sheep.

60. The treasury of the church is in the power of the keys given by Christ's merit.

62. The true treasure of the church is the holy gospel of the glory and grace of God.

71. Who speaks against the apostolic truth of indulgences, let him be anathema.

72. But who opposes the lust and licence of the preachers of pardons, let him be blessed.

The scandalous practices of those preachers will induce the laity to ask inconvenient questions, such as:

82. Why does not the Pope empty purgatory from charity?

92. Let all those prophets depart who say to the people of Christ, Peace, peace, where there is no peace.

93. But all those prophets do well who say to the people of Christ, Cross, cross, and there is no cross.

On the same day that he posted his Theses Luther wrote a letter of remonstrance to the prelate under whose sanction the indulgences had appeared, which still further explains his position.

TO ALBERT, ARCHBISHOP OF MAINZ
Wittenberg, October 31, 1517

Grace and the mercy of God and whatever else may be and is!

Forgive me, Very Reverend Father in Christ, and illustrious Lord, that I, the offscouring of men, have the temerity to think of a letter to your high mightiness. . . .

Papal indulgences for the building of St Peter's are hawked about under your illustrious sanction. I do not now accuse the sermons of the preachers who advertise them for I have not seen the same, but I regret that the people have conceived about them the most erroneous ideas. Forsooth these unhappy souls believe that if they buy letters of pardon they are sure of their salvation; likewise that souls fly out of purgatory as soon as money is cast into the chest; in short, that the grace conferred is so great that there is no sin whatever which cannot be absolved thereby, even if, as they say, taking an impossible example, a man should violate the mother of God. They also believe that indulgences free them from all penalty and guilt.

My God! thus are the souls committed, Father, to your charge, instructed unto death, for which you have a fearful and growing reckoning to pay. . . .

What else could I do, excellent Bishop and illustrious Prince, except pray your Reverence for the sake of the Lord Jesus Christ to take away your Instructions to the Commissioners altogether and impose some other form of preaching on the proclaimers of pardons, lest perchance someone should at length arise and confute them and their Instructions publicly, to the great blame of your Highness. This I vehemently deprecate, yet I fear it may happen unless the grievance is quickly redressed. . . .

Your unworthy son,
Martin Luther, Augustinian, Dr Theol.

On receipt of this letter, with the Theses enclosed, Albert began an 'inhibitory process' against the 'presumptuous monk', which was soon dropped on account of the action taken at Rome. The Archbishop promptly sent an account of the matters, with several of the Wittenberg professor's works, to the Curia.

The attack on indulgences was like a match touched to gunpowder. Everyone had been thinking what Luther alone was bold and clear-sighted enough to say, and almost everyone applauded him to the echo. Certain persons wrote exhorting him to stand fast and congratulating him on what he had done. The Theses had an immediate and enormous popularity. Luther himself was astonished at their reception, and before he knew it they were printed at Nuremberg both in Latin and German. The circle of humanists in the wealthy town received them warmly, the famous painter, Albrecht Dürer, sending the author a present of his own wood-cuts as a token of appreciation. These were forwarded to him by his friend Scheurl, who enclosed copies of the printed Theses. The answer explains the writer's position:

TO CHRISTOPHER SCHEURL AT NUREMBERG
Wittenberg, March 5, 1518

Greetings. I received both your German and Latin letters, good and learned Scheurl, together with the distinguished Albrecht Dürer's gift, and my Theses in the original and in the vernacular. As you are surprised that I did not send them to you, I reply that my purpose was not to publish them, but first to consult a few of my neighbours about them, that thus I might either destroy them if condemned or edit them with the approbation of others. But now that they are printed and circulated far beyond my expectation, I feel anxious about what they may bring forth; not that I am unfavourable to spreading known truth abroad—rather this is what I seek—but because this method is not that best adapted to instruct the public. I have certain doubts about them myself, and should have spoken far differently and more distinctly had I known what was going to happen. I have learned from their publication what is the general opinion about indulgences entertained everywhere by all, although they conceal it 'for fear of the Jews'. I have felt it necessary to write a defence of my Theses which I have not yet been able to print because my Lord Bishop of Brandenburg, to whom I referred it, has long kept me waiting for his opinion. If the Lord give me leisure I should like to publish a work in German on the virtue of indulgences to supersede my desultory Theses. For I have no doubt that people are deceived not by indulgences but by the use made of them. . . .

The defence of which Luther has just spoken was returned to him by the Bishop of Brandenburg with the advice not to print it. He did so, however, but the slowness of the printers prevented the appearance of the *Resolutions,* as the book was called, until September. In this he takes up the Theses one by one, explains and supports them by argument—in the case of the first, for example, citing the Greek to prove his statement. He dedicated the work to Pope Leo X in a letter written about the end of May, in which, while speaking as a submissive son of the church, he shows his opinions have only been confirmed by the attacks of enemies. The letter is well adapted to the man to whom it is addressed, a humanist, perhaps a freethinker, who would despise the writer more as an uncultured German than condemn him as a heretic. There is a fine irony in the words about the wonderful literary attainments of the age.

TO POPE LEO X
Wittenberg, May 30?, 1518

I have heard a very evil report of myself, Most Blessed Father, by which I understand that certain persons have made my name loathsome to you and yours, saying that I have tried to diminish the power of the keys and the authority of the Supreme Pontiff, and therefore accusing me of being a heretic, an apostate and a traitor, besides branding me with a hundred other calumnious epithets. My ears are horrified and my eyes amazed, but my conscience, sole bulwark of confidence, remains innocent and at peace. . . .

In these latter days a jubilee of papal judgement began to be preached, and the preachers, thinking everything allowed them under the protection of your name, dared to teach impiety and heresy openly, to the grave scandal and mockery of ecclesiastical powers, totally disregarding the provisions of the Canon Law about the misconduct of officials. . . . They met with great success, the people were sucked dry on false pretences . . . but the oppressors lived on the fat and sweetness of the land. They avoided scandals only by the terror of your name, the threat of the stake and the brand of heresy . . . if, indeed, this can be called avoiding scandals and not rather exciting schisms and revolt by crass tyranny. . . .

I privately warned some of the dignitaries of the church. By some the admonition was well received, by others ridiculed, by others treated in various ways, for the terror of your name and the dread of censure are strong. At length, when I could do nothing else, I determined to stop their mad career if only for a moment; I resolved to call their assertions into question. So I published some propositions for debate, inviting only the more learned to discuss them with me, as ought to be plain to my opponents from the preface to my Theses. Yet this is the flame with which they seek to set the world on fire! . . .

Now what shall I do? I cannot recall my Theses and yet I see that great hatred is kindled against me by their popularity. I come unwillingly before the precarious and divided judgement of the public, I, who am untaught, stupid and destitute of learning, before an age so fertile in literary genius that it would force into a corner even Cicero, no mean follower of fame and popularity in his day.

So in order to fulfil the desire of many and appease my opponents, I am now publishing a little treatise to explain my Theses. To protect myself, I publish it under the guardianship of your name and the shadow of your protection. . . .

And now, Most Blessed Father, I cast myself and all my possessions at your feet; raise me up or slay me, summon me hither or thither, approve me or reprove me as you please. I shall recognise your words as the words of

Christ, speaking in you. If I have deserved death, I shall not refuse to die. For the earth is the Lord's and the fulness thereof; blessed be he for ever. Amen. May he always preserve you. Amen.

Long before this letter was published, energetic steps had been taken against Luther in Rome. As previously stated, the Archbishop of Mainz, early in December, 1517, had forwarded to the Pope the monk's *Theses on Indulgences,* and those on scholastic philosophy, with other documents. Leo read the Theses, which he judged clever though animated by envy. At another time he professed to think they had been composed by a drunken German who would see the error of his ways when sober. It was, therefore, with no great apprehension that he ordered Gabriel della Volta, General of the Augustinians, 'to quiet that man, for newly kindled flames are easily quenched'.

Accordingly Volta instructed Staupitz to force the presumptuous brother to recant. The matter was brought before the general chapter of the Saxon province, held at Heidelberg, in April and May 1518. Luther refused to recant, but resigned his office of district vicar, to which his friend Lang was elected, Staupitz being again chosen provincial vicar. Far from recanting, the heretic expounded his fundamental ideas in a public debate on justification by faith and free will. 'The doctors', he writes to Spalatin on May 18, 'willingly heard my disputation and rebutted it with such moderation that I felt much obliged to them. My theology, indeed, seemed foreign to them, yet they skirmished with it effectively and courteously, all except one young doctor who moved the laughter of the audience by saying, "If the peasants heard you they would stone you to death."' Among the converts won by the new leader at this time was Martin Bucer, later one of the most prominent of the Protestant divines.

While at Heidelberg, Luther was received by the brother of the Elector Palatine in the splendid old castle, and shown all the armour and precious objects there collected.

Soon after his return to Wittenberg, Luther wrote the letter to the Pope last translated, which may have been forwarded to his Holiness by Staupitz.

In the meantime the Dominicans, represented in the person of Tetzel, sent urgent denunciations of the Wittenberg monk for heresy to the fiscal procurator (we should say attorney-general) of the Curia. Leo waited to see what would be the result of the efforts of Volta, but when it was known that these had entirely failed, he empowerd the procurator to begin a formal action 'for suspicion of heresy'. At the desire of this official, Perusco by name, the general auditor (supreme justice of the Curia), Jerome Ghinnucci, was charged with the conduct of the process, and Silvester Prierias, Master of the Sacred Palace, was requested to give an expert opinion on the Theses. As a Dominican and a Thomist he discharged his task thoroughly. His memorial, which he proudly printed with the title *The Dialogue*, takes the strongest ground of papal supremacy, and asserts that whoever denies that the infallible church has a right to do whatever she actually does is a heretic. On this advice Ghinnucci summoned Luther to appear at Rome within sixty days, sending the citation together with *The Dialogue*, which were received by the professor early in August. He answered the latter by a pamphlet asserting that both popes and councils could err, and this he sent to Prierias with a scornful letter:

> Your refutation seemed so trifling [he wrote] that I have answered it *ex tempore*, whatever came uppermost in my mind. If you wish to hit back, be careful to bring your Aquinas better armed into the arena, lest you be not treated so gently again.

Before Luther had time to decide whether to obey the summons to Rome or not, the Curia suddenly altered the method of procedure. On August 23 the Pope wrote to his agent in Germany, Cardinal Thomas de Vio of Gaeta, thence called Cajetan, to summon Luther to Augsburg at once, hear him, and if he did not recant, send him bound to Rome, or failing that to put him and his followers under the ban. This step was so surprising that many Germans believed it a breach of the Canon Law, which provides a much slower process against a *suspected* heretic. Such, however, was not the case. The Pope's action in expediting matters was due to Cajetan himself. This nuncio had been sent to Germany to attend the Diet of Augsburg (1518) and urge the cause of the Turkish war on the empire. From this vantage-point he had observed the immense commotion caused by the Theses and Resolutions, and was still more unfavourably impressed by a sermon on the ban published by the Wittenberg professor. Bans, said he, flew about like bats, and were not much more to be regarded than those blind little pests. Cajetan thought he would teach the scoffing preacher what a terrible thing a ban really was, and wrote to Rome warning Leo of the danger of allowing Luther to remain at large any longer, and pointing out the advantage of dealing with him at once at Augsburg. His letter was reinforced by one from the Emperor Maximilian—who disliked and feared the Elector Frederick—promising his help in quelling the schismatic.

These missives had their desired efffect. Ghinnucci, especially shocked by the flippant reference to the apostolic thunders as 'bats', concluded that Luther was already a *notorious* heretic, and that he was justified in using the summary process provided by the Canon Law against criminals of this class. The moment seemed favourable for a decisive blow, for Maximilian had promised his help. Hence the letter of August 23 written to Cajetan, and accompanied by one from Volta to the Augustinian Provincial of South Germany, Hecker, urging him to co-operate in securing the heretic's arrest.

At this critical juncture Luther was not left in the lurch by his powerful friends. The Elector of Saxony refused to allow him to appear without a safe-conduct from the Emperor, which was secured late and with difficulty. Staupitz and Link also went to Augsburg, where the interview was held, in order to use their influence against the employment of force. Fortified by this support, Luther went to Augsburg, where he arrived on October 7, but waited three days until the safe-conduct of Maximilian had reached him. During the interval he had a visit from an Italian, Urban de Serralonga, with whom he had the following conversation:

Urban—Your business here may be summed up in one word of six letters: Recant!

Luther—But may I not defend my position, or at least be instructed on it?

Urban—Do you think this is a game of running in a ring? Don't you know that it is all right to deceive people a little—as you say the preachers of indulgence do—to get their money? Do you think the Elector Frederick will take arms to protect *you*?

Luther—I hope not.

Urban—If not, where will you live?

Luther—Under heaven.

Urban—What would *you* do if you had the Pope and cardinals in your power?

Luther—I would show them all reverence and honour.

Urban—(with a scornful gesture) Hem!

Luther had three separate interviews with Cajetan, on October 12, 13, and 14 respectively. On the first day, having studied the etiquette of the occasion, he fell down on his face before his judge. Much pleased with this humility, the legate complimented him on his learning and bade him recant his errors. Asked what errors he meant, the prelate, who had been studying theology for two months, named two: first, the statement in the Theses that the treasury of the church (*thesaurus indulgentiarum*) consisted of the merits of Christ, and second, the assertion in the

Resolutions that the efficacy of the sacrament depended on the faith of the recipient. The selection was a clever one, both because on these two points there was most unanimity at Rome, and also because it was supposed that the accused would more readily retract these purely speculative points than other of a more practical bearing. That Luther did not recant, however, and that the altercation with his judge at times became hot and furious, he himself tells, in his own vivid way, in a letter to a friend at court:

TO GEORGE SPALATIN
Augsburg, October 14, 1518

Greetings. As I do not care to write directly to the Elector, dear Spalatin, do you, as his intimate friend, communicate the purport of my letter to him. This is now the fourth day that my lord the legate negotiates with me, or rather against me. He fairly promises, indeed, that he will do all mercifully and paternally, for the sake of the most illustrious Elector, but in reality he wishes to carry all before him with mere stubborn brute force. He would neither allow me to answer him in a public debate nor would he dispute with me privately. The one thing which he repeated over and over was: 'Recant. Admit your error; the Pope wishes it so, and not otherwise; you must willy nilly,' with other words to the same effect. He drew his most powerful argument against me from the decretal of Clement VI *Unigenitus.* 'Here,' said he, 'here you see that the Pope decides that the merits of Christ are the treasury of the church; do you believe or do you not believe?' He allowed no statement nor answer, but tried to carry his point with force of words and with clamour.

At length he was with difficulty persuaded by the prayers of many to allow me to present a written argument. This I have done today, having taken with me Fabian von Feilitzsch to represent the Elector, of whose request he again reminded the legate. After some time he threw aside my paper with contempt, and again clamoured for recantation. With a long and wordy argument, drawn from the foolish books of Aquinas, he thought to have conquered and put me to silence. I tried to speak nine or ten times, but every time he thundered at me, and continued the monologue. At length I, too, began to shout, saying that if he could show me that the decrees asserted that the merits of Christ were the treasury of the church, I would recant as he wished. Good heavens, what gesticulation and rude laughter this remark caused! He suddenly seized the book, read from it with breathless rapidity, until he came to the place where it is written that Christ by his passion acquired a treasure. Then I: 'O most reverend Father, consider this word "acquire". If Christ by his merits acquired a treasure, then his merits are not the treasure, but that which the merits merited, namely, the keys of the church, are the treasure. Therefore my conclusion was correct.' At this he was suddenly confused, but not wishing to appear so, suddenly jumped to another place, thinking it prudent not to notice what I had said. But I was hot and burst forth, certainly without much reverence: 'Do not think, most reverend Father, that we Germans understand no grammar; it is a different thing to *acquire* a treasure and to *be* a treasure.' Having thus broken his self-confidence, as he still clamoured for recantation, I went away. He said: 'Do not return to me again unless you wish to recant.'

But lo! as soon as he had finished dinner he called our reverend vicar, Father Staupitz, and used his blandishments on him to try to get him to persuade me to recant. The legate even asserted, as I was absent, that I had no better friend than he. When Staupitz answered that he had always advised me, and still did so, to submit humbly to the church, and that I had declared publicly that I would do so, Cajetan even confessed that he was, in his own opinion, inferior to me in theological learning and in talent, but that, as the representative of the Pope and of the prelates, it was his duty to persuade me to recant. At length they agreed that he should suggest an article for me to revoke.

Thus the business stands. I have no hope nor confidence in him. I am preparing an appeal, resolved not to recant a syllable. If he proceeds as he has begun, by force, I shall publish my answer to him, that he may be confounded throughout the whole world.

Farewell in haste,
Brother Martin Luther, Augustinian

As indicated in this letter, Staupitz and Link were far more amenable to pressure than was Luther. They hoped that all might be settled peaceably, in a way which would satisfy the legate without compromising their brother. Finding that he was immovable, Staupitz absolved him from the vow of obedience, partly to relieve himself from responsibility, and partly, no doubt, to guard him against molestation from Hecker and Volta. Staupitz and Link then judged it best to retire from the city without giving the nuncio notice of their intention.

On October 16, Luther drew up an appeal requesting that the badly informed Pope be better informed, and the next day wrote Cajetan a courteous but firm letter. Notwithstanding all precautions, the accused man stood in considerable danger, for safe-conducts to heretics had been broken before. The moment was almost as decisive as the later one at Worms, and here, as there, the heroic monk stood like iron against the threats of foes and the supplication of friends alike, resolved to do nothing against his conscience.

TO CARDINAL CAJETAN AT AUGSBURG
Augsburg, October 17, 1518

Very Reverend Father in Christ, I come again, not personally but in writing; deign to hear me mercifully.

My reverend and beloved father in Christ, our Vicar,

John Staupitz, has pleaded with me to think humbly of my own opinion and to submit, and has persuaded me that your Reverence is favourably disposed towards me. . . . So that my fear has gradually passed away, or rather changed into a singular love and true, filial veneration for your Reverence.

Now, Most Reverend Father in Christ, I confess, as I have before confessed, that I was assuredly unwise and too bitter, and too irreverent to the name of the Pope. And although I had the greatest provocation, I know I should have acted with more moderation and humility, and not have answered a fool according to his folly. For so doing I am most sincerely sorry, and ask pardon, and will say so from the pulpit, as I have already done several times, and I shall take care in future to act and speak differently, by God's mercy. Moreover, I am quite ready to promise never to speak of indulgences again and to maintain silence, provided only the same rule, either of speaking or of keeping silence, be imposed on those men who have led me into this tragic business.

For the rest, most reverend and now beloved Father in Christ, as to the truth of my opinion, I would most readily recant, both by your command and the advice of my vicar, if my conscience in any way allowed it. But I know that neither the command nor the advice nor the influence of anyone ought to make me do anything against conscience or can do so. For the arguments [you cite] from Aquinas and others are not convincing to me, although I have read them over in preparation for my debates and have thoroughly understood them. I do not think their conclusions are drawn from correct premises. The only thing left is to overcome me with better reasons, in which I may hear the voice of the Bride which is also the voice of the Bridegroom.

I humbly implore your Reverence to deign to refer this case to our Most Holy Lord Leo X, that these doubts may be settled by the church, so that he may either compel a just withdrawal of my propositions or else their just affirmation. I wish only to follow the church, and I know not what effect my recantation of doubtful and unsettled opinions might have, but I fear that I might be reproached, and with reason, for not knowing either what I asserted or what I withdrew. May your Reverence deign to receive my humble and suppliant petition, and to treat me with mercy as a son.

Your Reverence's devoted son,
Brother Martin Luther, Augustinian

After waiting in vain for three days for an answer, Luther left Augsburg secretly at night and returned to Wittenberg. The first thing he did there was to write out the account of the interview of which he had spoken to Spalatin, and to publish it as the *Acta Augustana.* In the preface to the reader he says:

They vexed Reuchlin a long time for some advice he gave them, now they vex me for proposing questions for debate. Who is safe from the teeth of this Behemoth? . . .

I see that books are published and various rumours scattered abroad about what I did at Augsburg, although truly I did nothing there but lose the time and expense of the journey . . . for I was instructed there that to teach the truth is the same as to disturb the church, but to flatter men and deny Christ is considered the same as pacifying and exalting the church of Christ.

Foiled of his purpose, Cajetan wrote to the Elector Frederick asking him to arrest Luther and send him to Rome. The peace-loving prince may have wavered for an instant. According to the story he summoned his counsellors and asked their advice. One of them, Fabian von Feilitzsch, related the fable of the sheep, who, at the advice of the wolves, sent away the watchdogs. If we give up Luther, he concluded, we shall have no one to write in our defence, but they will accuse us all of being heretics. It is probable that Frederick never seriously considered the surrender of his subject, but he did ponder a plan to hide him in a castle, as he later did in the Wartburg. Early in December Spalatin and Luther had a meeting at Lichtenberg to discuss this project, which was not adopted. On December 8 the Elector wrote a diplomatic letter to the cardinal, saying that he was not convinced that the accused was a heretic, but had rather been informed by learned men that his doctrines were only objectionable to those whose pecuniary interests were involved. He wished only to act as a Christian prince, but could not compromise his university by sending an uncondemned man to Rome.

Cajetan had been convinced by his interview that it would be difficult to convict Luther of heresy. He therefore requested Leo to settle the points in dispute once for all by an *ex cathedra* declaration. This was done in a bull of November 9, which, without mentioning names, condemned the errors of certain monks on indulgences and other points. The claim could now no longer be made that the matters in question were not decided authoritatively.

Immediately upon the failure of Cajetan to arrest the heretic, the Pope dispatched a special nuncio to Germany for this purpose, Charles von Miltitz. Hoping to win the Elector to his side, Leo sent him a long-coveted honour, the anointed golden rose, with flattering letters both to him and to his principal counsellors. On the other hand, Miltitz was furnished with a ban against Luther and power to declare the interdict (i.e., suspension of all ministrations of the church except baptism and supreme unction) against Saxony. Cajetan had not thought it wise to excommunicate a man whom he had not been able to convict, but now it was felt that there would be no more excuse for delay, and that the disturber of the church's peace would be brought to terms at once.

The plan of Rome was wrecked partly by the resistance of Frederick, partly by the conduct of Miltitz, a Saxon by birth, and a vain, frivolous person, who forgot his instructions as soon as he arrived in Germany, hoping that instead of using force he could set everything right by gentle means. He accordingly arranged for a personal interview with the Augustinian friar, whom he expected to cajole into recantation; this took place at Altenberg, the capital of Electoral Saxony, early in January 1519. The result of the first day's negotiations is thus related in a letter:

TO FREDERICK, ELECTOR OF SAXONY
Altenberg, January 5 or 6, 1519

Most serene, highborn Prince, most gracious Lord! It overwhelms me to think how far your Grace has been drawn into my affairs, but as necessity and God so dispose it, I beg your Grace to be favourable still.

Charles von Miltitz yesterday pointed out with care the crimes I had committed against the Roman church, and I humbly promised to make what amends I could. I beg your Grace to attend to the plan I proposed, for by it I meant to please your Grace.

First, I agreed to let the matter alone henceforth, until it bleeds to death of itself, provided my opponents also keep silence. . . .

Secondly, I agreed to write to his Holiness the Pope, humbly submitting and recognising that I had been too hot and hasty, though I never meant to do aught against the Holy Roman church, but only as her true son to attack the scandalous preaching whereby she is made a mockery, a byword, a stumbling-block, and an offence to the people.

Thirdly, I promised to send out a paper admonishing everyone to follow the Roman church, obey and honour her, and explaining that my writings were not to be understood in a sense damaging to her. . . .

Fourthly, Spalatin proposed, on the recommendation of Fabian von Feilitsch, to leave the case to the Archbishop of Salzburg. I should abide by his judgement, with that of other learned and impartial men, or else return to my appeal. Or perhaps the matter might remain undecided and things be allowed to take their natural course. But I fear the Pope will allow no other judge but himself, nor can I tolerate his judgement; if the present plan fails, we shall have to go through the farce of the Pope writing a text and my writing the commentary. That would do no good.

Miltitz thinks my propositions unsatisfactory, but does not demand recantation. . . .

Your Grace's obedient chaplain,
Doctor Martin

In accordance with this plan Luther drew up a very humble letter to the Pope, but as it did not satisfy Miltitz he never sent it. On the second day of the conference for the agreement here proposed there was substituted a much simpler one.

TO FREDERICK, ELECTOR OF SAXONY
Altenberg, January 6 or 7, 1519

Serene, highborn Prince, gracious Lord! Let me humbly inform your Grace that Charles von Miltitz and I have at last come to an agreement, and concluded our negotiations with two articles.

1. Both sides shall be inhibited from preaching, writing, and acting further in the matter.

2. Miltitz will write to the Pope at once, informing him how things stand, and asking him to recommend the matter to some learned bishop, who will hear me and point out the errors I am to recant. For when I have learned my mistakes, I will gladly withdraw them, and do nothing to impair the honour and power of the Roman church.

The letter of Miltitz to the Pope was couched in somewhat too sanguine terms. He represented that Luther was ready to recant everything. Leo was so pleased to hear it that he dispatched a very friendly missive to the Wittenberg monk (March 29, 1519) inviting him to Rome to make his confession, and even offering him money for the journey.

That he was able to take no further action for a time was due to the political situation. In January 1519, the Emperor Maximilian died. Among the candidates for the position were King Charles of Spain, King Francis of France, and the Elector Frederick. The interest of the papacy in this election overshadowed all other matters for a time, and the cautious policy necessary prevented too much pressure being brought to bear on Frederick. The process for heresy was consequently suspended for fourteen months.

If Miltitz had been satisfied with his interview, Luther was not. When they parted with the kiss of peace he felt that it was a Judas kiss and that the envoy's tears were crocodile's tears. He tried, nevertheless, to live up to the spirit of the agreement. In fulfilment of the third proposition in the first day's interview, he published *An Instruction on Certain Articles*. In this he explains his position on a number of points. Prayers for the dead in purgatory he thinks are allowable. Of indulgences it is enough for the common man to know that indulgence is a relaxation of the satisfaction for sin, but is a much smaller thing than a work of charity, for it is free; no one sins in not buying a papal pardon, but if he buys one instead of giving to the poor or helping his neighbour, he sins, mocking himself and God. The church's commands, he says, are to be obeyed, yet one should place God's commands higher. In conclusion he adds that there is no doubt that God has honoured the Roman church above all others.

The first article of the agreement, that both sides should maintain silence, came to nothing, for neither party observed the truce, and the whole controversy was soon given an even wider publicity than it had yet attained, by an event of the first importance, the great debate with John Eck at Leipzig.

6

The Leipzig Debate, 1519

The ablest and most persistent opponent Luther ever had was John Eck. From 1517 to 1543 this champion of the church met him at every turn and did everything in his power to foil the great heresiarch. Like the Wittenberger, Eck was a peasant by extraction and a monk by profession, a theologian of no mean ability and a man of energy and resource. Before 1517 he had distinguished himself in debates at Vienna and elsewhere, and burned to make himself still more famous in this line. Just before Luther crossed his path, he charged Erasmus—the foremost scholar of the day—with something very like heresy because the latter had said that the Greek of the New Testament was not as good as that of Demosthenes.

The publication of the *Ninety-Five Theses* gave him a more substantial object to attack, and he at once assailed them in a pamhplet called *Obelisks* (literally the small daggers with which notes are marked). Of it Luther wrote, on March 24, 1518, to his friend John Silvius Egranus of Zwickau:

> A man of signal and talented learning and of learned talent has recently written a book against my Theses. I mean John Eck, doctor of theology, chancellor of the university of Ingolstadt, canon of Eichstätt and preacher

at Augsburg, a man already famous and widely known as an author. What cuts me most is that we had recently formed a great friendship. Did I not already know the machinations of Satan, I should be astonished at the fury with which Eck has broken that sweet amity without warning or letter of farewell.

In his *Obelisks* he calls me a fanatic Hussite, heretical, seditious, insolent and rash, not to mention such slight abuse as that I am dreaming, clumsy, unlearned, and a despiser of the Pope. In short the book is nothing but the foulest abuse, expressly mentioning my name and directed against my Theses. It is nothing less than the malice and envy of a maniac. I would have swallowed this sop for Cerberus, but my friends compelled me to answer it.

The answer was a pamphlet called *Asterisks,* circulated in manuscript.

Before the altercation had progressed any further, it was taken out of Luther's hands by another Wittenberg professor, John Bodenstein of Carlstadt, a man destined to play an important part in the Protestant revolt. Though careful to incur no great danger, he was by nature a revolutionary, and longed to out-Luther Luther. While the latter was away at Heidelberg in the spring of 1518, Carlstadt came forward with a set of theses against Eck on free will and the authority of scripture. The Ingolstadt professor answered these with some counter-theses, in which an extreme view of the papal supremacy was maintained. Carlstadt, who held a benefice directly from the Pope, was not prepared to answer this point, but Luther had no such scruples, and towards the end of the year he published twelve propositions directed against Eck. Of these the most important was the twelfth:

The assertion that the Roman church is superior to all other churches is proved only by weak and vain (*frigidis*) papal decrees of the last four hundred years, against which militate the accredited history of eleven hundred years, the Bible, and the decree of the Nicene Council, the holiest of all councils.

This unheard-of attack on the power of the Roman see made an immense sensation. Eck could not leave it unnoticed, nor did he wish to, and therefore arranged that he should debate with both Wittenberg professors. A letter from Luther—according to modern notions a very rude one—written during the course of negotiations, is illuminating:

TO JOHN ECK AT INGOLSTADT
Wittenberg, February 18, 1519

I wish you salutation and that you may stop seducing Christian souls. I regret, Eck, to find so many reasons to believe that your professed friendship for me is hypocritical. You boast that you seek God's glory, the truth, the salvation of souls, the increase of the faith, and that you teach of indulgences and pardons for the same reasons. You have such a thick head and cloudy brain that, as the apostle says, you know not what you say. . . .

I wish you would fix the date for the disputation or tell me if you wish me to fix it. More then. Farewell.

Leipzig was finally chosen as the ground for the debate. The faculty of that university made some difficulties, fearing to become involved, but Duke George of Albertine Saxony, maintaining that the advancement of Christian truth was the chief end of the university, forced them to yield. During the next six months Luther's principal occupation was the preparation for the battle, for which he plunged eagerly into the study of church history and especially of the Canon Law. The results of these researches, which left a lasting influence on his mind, are brilliantly portrayed in two letters written on the same day to his best friend:

TO GEORGE SPALATIN AT ALTENBERG
Wittenberg, about February 24, 1519. (Letter no. 1)

Greetings. I beseech you, dear Spalatin, be not fearful nor let your heart be downcast with human cares. You know that if Christ did not rule me, I should have perished long ago, either at the first controversy about indulgences, or when my sermon on them was published, or when I promulgated my Resolutions, or when I answered Prierias, or recently in the interview at Augsburg, especially as I went thither. What mortal man was there who did not either fear or hope that I would cause my death by one of these things? In fact Olsnitzer recently wrote from Rome to our honorary chancellor, the Duke of Pomerania, that my Resolutions and Answer to Prierias had so perturbed the Roman church that they were at a loss how to suppress them, but that they intended to attack me not by law, but by Italian subtlety—these were his very words. I understand this to mean poison or assassination.

I repress much for the sake of the Elector and university which otherwise I should pour out against that spoiler of the Bible and the church, Rome, or rather Babylon. For the truth of the scripture and of the church cannot be spoken, dear Spalatin, without offending that beast. Do not therefore hope that I shall be quiet or safe in future unless you wish me to give up theology altogether. Let my friends think me mad. For the thing will not be ended (if it be of God) even should all my friends desert me as all Christ's disciples and friends deserted him, and the truth be left alone to save herself by her own might, not by mine nor by yours nor by any man's. I have expected this hour from the first.

My twelfth proposition was extorted from me by Eck, but, as the Pope has defenders enough, I do not think they ought to take it ill unless they forget the freedom of debate. At all events, even should I perish, nothing will be lost to the world. For my friends at Wittenberg have now progressed so far, by God's grace, that they do not need me at all. What will you? I fear I am not worthy to suffer and die for such a cause. That will be the blessed lot of better men, not of so foul a sinner. . . .

TO GEORGE SPALATIN AT ALTENBERG
Wittenberg, about February 24, 1519. (Letter no. 2)

Greetings. I had just finished my last letter, dear Spalatin, when Carlstadt gave me the letter which you sent him, full of such complaints that I was almost moved to rage. You urge me to tell my plan. I am not unwilling for you to know what I intend, but I know the best way to defeat a plan is to tell it, especially if the matter be of God, who does not like his plans to be laid bare before they are fulfilled. . . .

You know that I have to do with a crafty, arrogant, slippery, loud-mouthed sophist, whose one aim is to traduce me publicly and hand me over to the Pope devoted to all the furies. You will understand his iniquitous snares if you read his twelfth proposition. Wherefore, considering his craft, and seeing that I was about to be ruined by his arts, I carefully prepared *my* twelfth proposition, that he may imagine that he has most certainly triumphed, and while singing a paean of joy, shall forthwith expose himself to the scorn of all, God willing. For I know that at this stage of the debate he will burst forth passionately gesticulating and shouting that I cannot prove my assertion, but have made a mistake in reckoning time (as you also think), and that it is much more than four hundred years ago, more than a thousand, since the time of Pope Julius I, directly after the Nicene Council, that the Roman church published decrees asserting that she was the superior of all and that no council could be called without her assent. Relying on these statements he will even laugh, I hope, at my incredible folly and rashness.

Then I shall say that these decrees were not then

received, and that if Gregory IX, the first collector of the decretals (who in the time of Frederick II canonised St Francis, St Dominic, and our own St Elizabeth, i.e. is not yet dead four hundred years), and if Boniface VIII, author of the sixth book of decretals, and Clement V, author of the Clementines, had not collected these decretals and published them, Germany would doubt-less never have known them. Therefore it is to be attri-buted to these three popes that the decretals of the Roman pontiffs were spread abroad and the Roman tyranny was established.

To what conclusion do these arguments tend? I deny that the Roman church is superior to all churches, but not that she is our superior, as she now is *de facto*. How will Eck prove that the church of Constantinople, or any Greek church, or that of Antioch or Alexandria or Africa or Egypt, was ever under the Roman church or received bishops confirmed by her? . . .

We Germans established the authority of the popes as much as we could when the empire was transferred to us, and in return we have borne them as a punishment of the furies, headsmen and tormentors and blood-suc-kers of archbishoprics and bishoprics.

I call the decretals 'vain' because they twist scriptural texts to their own purposes, texts which speak nothing of government but only of scriptural food and faith. . . .

I count the papal power as a thing indifferent, like wealth or health or other temporal goods, and am very sorry that so much is made of temporal matters, which are insisted on as if by the command of God, though he always teaches that they should be despised. How can I bear with equanimity this perverse interpretation of God's Word and that wrong opinion, even if I allow the power of the Roman church as a thing convenient?

Farewell.
Brother Martin Luther, Augustinian

Of the sojourn in Leipzig (June 27–July 18), the reception there and the debate itself, the best account is given by Luther in the letter next translated. The encounter was held in a richly decorated hall of the Pleissenburg, a castle only recently torn down to make way for the new Rathaus. A large and distinguished audience had gathered, including Duke George, later one of the most determined opponents of the new doctrine.

An eyewitness has left us the first description of Luther as he appeared on this occasion, and one which agrees well with Cranach's earliest portrait of him, the wood-cut of 1520. He was of middle height, so emaciated that one could almost count his bones, yet he seemed in the vigor of manhood. His voice was clear and distinct. Polite and cheerful in society, he affected no stoicism, but gave each hour its due. His serene countenance was never disturbed. The richness and fluency of his Latin diction was noticed, as was his careful preparation of the material.

Only contemporaries could appreciate the ability of the speakers in this debate, full notes of which have been preserved. In learning and force of argument the honours seem to be about equal. Eck manoeuvred skilfully to make Luther's opinions appear identical with those of Huss. The latter took up the challenge, and on the second day of the combat boldly asserted: 'It is certain that among the articles of John Huss and the Bohemians there are many which are most Christian and evangelical, which the universal church is not able to condemn.' These words sent a thrill through the audience: Duke George put his arms akimbo, shook his head, and said loudly, 'That's the plague.'

Eck had accomplished his point in driving Luther to a position of universally acknowledged heresy. He played his advantage with great skill, taxing his opponent over and over with being a Hussite, Luther often interrupting him with 'It is false,' or, 'He lies impudently.'

After the question of the papal supremacy was put aside

for other points, the debate, which continued until July 14, was comparatively tame. Let us now hear what Luther has to say about it:

TO GEORGE SPALATIN AT ALTENBERG
Wittenberg, July 20, 1519

... I should have written long ago about this famous debate of ours, but I had neither the time nor place to do it. Certain men of Leipzig, neither candidly nor justly, triumph with Eck and babble of his fame, but you can judge of it from my account.

Almost the instant that we came, before we had descended from our wagons, the Inhibition of the Bishop of Merseburg was fixed to the doors of the churches, alleging against the debate some new points, declaratory and other. This was disregarded, and he who had posted the notice was thrown into chains by the Town Council because he had done it without their knowledge.

Accomplishing nothing by this trick, they resorted to another. Having called Carlstadt aside, they urged him (at Eck's desire) to agree that the debate should not be reported in writing, for he hoped to get the better of us by shouting and gesticulating, in which points indeed he is our superior. Carlstadt said that the agreement had already been made and must be adhered to, and that the debate should be reported. At length, to obtain this point at all, he was forced to consent that the report of the debate should not be published prior to the decision of the judges. Then a new dispute arose about choosing them. At length they forced him to consent that the judges should be chosen after the disputation was finished, otherwise they would not debate at all. Thus they put us on the horns of a dilemma, so that in either case we should have the worst of it, whether we refused to debate on these terms, or recognised the necessity of submitting to unjust judges. See how plain is their guile by which they would filch the freedom we had agreed upon! For we know that the universities and the Pope will either never decide or will decide against us, which is just what they desire.

The next day they called me aside and proposed the same thing. I refused their conditions, fearing the Pope. Then they proposed the universities as judges without the Pope. I asked that the conditions agreed be observed, and when they refused I withdrew and declined to debate. At once an uncontradicted report went abroad that I dared not, and what was worse would allow no judge. The affair was bandied about and interpreted in the most odious and malignant light, so that they even won over our best friends and bequeathed a lasting shame to our university. So I went to them with conciliatory friends, and accepted their conditions, even though indignant at them. But I reserved my power of appeal and excluded the Roman Curia, so that there might be no prejudice to my case.

Eck and Carlstadt debated a week on free will. Carlstadt with God's help advanced splendid and copious arguments and citations and brought books to prove his points. A chance was thus given Eck to oppose Carlstadt; he refused to debate unless the books were left at home, because by them Carlstadt could prove the correctness of his own quotations from the Bible and the Fathers and the inaccuracy of Eck's. So another tumult arose. At length it was decided for Eck that the books should be left at home, but who cannot see that when a question of truth is at stake it is desirable to have the books at hand? Never did hatred and ambition show themselves more impudently than here.

At last the man of guile conceded all that Carlstadt argued for, although he had violently opposed it, and agreed with him in all, boasting that *he* had brought Carlstadt over to *his* opinion. He abandoned Scotus and the Scotists, Capreolus and the Thomists, saying that the schoolmen had thought and taught the same as Carlstadt. Then and there fell Scotus and Capreolus with their respective schools!

The next week he debated with me—at first sharply about the primacy of the Pope. His strength lay in the words, 'You are Peter', 'Feed my lambs', 'Follow me', and 'Strengthen thy brethren', together with a lot of quotations from the Fathers. (You will soon see what I answered.) Then, resting his whole weight on the Council of Constance, which had condemned the assertion of Huss that the papacy was dependent on the Emperor, he went to the extreme length of saying that it bore sway by divine right. Thereupon, as if entering the arena, he cast the Bohemians in my teeth, and charged me with being an open heretic and an ally of the Hussites. For the sophist is no less insolent than rash. These charges tickled the Leipzig audience more than the debate itself.

In rebuttal I pointed to the Greeks for a thousand years, and to the ancient Fathers who had not been under the sway of the Roman pontiff to whom I did not deny a precedence of honour. Then I discussed the authority of a council. I said openly that some articles had been wrongly condemned [sc. by the Council of Constance], as they had been taught in the plainest words by Paul, Augustine, and even Christ himself. At this point the reptile swelled up, painted my crime in the darkest colours, and almost drove the audience wild with his rhetoric. At length I proved from the words of that council that not all the articles there condemned were heretical and erroneous, so that his mode of proof accomplished nothing. And thus the matter rested.

The third week we debated penance, purgatory, indulgences, and the power of a priest to absolve. For he did not care about his dispute with Carlstadt, but only that with me. Indulgences fell through completely and he agreed to almost all I said, so that their use was turned to scorn and mockery. He hoped this would be

the subject of a future debate with me, as he said in public, that people might understand that he made no great
matter of indulgences. He is said to have granted that
had I not disputed the power of the Pope he would have
agreed with me easily on all points. He even confessed to
Carlstadt: 'If I could only agree with Luther as much as I
do with you, I would go home with him at once.' The
man is fickle and subtle, ready to do anything. He who
once said to Carlstadt that the schoolmen taught the
same as he, said to me that Gregory of Rimini was the
only one who supported me against all others. Thus he
thinks it no fault to assert and deny the same thing at
different times. Nor do the men of Leipzig grasp this, so
great is their stupidity. And what is still more monstrous,
he asserts one thing in the academy and another in the
church to the people. Asked by Carlstadt why he did
this, the man shamelessly replied that the people ought
not to be taught points on which there was doubt.

My part thus ended, he debated the last three days
with Carlstadt, agreeing to and yielding all: that spontaneous action is sin; that free will without grace can do
nothing but sin; that there is sin in every [natural] good
work; that it is only grace which enables a man to do
what he can for the Disposer of grace—all of which the
schoolmen deny. So in the whole debate he treated nothing as it deserved except my thirteenth proposition. In
the meantime he congratulates himself, triumphs and
reigns, but only until we shall have published our side.
As the debate turned out badly, I shall draw up additional propositions.

The citizens of Leipzig never greeted us nor visited us,
but acted like the bitterest enemies; but Eck they followed and clung to and invited to dinners in their
houses and gave him a robe and a chamois-hair gown.
They escorted him around on horseback; in fact they
tried everything they could think of to insult us.
Moreover, they persuaded Caesar Pflug and Duke

George to let these things pass. They did give us one thing, the customary present of wine, which perhaps it would not have been safe for them to omit. The few who favoured us came to us clandestinely, but Dr Stromer of Auerbach, a man of upright mind, invited us and so did Professor Pistorius. Duke George himself invited three of us together. Likewise the most illustrious Duke summoned me by myself and talked much with me about my writings, especially that on the Lord's Prayer, and mentioned that the Hussites expected much from me, and that I had raised doubts in many consciences about the Lord's Prayer, so that many complained that they would not be able to say one paternoster in four days if they thought they ought to believe me, and much else to the same effect. Nor was I so stupid as not to know the difference between a fife and a f—; I regretted that the excellent and pious prince should represent and comply with the feelings of others when I saw he was so clever in speaking like a prince about his own.

The last exhibition of hatred was this: when on the day of St Peter and St Paul [June 29] I was asked by our rector, the Duke of Pomerania, to read the gospel in the chapel of the castle, suddenly the report of my preaching filled the city, and such a vast concourse of men and women came to hear me that I was compelled to preach in the debating-hall, with all the professors and other hostile listeners sitting around. The gospel for the day [Matthew 16:13–19] clearly takes in the subject of both debates, and so I was forced to expound the substance of the disputations to all, to the great annoyance of Leipzig.

Stirred up by this, Eck preached four times thereafter in different churches, reviling me and attacking all I had said. Thus those would-be theologians bade him do. But *I* was not allowed to preach again, although many asked it. I was only to be accused and criminated without a chance to defend myself. They acted on the same principle in the debate, so that Eck, although in the negative, had the last word, which I could not refute.

When Caesar Pflug heard that I had preached (for he was not then present), he said, 'I wish Dr Luther would save his sermons for Wittenberg.' In short, I have known hatred before, but never more shameless nor more impudent.

Here you have the whole tragedy. Dr Planitz will tell you the rest, for he was present in person. Because Eck and Leipzig sought their own glory and not the truth, it is no wonder that they began badly and ended worse. For whereas we hoped to make peace between Wittenberg and Leipzig, they acted so odiously that I fear it will rather seem that discord and mutual dislike are now first born. I, who try to bridle my impetuosity, am not able to banish all dislike of them, because I am flesh and their impudent hatred and malignant injustice were overbearing in so sacred and divine a cause.

Farewell and commend me to the most illustrious Elector. . . .

Yours,
Martin Luther

It is plain from this letter that the writer was smarting under the sense of outrage. If he had not been defeated, he had been out-manoeuvred. Such debates, of course, decide nothing. Each party remained strengthened in its own opinion. In this case, too, the universities, to whom the decision was submitted, put off giving it for one reason or another.

Yet the disputation at Leipzig was a turning-point. It showed that the Wittenberg monk was no longer in a position where reconciliation with the church was possible. In the train of one combat followed a cloud of polemics, half the Germans who could write taking sides against the new leader, and the other half for him. As this bickering—for that is what most of it was—left little permanent result, it need not find a large place in the biography of Luther, even though he took an active part in the controversy.

7

The Burning of the Canon Law and of the Pope's Bull, 1520

The action against Luther for heresy at Rome had been allowed to sleep since the beginning of 1519 on account of the exigencies of politics. The death of the Emperor Maximilian in January of that year made necessary the election of a successor. Of the three principal candidates Leo X preferred the Elector of Saxony, who, it was thought, would make both the weakest and most docile Emperor. Frederick was so highly esteemed for his personal qualities that he might have stood a good chance of the election, but feeling that the position would be too great for his resources, he did not press his own cause, but threw his great weight into the scale for the Hapsburg candidate against the Valois. It was, perhaps, largely due to his efforts that on June 28, 1519, Charles of Spain was chosen.

After these events had wrecked the hopes of the Curia, and especially after the Leipzig debate had brought Luther's heresy into a stronger light than ever before, the process against the Saxon was renewed. Another effort was made to induce the Elector to give him up; indeed Saxony was threatened with the interdict in case he did not comply, though later events showed that the Pope hardly dared use such a drastic measure. The threat did not succeed; Frederick replied in his usual courteous and procrastinating style that Miltitz had undertaken to bring Luther's case before the Archbishop of Trier for judgement, and that the Curia had no right to threaten the ban and interdict before the result of this attempt at reconciliation was known.

This letter worked like a declaration of war. A consistory was held at Rome on January 9, 1520, in which Ghinnucci, who had charge of Luther's case, thundered against the peaceful, pious prince as a raging tyrant, the enemy not only of the clergy but of the whole Christian religion.

The Pope at once appointed a commission, consisting of Cajetan, Accolti, the generals and procurators of the Dominican and Franciscan order, and others, to draw up a bull against the heretic. Except the first two they were all poor theologians, but making up in zeal what they lacked in knowledge, they proceeded in short order to damn *all* Luther's propositions as rank heresy. Leo, being advised by the wiser heads among the cardinals that such a sweeping position would be untenable, dissolved the first commission in February and appointed a second, consisting of Cajetan, Accolti, the generals of the orders, and some of the best theologians in Rome. This body, proceeding more cautiously, drew up a report carefully distinguishing a number of propositions as 'partly heretical, partly scandalous, and partly offensive to pious ears'. They recommended that a bull be drawn up condemning these propositions without mentioning Luther's name, and that a final summons be sent him to come to Rome and recant. In other words, they held that a peaceful solution of the problem was still possible. Following their advice, Leo commanded Volta to write to Staupitz asking him to force his brother to recant. Whether Staupitz tried to obey this letter of March 15, 1520, is not known; but in the following August he resigned his office in the order and shortly after secured a dispensation to become a Dominican.

Towards the end of March a sudden and decisive

change in the papal policy was caused by the arrival of Eck. Since the great debate this zealous Catholic had been busy going around to the universities trying to get them to decide in his favour and condemn Luther; two of them, Cologne and Louvain, did so. Eck then turned his steps to Rome, where he painted his enemy's heresy in such black colours that Leo decided there was nothing left but to condemn him, and accordingly appointed a third commission, of Cajetan, Eck, Accolti, and the Spanish Augustinian Johannes, with orders to draft a bill for this purpose. Accolti was the draftsman for the committee; the theological material was largely supplied by Eck from the condemnation of Luther's doctrines by the University of Louvain.

The bull was presented for ratification before a consistory held on May 21, which decided, before promulgating the document, to hear the theologians who had drawn it up. This was done in three sittings of May 23, May 25, and June 1. No record of debates in these consistories has been published, but the fact is recorded that there were long arguments before the bull received the assent of the College of Cardinals. It is possible that a peace party was against the use of force even at this late stage, but it is more probable that the opposition came from a Spanish cardinal, Carvajal, who belonged to the conciliar party in the church and was offended by the designation of Luther's appeal to a council as heretical. Whatever opposition there was, however, was finally overcome, the bull was ratified and signed by Leo at his hunting lodge at Magliana on June 15.

According to the provision of the Canon Law, that before a heretic is finally condemned he must be given a fatherly warning, this bull, *Exsurge Domine*, does not excommunicate Luther, but only threatens this penalty in case he does not recant within sixty days after its publication in Germany. Beginning with the words: 'Arise, Lord, plead thine own cause, arise and protect the vineyard thou gavest Peter from the wild beast who is devouring it,' the bull sets forth some of the professor's opinions, quoted apart from their context, designates them as 'either heretical, or false, or scandalous, or offensive to pious ears, or misleading to the simple', and condemns them. If, after all the Pope's fatherly care and admonition, Luther does not recant within sixty days after the posting of the bull in Germany, he is to be declared a stiff-necked, notorious, damned heretic, and must expect the penalties due to his crime.

Before this document was ratified, Cardinal Raphael Riario had written to the Elector, on May 20, urging him to force the heretic to recant or expect the consequences. The letter only arrived on July 6, and, as we have seen, made a great impression upon the Wittenberg professor. Frederick answered it quite promptly, enclosing *An Offer or Protestation* (*Oblatio sive Protestatio*), drawn up by Luther, proposing to leave his doctrine to the arbitrament of impartial judges. This arrived in Rome by the end of July.

Eck, who had been so instrumental in drawing up the bull, was commissioned to post it in Germany. Before he had done so, however, the document had been published there (August) by Ulrich von Hutten, who judged that it would injure the church more than her enemy. Eck posted it officially at Meissen, Merseburg, and Brandenburg near the end of September. He also tried to force it on the universities of Germany, many of whom declined to receive it on technical grounds. At Wittenberg the faculty would have nothing to do with it, and at Erfurt the students seized all the printed copies and threw them into the river.

Having threatened the heretic with excommunication, Rome left no stone unturned to secure his condemnation by the empire. Charles was coming from Spain to be crowned in October 1520, and to hold his first diet at Worms early in 1521. To him and to the nation Leo despatched two nuncios, Aleander and Caracciola. Leaving Rome on July 27, 1520, Aleander arrived in Cologne, where he published the bull on September 22. Four days later he was in Antwerp, and on September 28 he had an audience with Charles and secured from him the first decree against Luther and his followers in the Netherlands. On October 8, the indefatigable legate published the bull at Louvain and solemnly burned the condemned books, at the same time making a speech violently attacking Erasmus, who lived there, for supporting the heretic. For this Aleander was hurt in a bitter anonymous satire— the *Acta Academiae Lovaniensis*—which may have come from the pen of the great humanist. On October 17, the nuncio did at Liège what he had done at Louvain.

Charles was crowned Emperor at Aix-la-Chapelle on October 23. The plague breaking out in the overcrowded town, the royal suite, including the legate, was forced to leave soon after, and went to Cologne, where they arrived on October 28. Here they found the Elector Frederick, who, having started out to attend the coronation, had been detained by an attack of gout. He had posted up Luther's *Offer or Protestation,* and had with him a letter from the monk to the Emperor, written about August 31. It is a humble appeal:

> That I dare to approach your Most Serene Majesty with a letter, most excellent Emperor Charles, will rightly cause wonder to all. A single flea dares to address the king of kings. But the wonder will be less if the greatness of the cause is considered, for as truth is worthy to approach the cause of celestial Majesty, it cannot be unworthy to appear before an earthly prince. It is a fair thing for earthly princes, as images of the heavenly Prince, to imitate him, as they also sit on high, but must have respect for the humble things of the earth and raise up the poor and needy from the mire. Therefore I, poor and needy, the unworthy representative of a most worthy cause, prostrate myself before the feet of your Most Serene Majesty.
>
> I have published certain books, which have kindled

the hatred and indignation of great men against me, but I ought to be protected by you for two reasons: first, because I came unwillingly before the public, and only wrote when provoked by the violence and fraud of others, seeking nothing more earnestly than to hide in a corner, and secondly, because, as my conscience and the judgement of excellent men will testify, I studied only to proclaim the gospel truth against the superstitious traditions of men. Almost three years have elapsed, during which I have suffered infinite wrath, contumely, danger, and whatever injuries they can contrive against me. In vain I seek respite, in vain I offer silence, in vain propose conditions of peace, in vain beg to be better instructed; the only thing that will satisfy me is for me to perish utterly with the whole gospel.

When I had attempted all in vain, I hoped to follow the precedent of Athanasius and appeal to the Emperor. . . . So I commend myself, so I trust, so I hope in your Most Sacred Majesty, whom may our Lord Jesus Christ preserve to us and magnify for the eternal glory of his gospel. Amen.

Again on October 3, 1520, Luther had written to Spalatin:

Many think I should ask the Elector to obtain an imperial edict in my favour, declaring that I should not be condemned nor my books prohibited except by warrant of scripture. Please find out what is intended; I care little either way, because I rather dislike having my books so widely spread, and should prefer to have them all fall into oblivion together, for they are desultory and unpolished, and yet I do want the matters they treat of known to all. But not all can separate the gold from the dross in my works, nor is it necessary, since better books and Bibles are easily obtainable.

It was in accordance with the plan here indicated that on October 31 the Elector had a conference with the Emperor in the sacristy of the cathedral, and the latter promised that he would allow Luther the way of the law which the professor himself had proposed.

On Sunday, November 4, the legates also obtained an audience with Frederick. Aleander handed him a letter certifying that he was commissioned by the Pope, and demanded, first, that the heretic's books be burned, and second, that he be either punished by Frederick or delivered up bound. The next day the Elector sent for Erasmus, who happened to be in the city, and asked him if Luther had erred. For answer he received the winged word, which flew to the farthest ends of Germany: 'Yes. He has erred in two points, in attacking the crown of the Pope and the bellies of the monks.' The learned humanist drew up twenty-two short propositions which he called *Axioms*, stating the best solution to the difficulty would be for the Pope to recommend the decision on this matter to a tribunal of learned and impartial men. On a second interview with the nuncios on November 6, Frederick refused their requests and insisted on such a court as Erasmus had recommended.

The time given Luther to recant expired on one of the last days of November. Instead of doing so, however, he hit back at his oppressors with his usual spirit. He first published two short manifestos, *Against the New Bull Forged by Eck*—for like Erasmus he doubted the genuineness of the document—and *Against the Execrable Bull of Antichrist*. But his most dramatic answer was solemnly to burn the bull along with the whole Canon Law. The notice to the students, drawn up and posted by Melanchthon early on the morning of December 10, reads as follows:

Let whosoever adheres to the truth of the gospel be present at nine o'clock at the church of the Holy Cross outside the walls, where the impious books of papal decrees and scholastic theology will be burned according to ancient and apostolic usage, inasmuch as the boldness of the enemies of the gospel has waxed so great that they daily burn the evangelical books of Luther. Come, pious and zealous youth, to this pious and religious spectacle, for perchance now is the time when the Antichrist must be revealed!

At the set time a large crowd gathered just outside the Elster gate, near the Black Cloister, but beyond the walls; the students built a pyre, a certain 'master', probably Melanchthon, lit it, and Luther threw on the whole Canon Law with the last bull of Leo X, whom he apostrophised in these solemn words: 'Because thou hast brought down the truth of God, he also brings thee down into this fire today. Amen.' Others threw on the works of the schoolmen and some of Eck and Emser. After the professors had gone home, the students sang funeral songs and disported themselves at the Pope's expense.

Luther now justified his act by publishing an *Assertion of All the Articles Condemned by the Last Bull of Antichrist*, which appeared in Latin in December 1520, and in German in March 1521. In this he states that his positions have not been refuted by scripture in the bull—whether that document is genuine or not. But if one cannot found his creed on the Bible now, he adds, why did Augustine have the right to do it eleven hundred years ago? He then takes up, one by one, the forty-one articles condemned, and proves that they are right. In view of later developments the most interesting of these proofs is that of the 36th article, on free will. Since the fall of man, says the Wittenberg professor, free will is simply a name; when a man does what is in him he sins mortally. He cites Augustine to the effect that free will without grace is able to do nothing but sin. He quotes many texts of the Bible to prove this point and argues it at length.

Nothing was now left to the church but to excommunicate the rebel and fulfil the threat of the *Exsurge Domine*. The 'holy curse' was drawn up and signed at Rome on

January 3, 1521, and sent to Aleander to publish in Germany. It banned not only Luther but Hutten, Pirkheimer, and Spengler, and denounced the Elector Frederick. The wise legate received the terrible document at the Diet of Worms, and rightly fearing that in this form 'it would prove destructive to the cause of the church', sent it back with a recommendation to modify it. This was done; in its final form the bull *Decet Pontificem Romanum* confined itself to excommunicating the heresiarch, and was then, on May 6, published at Worms, three weeks after he had already been heard by the Diet.

8

The Diet of Worms, 1521

From Cologne Charles V proceeded to Worms, where he was about to open his first diet. The varied programme of the national assembly included the drafting of a constitution for the empire and the formulation of grievances against the tyranny of the Roman hierarchy. It could hardly hope to avoid the religious question then agitating the whole nation, but the unprecedented course of summoning the heretic to answer before the representatives of his nation was not decided on until after the estates had been sitting for a month.

Luther himself, in appealing to the Emperor, did not expect to be called before the Diet; he hoped to be allowed to defend his doctrines before a specially appointed tribunal of able and impartial theologians. This plan was pressed quietly but vigorously by Erasmus, the foremost living man of letters. Besides his action in urging Frederick to insist on such a trial for his subject, the great humanist had, at Cologne, handed to the counsellors of the Emperor a short memorial, *Advice of One Heartily Wishing the Peace of the Church,* proposing the appointment of such a commission. He partly won over the Emperor's confessor, Glapion, but Chièvres and Gattinara, the real powers behind the imperial throne, remained in opposition. A little later at Worms, John Faber, a Dominican friar, came forward with a similar plan, composed with the help of Erasmus.

Such a solution of the difficulty would have been most distasteful to the Curia. Regarding the Wittenberg professor's opinions as *res adjudicatae*, the Romanists saw no reason for giving him a chance to defend them, and wished only to punish the man already condemned. This course was urged by Aleander, an extremely able and unscrupulous diplomat. His chief support was the young Emperor, whose formal, backward mind failed to comprehend and even detested any variation from the faith in which he had been brought up. Though by no means a fool, he was a dull man, slow to learn and slow to forget, but possessed of two extremely valuable qualities, moderation and persistence. Of the Lutheran affair he had no understanding whatever. Not being able to speak German, he was unable to sympathise with even the nationalist side of the formidable movement. On May 12, 1520, Manuel, his ambassador at Rome, suggested that he use Luther as a lever to wring concessions from the Pope, but the idea found no root in his mind; from the first his opposition to the schismatic was a foregone conclusion.

Aleander worked with admirable diligence and consummate ability to win powerful supporters among the electors and great men of Germany. By skilful negotiation and concession he secured the adhesion of Joachim I of Brandenburg, for many years the leader of the Catholic party in Germany. He tried hard to get the unqualified backing of Albert of Mainz by the same means, but failed, partly because of the counter-negotiations of Erasmus and his friend Capito. The Elector of Mainz therefore represented a mediating policy.

Aleander's strongest opponent was Frederick of Saxony, 'that fox and basilisk', as he called him, a crafty statesman who knew well how to protect his obnoxious subject without too deeply involving himself. Among the other members of the college, the Elector Palatine was not unfavourable to Luther.

The common people were strongly in favour of Luther. 'Nine tenths of the Germans', wrote Aleander, 'shout "Long live Luther," and the other tenth "Death to Rome."' Foremost among his adherents was Hutten, who with his followers hung like a cloud near Worms, threatening to burst and sweep away the Papists should any harm come to the bold monk of Saxony.

When the alternative plan of Aleander was announced to Luther in Wittenberg—to summon him not before an impartial tribunal to discuss his doctrines but before the estates to recant—he wrote as follows:

TO GEORGE SPALATIN AT ALLSTEDT
Wittenberg, December 21, 1520

Greetings. Today I received copies of your letter from Allstedt and also of that from Kindelbrück asking me what I would do were I summoned before the Emperor Charles as my enemies wish, in case I could go without danger to the gospel and the public safety.

If I am summoned I will go if I possibly can; I will go ill if I cannot go well. For it is not right to doubt if I am summoned by the Emperor I am summoned by the Lord. He lives and reigns who saved the three Hebrew children in the furnace of the king of Babylon. If he does not wish to save me, my life is a little thing compared to that of Christ, who was slain in the most shameful way, to the scandal of all and the ruin of many. Here is no place to weigh risk and safety; rather we should take care not to abandon the gospel which we have begun to preach to be mocked by the wicked, lest we give cause to our enemies of boasting that we dare not confess what we teach and shed our blood for it. May Christ the merciful prevent such cowardice on our part and such a triumph on theirs. Amen. . . .

It is certainly not for us to determine how much danger to the gospel will accrue by my death. . . .

One duty is left for us: to pray that the empire be

saved from impiety and that Charles may not stain the
first year of his reign with my blood or with that of any
other. I should prefer, as I have quite often said, to
perish only at the hands of the Romanists so that the
Emperor may not be involved in my cause. You know
what nemesis dogged Sigismund after the execution of
Huss; he had no success after that and he died without
heirs, for his daughter's son Ladislaus perished, so that
his name was wiped out in one generation and moreover
his queen Barbara became infamous as you know,
together with the other misfortunes which befell him.
Yet if it be the Lord's will that I must perish at the hands
not of the priests but of the civil authorities, may his will
be done. Amen.

Now you have my plan and purpose. You may expect
me to do anything but flee or recant; I will not flee,
much less will I recant. May the Lord Jesus strengthen
me in this. For I can do neither without peril to religion
and to the salvation of many.

In similar tone Luther wrote a month later to his best
patron.

TO THE ELECTOR FREDERICK OF SAXONY
AT WORMS

Wittenberg, January 25, 1521

Most serene, highborn Prince, most gracious Lord!
My poor prayers and humble obedience are always at
your Grace's service.

I have received with humble thankfulness and pleasure your Grace's information about his Imperial and
Royal Majesty's intentions regarding my affair, and I
humbly thank his Imperial Majesty and your Grace for
your favour. I rejoice from my heart that his Imperial
Majesty proposed to take up this business, which is
rather God's, Christendom's, and the German nation's
than mine or that of any individual.

I am humbly ready, as I always have been, and as I

have often said I would be (especially in a pamphlet recently published of which I am sending your Grace a copy), to do and allow all that may be done with God and Christian honour, or all which I shall be convinced by honourable, Christian, and sufficient reasons of Holy Writ that I ought to do or allow.

Therefore I humbly pray your Grace to pray to his Imperial Majesty to provide me with sufficient protection and a free safe-conduct for all emergencies, and that his Imperial Majesty should command the business to be recommended to pious, learned, impartial Christian men, both clerical and lay, who are well grounded in the Bible, and have understanding of the difference between human laws and ordinances. Let such men try me, and, for God's sake, use no force against me until I am proved unchristian and wrong. Let his Majesty, as the temporal head of Christendom, in the meantime restrain my adversaries, the papists, from accomplishing their raging, unchristian plans against me, such as burning my books and grimly laying snares for my body, honour, well-being, life, and salvation, although I am unheard and unconvicted. And if I, more for the protection of the divine, evangelical truth, than for the sake of my own little and unworthy person, have done aught against them, or shall be compelled to do aught, may his Majesty graciously excuse my necessary means of protection, and keep me in his gracious care to save the divine word. I now confidently commit myself to the virtue and grace of his Majesty, and of your Grace and all Christian princes, as to my most gracious lords.

And so I am, in humble obedience, ready, in case I obtain sufficient surety and a safe-conduct, to appear before the next Diet at Worms and before learned, pious, and impartial judges, to answer to them with the help of the Almighty, that all men may know in truth that I have hitherto done nothing from criminal, reckless, disordered motives, for the sake of worldly honour and profit, but that all which I have written and taught has been according to my conscience and sworn duty as a teacher of the Holy Bible, for the praise of God and for the profit and salvation of all Christendom and the advantage of the German nation, in order to extirpate dangerous abuses and superstitions and to free Christendom from so great, infinite, unchristian, damnable, tyrannical injury, molestation, and blasphemy.

Your Grace and his Majesty will have an eye and a care to the much troubled state of all Christendom; as your Grace's chaplain I am humbly and dutifully bound to pray God for his mercy and favour on you and his Imperial Majesty at all times.

Your Grace's obedient, humble chaplain,
Martin Luther

Now, if ever, Luther's plain heroism showed itself. Daily expecting an awful crisis not only in his own life but in all that he held dear, he went quietly about his business, teaching, preaching, and doing whatever his hand found to do. While writing polemics 'against ten hydras' his deeply untroubled spiritual life found expression in a tract on the Magnificat, in which Mary's canticle became again the song of the triumph of the lowly and the meek. His determination to stand fast never wavered; he often quoted Christ's words that whoso denied his Lord before men would be denied by him before his heavenly Father. While so firm himself, he was much saddened by the irresolution of some of his friends, especially of his still beloved and revered Staupitz. After laying down his office as Vicar of the Augustinians, the old man had retired to distant Salzburg, where the learned and orthodox archbishop, Cardinal Lang, received him warmly. But even here he could not escape the tumult of the battle; for Lang tried hard to get him to denounce Luther openly. On January 4, 1521, Staupitz wrote pathetically to Link, acknowledging that 'Martin has undertaken a hard task and acts with great courage illuminated by God; I stammer and am a child needing milk.' Nevertheless, but a little later he wrote an open letter submitting himself to the judgement of the Pope, a document intended as a compromise and as non-committal, but one which was generally taken as a renunciation of the reformed teaching. On seeing the declaration, Luther wrote Staupitz a letter equally solemn and gentle; he does not judge his old friend, but it is impossible not to feel all the more strongly the contrast between the irresolution of the one man and the unyielding courage of the other.

TO JOHN STAUPITZ AT SALZBURG
Wittenberg, February 9, 1521

Greetings. I wonder, reverend Father, that my letters and pamphlets have not reached you, as I gather from your letter to Link that they have not. Conversations with men take so much of my time that preaching unto others I have myself become a castaway. . . .

At Worms they have as yet done nothing against me, although the papists contrive harm with extraordinary fury. Yet Spalatin writes the evangelical cause has so much favour there that he does not expect I shall be condemned unheard. . . .

I have heard with no great pain that you are attacked by Pope Leo, for thus the cross you have preached to others you may exemplify yourself. I hope that wolf, for you honour him too much to call him a Lion (Leo), will not be satisfied with your declaration, which will be interpreted to mean that you deny me and mine, inasmuch as you submit to the Pope's judgement.

If Christ love you he will make you revoke that declaration, since the Pope's bull must condemn all that you have hitherto taught and believed about the mercy of God. As you knew this would be the case, it seems to me that you offend Christ in proposing Leo for a judge, whom you see to be an enemy of Christ running wild (*debacchari*) against the word of his grace. You should have stood up for Christ and have contradicted the Pope's impiety. This is not the time to tremble but to cry aloud, while our Lord Jesus is being condemned, burned, and blasphemed. Wherefore as much as you exhort me to humility I exhort you to pride. You are too yielding, I am too stiff-necked.

Indeed it is a solemn matter. We see Christ suffer. Should we keep silence and humble ourselves? Now that our dearest saviour, who gave himself for us, is made a mock in the world, should we not fight and offer our lives for him? Dear father, the present crisis is graver than many think. Now applies the gospel text: 'If anyone is ashamed of me and my words, the Son of Man will be ashamed of him when he comes in his glory and in the glory of the Father and of the holy angels' [Luke 9:26]. May I be found guilty of pride, avarice, adultery, murder, opposition to the Pope, and all other sins rather than be silent when the Lord suffers and says: 'I looked on my right hand and beheld, but there was no man that would know me: refuge failed me; no man cared for my soul.' By confessing him I hope to be absolved from all my sins. Wherefore I have raised my horns with confidence against the Roman idol, and the true Antichrist. The word of Christ is not the word of peace but the word of a sword. But why should I, a fool, teach a wise man?

I write this more confidently because I fear you will take a middle course between Christ and the Pope, who are now, you see, in bitter strife. But let us pray that the Lord Jesus with the breath of his mouth will destroy this son of perdition. If you do not wish to, at least let me go and be bound. With Christ's aid I will not keep still about this monster's crimes before his face.

Truly your submission has saddened me not a little, and has shown me that you are different from that Staupitz who was the herald of grace and of the cross. If you had said what you did, before you knew of the bull and of the shame of Christ, you would not have saddened me.

Hutten and many others write strongly for me and daily those songs are sung which delight not that Babylon. Our elector acts as constantly as prudently and faithfully, and at his command I am publishing my *Defence* in both languages. . . .

In the meantime Luther's enemies were not idle. Aleander addressed the Diet on February 18, painting the new heresy in the blackest colours, touching lightly on the points with which the Germans would sympathise, but bearing his whole weight on certain opinions relative to the sacrament which would shock most of them, and demanding, in conclusion, that proper steps be taken to extirpate the impending schism and its author. After a stormy debate the Estates decided to summon Luther to recant the objectionable heresies, and to be questioned on certain other points, namely, those relative to the power of the Pope and the grievance of the German nation. The Emperor accordingly drew up a formal summons, addressing the excommunicated man as 'honourable, dear, and pious', giving as the purpose of the citation 'to obtain information about certain doctrines originating with you and certain books written by you', and assuring certain safe-conduct to and from the Diet. Charles also endeavoured to get the Diet to pass a decree for the burning of the heretic's books, but failing in this, he issued a mandate on his own responsibility directing that they be delivered up to the magistrate and no more copies be printed.

Even now an attempt was made by the party of mediation to obtain a declaration from Luther which would obviate the necessity of his appearance before the Diet. Glapion, the Emperor's confessor, possibly acting at the suggestion of Erasmus, held a friendly interview with Spalatin in which he pointed out that all might be amicably settled if Luther would repudiate a few articles. These he had drawn from the *Assertion of all the Articles Wrongly Condemned*, and from the *Babylonian Captivity;* the latter he thought might be the more easily given up, as the book had appeared anonymously. When these articles were forwarded by Spalatin, the Wittenberg professor replied as follows:

TO GEORGE SPALATIN AT WORMS
Wittenberg, March 19, 1521

Greetings. I have received the articles they ask me to recant, with the list of things they want me to do. Doubt not that I shall recant nothing, as I see that they rely on no other argument than that I have written (as they pretend) against the usages and customs of the church. I shall answer the Emperor Charles that if I am summoned solely for the sake of recantation I shall not come, seeing that it is all the same as if I had gone thither and returned here. For I can recant just as well here if that is their only business. But if he wishes to summon me to my death, holding me an enemy of the empire, I shall offer to go. I will not flee, Christ helping me, nor abandon his word in the battle. I am assuredly convinced that those bloody men will never rest until they slay me. I wish if it were possible that only the Pope's followers should be guilty of my blood. We are turned again as we were before Christ, so firmly does Antichrist hold the kingdoms of this world captive in his hand. The Lord's will be done. Use your influence, where you can, not to take part in this council of the ungodly. . . .

Martin Luther, Augustinian

The expected summons and safe-conduct reached Luther on March 26. After quietly finishing some literary work, he set out, on April 2, accompanied by his colleague Amsdorf, a brother monk, and a talented young student named Swaven. Horses and wagon were provided by the town, and the university voted twenty gulden to cover the necessary expenses. The journey was a triumphal progress; the people thronged to see the bold asserter of the rights of conscience. At Erfurt, where Luther preached, he was given a rousing reception by the students and their professor, the humanist Eoban Hess. Notwithstanding popular sympathy, there was considerable danger in going to Worms: in spite of an imperial safe-conduct, Huss had been burned. When Spalatin wrote reminding his friend of this precedent, he received the following answer:

TO GEORGE SPALATIN AT WORMS
Frankfurt am Main, April 14, 1521

I am coming, dear Spalatin, even if Satan tries to prevent me by a worse disease than that from which I am now suffering, for I have been ill all the way from Eisenach, and am yet ill, in a way I have not hitherto experienced.

I know that the mandate of Charles has been published to terrify me. Truly Christ lives and I shall enter Worms in the face of the gates of hell and the princes of the air. I send copies of the Emperor's summons. I think it better not to write more until I can see on the spot what is to be done, lest perchance I should puff up Satan, whom I propose rather to terrify and despise. Therefore prepare a lodging.

Martin Luther

Finding that Luther was not to be intimidated, the Catholics, who were more frightened than he was, tried by a stratagem to prevent his appearance or at least to delay it until the time granted had expired. The Emperor's confessor, Glapion, in an interview with Sickingen, Hutten, and Bucer, assumed a friendly attitude, and proposed that instead of exposing himself to the danger of an appearance the heretic should hold a private conference with himself in a neighbouring castle. Bucer was dispatched with this proposition. Luther knew no way but the direct one, however, and proceeded.

On the morning of April 16 he arrived at his destination, greeted by a vast concourse of people, and took up his abode in the hostel of the Knights of St John. He was summoned to the Diet the next day at four o'clock, though he was not admitted until nearly six.

Few moments in history have been at once so dramatic and so decisive as that in which Luther appeared before the Emperor and Diet at Worms. In the greatness of the tribunal, of the accused, and of the issues involved, nothing is lacking to impress a thoughtful mind. In the foreground of the assembly sat the young Emperor, on whose brows were united the vast, if shadowy, pretensions to Roman dominion and the weight of actual sovereignty over a large collection of powerful states. Around him were the representatives of the Free Cities of Germany. The nuncios, representing the supreme power of the church, were conspicuous by their absence; the Pope would not even hear the rebel in his own defence.

The son of peasants now stood before the son of Caesars: the poor and till lately obscure monk before a body professing to represent the official voice of united Christendom. To challenge an infamous death was the least part of his courage: to set up his own individual belief and conscience against the deliberate, ancient, almost universal opinion of mankind required an audacity no less than sublime.

And how much depended on his answer! The stake he played for was not his own life, nor even the triumph of this religion or of that: it was the cause of human progress. The system against which he protested had become the enemy of progress and of reason: the church had become hopelessly corrupt and had sought to bind the human mind in fetters, stamping out in blood all struggles for freedom and light. Hitherto her efforts had been successful: the Waldenses had perished; Wycliffe had spoken and Huss had died in vain. But now the times were ripe for a revolution; men only needed the leader to show them the way.

The proceedings were short and simple. An officer first warned the prisoner at the bar that he must say nothing except in answer to the questions asked him. Then John Eck, Official of Trier (not to be confused with the debater of the same name), asked him if the books lying on the table were his and whether he wished to hold to all that he had said in them or to recant some part. At this point Jerome Schurf, a jurist friendly to the Wittenberg monk, cried out: 'Let the titles of the books be read.' When this had been done, Luther replied:

His Imperial Majesty asks me two things, first whether these books are mine, and secondly, whether I will stand by them or recant part of what I have published. First, the books are mine, I deny none of them. The second question, whether I will reassert all or recant what is said to have been written without warrant of scripture, concerns faith and the salvation of souls and the divine word, than which nothing is greater in heaven or on earth, and which we all ought to reverence; therefore it would be rash and dangerous to say anything without due consideration, since I might say more than the thing demands or less than the truth, either of which would bring me in danger of the sentence of Christ, 'If anyone is ashamed of me and my words, the Son of Man will be ashamed of him.' Wherefore I humbly beg your Imperial Majesty to grant me time for deliberation, that I may answer without injury to the divine word or peril to my soul.

After consulting the Emperor and his advisers, Eck replied:

Although, Martin, you knew from the imperial mandate why you were summoned, and therefore do not deserve to have a longer time given you, yet his Imperial Majesty of his great clemency grants you one day more, commanding that you appear tomorrow at this time and deliver your answer orally and not in writing.

Though Luther knew the general reason of his summons, he had been surprised by the form in which the question was put to him. He had expected that certain articles would be brought forward and that he would have an opportunity to state the reasons why he held them and to defend them in debate. When he was required to recant point-blank, without any chance to present his case and without hearing what particular things he was to recant, he was taken unprepared. Seeing how necessary it was to have his answer in exact form, he had only done the wisest thing. Some, however, inferred from this request and from the low tone in which it was uttered, that his spirit was broken. How little this was the case may be seen by a letter written the same evening to an imperial counsellor and humanist at Vienna, John Cuspinian. After leaving the assembly hall, Luther went to his lodgings, where he was visited by nobles and others who wished him well. Among them was George Cuspinian, a canon of Würzberg, who had followed his bishop to the Diet. He gave such warm assurances of good-will from his cousin, the more noted John, that the Reformer found time to acknowledge them:

TO JOHN CUSPINIAN AT VIENNA
Worms, April 17, 1521

Greetings. Your brother, most famous Cuspinian, has easily persuaded me to write to you from the midst of this tumult, since I have long wished to become person-ally acquainted with you on account of your celebrity. Take me, therefore, into the register of your friends, that I may prove the truth of what your brother has so generously told me of you.

This hour I have stood before the Emperor and Diet, asked whether I would revoke my books. To which I answered that the books were indeed mine, but that I would give them my reply about recanting tomorrow, having asked and obtained no longer time for consider-ation. Truly, with Christ's aid, I shall never recant one jot or tittle. Farewell, my dear Cuspinian.

The following day he appeared at the same hour before

the august assembly. Eck addressed him in an oration of which the following summary is given by one present, probably Spalatin:

His Imperial Majesty has assigned this time to you, Martin Luther, to answer for the books which you yesterday openly acknowledged to be yours. You asked time to deliberate on the question whether you would take back part of what you had said or would stand by all of it. You did not deserve this respite, which has now come to an end, for you knew long before why you were summoned. And everyone —especially a professor of theology—ought to be so certain of his faith that whenever questioned about it he can give a sure and positive answer. Now at last reply to the demand of his Majesty, whose clemency you have experienced in obtaining time to deliberate. Do you wish to defend all of your books or to retract part of them?

Luther, now certain of what to say, made a great oration, at first in German and then in Latin, the substance of which, as written down by himself immediately afterwards, is here translated:

Most Serene Emperor, Most Illustrious Princes, Most Clement Lords! At the time fixed yesterday I obediently appear, begging for the mercy of God, that your Most Serene Majesty and your Illustrious Lordships may deign to hear this cause, which I hope may be called the cause of justice and truth, with clemency; and if, by my inexperience, I should fail to give anyone the titles due to him, or should sin against the etiquette of the court, please forgive me, as a man who has not lived in courts but in monastic nooks, one who can say nothing for himself but that he has hitherto tried to teach and to write with a sincere mind and single eye to the glory of God and the edification of Christians.

Most Serene Emperor, Most Illustrious Princes! Two

questions were asked me yesterday. To the first, whether I would recognise that the books published under my name were mine, I gave a plain answer, to which I hold and will hold for ever, namely, that the books are mine, as I published them, unless perchance it may have happened that the guile or meddlesome wisdom of my opponents has changed something in them. For I only recognise what has been written by myself alone, and not the interpretation added by another.

In reply to the second question I beg your Most Sacred Majesty and your lordships to be pleased to consider that all my books are not of the same kind.

In some I have treated piety, faith, and morals so simply and evangelically that my adversaries themselves are forced to confess that these books are useful, innocent, and worthy to be read by Christians. Even the bull, though fierce and cruel, states that some things in my books are harmless, although it condemns them by a judgement simply monstrous. If, therefore, I should undertake to recant these, would it not happen that I alone of all men should damn the truth which all, friends and enemies alike, confess?

The second class of my works inveighs against the papacy as against that which both by precept and example has laid waste all Christendom, body and soul. No one can deny or dissemble this fact, since general complaints witness that the consciences of all believers are snared, harassed, and tormented by the laws of the Pope and the doctrines of men, and especially that the goods of this famous German nation have been and are devoured in numerous and ignoble ways. Yet the Canon Law provides (e.g., distinctions 9 and 225, questions 1 and 2) that the laws and doctrines of the Pope contrary to the gospel and the Fathers are to be held erroneous and rejected. If, therefore, I should withdraw these books, I would add strength to tyranny and open windows and doors to their impiety, which would then flourish and burgeon more freely than it ever dared before. It would come to pass that their wickedness would go unpunished, and therefore would become more licentious on account of my recantation, and their government of the people, thus confirmed and established, would become intolerable, especially if they could boast that I had recanted with the full authority of your Sacred and Most Serene Majesty and of the whole Roman Empire. Good God! In that case I would be the tool of iniquity and tyranny.

In a third sort of books I have written against some private individuals who tried to defend the Roman tyranny and tear down my pious doctrine. In these I confess I was more bitter than is becoming to a minister of religion. For I do not pose as a saint, nor do I discuss my life but the doctrine of Christ. Yet neither is it right for me to recant what I have said in these, for then tyranny and impiety would rage and reign against the people of God more violently than ever by reason of my acquiescence.

As I am a man and not God, I wish to claim no other defence for my doctrine than that which the Lord Jesus put forward when he was questioned before Annas and smitten by a servant: he then said: If I have spoken evil, bear witness of the evil. If the Lord himself, who knew that he could not err, did not scorn to hear testimony against his doctrine from a miserable servant, how much more should I, the dregs of men, who can do nothing but err, seek and hope that someone should bear witness against my doctrine. I therefore beg by God's mercy that if your Majesty or your illustrious Lordships, from the highest to the lowest, can do it, you should bear witness and convict me of error and conquer me by proofs drawn from the gospels or the prophets, for I am most ready to be instructed and when convinced will be the first to throw my books into the fire.

From this I think it is sufficiently clear that I have carefully considered and weighed the discords, perils, emulation, and dissension excited by my teaching, concerning which I was gravely and urgently admonished yesterday. To me the happiest side of the whole affair is that the Word of God is made the object of emulation and dissent. For this is the course, the fate, and the result of the Word of God, as Christ says: 'I am come not to send peace but a sword, to set a man against his father and a daughter against her mother.' We must consider that our God is wonderful and terrible in his counsels. If we should begin to heal our dissensions by damning the word of God, we should only turn loose an intolerable deluge of woes. Let us take care that the rule of this excellent youth, Prince Charles (in whom, next to God, there is much hope), does not begin inauspiciously. For I could show by many examples drawn from scripture that when Pharaoh and the king of Babylon and the kings of Israel thought to pacify and strengthen their kingdoms by their own wisdom, they really only ruined themselves. For he taketh the wise in their own craftiness and removeth mountains and they know it not. We must fear God. I do not say this as though your lordships needed either my teaching or my admonition, but because I could not shirk the duty I owed Germany. With these words I commend myself to your Majesty and your Lordships, humbly begging that you will not let my enemies make me hateful to you without cause. I have spoken.

Eck replied with threatening mien:

Luther, you have not answered to the point. You ought not to call in question what has been decided and condemned by councils. Therefore I beg you to give a simple, unsophisticated answer without horns (*non cornutum*). Will you recant or not?

Luther retorted:

Since your Majesty and your Lordships ask for a plain answer, I will give you one without either horns or teeth. Unless I am convicted by scripture or by right reason (for I trust neither in popes nor in councils, since they have often erred and contradicted themselves)—unless I am thus convinced, I am bound by the texts of the Bible, my conscience is captive to the word of God, I neither can nor will recant anything, since it is neither safe nor right to act against conscience. God help me. Amen.

The Spaniards in the audience broke into groans and hisses, the Germans into applause, and Luther was conducted from the hall amid an incipient tumult. When he reached his lodgings, he joyfully exclaimed: 'I am through! I am through!' He had indeed done the great deed he had set out to do and spoken the words which will ring through ages.

But his business at Worms was not yet over. The moderate Catholics, hoping that something could yet be accomplished, held a series of conferences with him. Their representatives were Cochlaeus, later one of the bitterest enemies of the Evangelical church, Dr Vehus, chancellor of the Margrave of Baden, and the Archbishop Elector of Trier. But nothing came of the negotiations. Luther hardened himself, as one of his opponents expressed it, like a rock.

On April 26 he left Worms. Two days later he reached Frankfurt where he wrote an interesting letter to Lucas Cranach, his warm friend, the Wittenberg artist. In 1520 the monk had stood godfather to the painter's little daughter, and in return Cranach made two woodcuts of him, the one in 1520, the other in March 1521. This last, giving him so plain an impression of iron will and strength of character that all who run may read, is perhaps the best portrait of the Reformer in existence.

TO LUCAS CRANACH AT WITTENBERG
Frankfurt am Main, April 28, 1521

My humble greetings to you, dear friend Lucas. I bless and commend you to God. I am going somewhere to hide, though I myself do not yet know where. I should indeed suffer death at the hands of the tyrants, especially at those of furious Duke George, but I must not despise the advice of good men nor die before the Lord's time.

They did not expect me to come to Worms, and what my safe-conduct was worth you all know from the mandate that went out against me. I thought his Majesty the Emperor would have brought together some fifty doctors to refute the monk in argument, but in fact all they said was: 'Are these books yours?'—'Yes.'—'Will you recant?'—'No!'—'Then get out.' O we blind Germans, we act so childishly and let ourselves be fooled by the Romanists.

God bless you and keep your mind and faith in Christ against the Roman wolves and serpents and their adherents. Amen.

Dr Martin Luther

On May 1 he reached Hersfeld, where he was royally welcomed by the abbot of the Benedictine monastery and where he preached. On May 2 he entered his dear old Eisenach, where he also delivered a sermon the next day. On the third he drove through the beautiful forests to Möhra, his father's early home, and visited his uncle Heinz Luther. On the morning of May 4 he preached in the open air, and after dinner set out in the direction of Schloss Altenstein with Amsdorf and a brother monk. In the heart of the forest, in a place now marked by a monument, according to a preconcerted plan some masked riders appeared, captured the banned heretic, and rode with him back in the direction of Eisenach to the Wartburg, the castle in which the Elector had decided to keep him.

In this charming spot Luther remained hidden almost a year, obeying the command of his wary sovereign. The room assigned to him was not in the main building, but in a small one. It was reached by a narrow flight of stairs which led immediately from the entrance to the chamber. It has been preserved as it was in his day, with the old stove, bedstead, table, and stump which served as a stool. As he sat by the leaded-glass window, his eye swept the wild landscape for many miles towards the west.

In the meantime great events were happening at Worms. Charles had been sincerely shocked at the audacity of the rebel monk. The usually reserved young man immediately drew up a paper, perhaps the one frank and spontaneous action of his whole career, stating that he had resolved to stake life, lands, and all on the maintenance of the Catholic faith of his fathers. Aleander, thinking that all was settled, was delighted. After waiting until the Elector of Saxony and other supporters of the new leaders had left Worms, Charles drafted an edict, submitted it for approval to four electors and a few remaining members of the Diet, and signed it May 26—although it was officially dated May 8. The Edict of Worms described Luther's doctrine in the strongest terms as a cesspool of heresies old and new, put him under the ban of the empire, forbade any to shelter him and commanded all, under strong penalties, to give him up to the authorities. It was also forbidden to print, sell, or read his books.

When the news of Luther's disappearance spread throughout Europe a cry of dismay arose from all who had his cause at heart. Albrecht Dürer, the painter of Nuremberg, an ardent admirer of the Reformer, then on a visit to Antwerp, heard the news on May 17.

I know not whether he yet lives or is murdered [wrote he in his diary], but in any case he has suffered for the Christian truth. . . . If we lose this man who has written more clearly than anyone who has lived for one hundred and forty years, may God grant his spirit to another. . . . His books are to be held in great honour and not burned as the Emperor commands, but rather the books of his enemies. O God, if Luther is dead, who will henceforth expound to us the gospel? What might he not have written for us in the next ten or twenty years?

9

The Wittenberg Revolution, 1521–1522

While Luther was in retirement at the beautiful old castle near Eisenach, the movement started by him was carried on with accelerated velocity at Wittenberg. Carlstadt's attack on sacerdotal celibacy was only the first step in a revolution. In this movement two distinct factors combined, the one of constructive reform, the other of popular tumult; the best elements of the first were due to Luther, who, while absent, kept up a constant correspondence with Wittenberg; for the second element other leaders were responsible, Carlstadt, Zwilling, and the Zwickau prophets.

The constructive reform was embodied in two city ordinances, the first of November, 1521, the second of January 24, 1522. The earlier bit of legislation provided for 'a common purse', that is, for the public care of the worthy poor, on new principles, deduced from the *Address to the Nobility* and the larger *Sermon on Usury*. It will be remembered how in his great pamphlet the author proposes that begging be prohibited. This was now done by the town of Wittenberg, while the deserving poor, i.e., those who could not support themselves, were provided for from funds voluntarily contributed to the parish church. That not only the ideas but the form of this ordinance proceeded from Luther has been proved from a first draft of the document in his hand recently discovered.

The second decree passed by the town council two months after the first was an extension of the other on more radical lines, doubtless due to the active influence of Zwilling and Carlstadt. It provided that to the common fund should be applied the income from the property of the twenty-one resident brotherhoods, and especially from endowed masses, now regarded as an abomination. The expenses of the common treasury were also greatly enlarged; orphans were to be cared for, students at the schools and university to be helped, poor girls to be supplied with dowries, and workmen loaned capital at four per cent. The laws against begging were re-enacted with additional penalties. A police charged with the surveillance of morals and especially with the suppression of houses of ill-repute was instituted. Finally, a new form of divine service was introduced, by which all pictures and superfluous altars were to be torn down, communion was to be administered in both kinds, and the government bound itself to see that ministers preached only the pure gospel. All the provisions of this comprehensive decree, except the last on public worship, were suggested by Luther.

These reforms, for the most part salutary, were accompanied by others, which, even when unobjectionable in themselves, were carried through with mob violence. The riots began about the first of October, when Gabriel Zwilling, an Augustinian monk, began to preach against the mass and the canonical hours. At his insistence these services were stopped by the monks on October 6 or 7; he then began a campaign against the monastic life itself, not only leaving it free to his brothers to quit the cloister, but forcing them to do so with insults and threats.

Carlstadt now began to attack the mass, and with such success that the priests celebrating it in the parish church on December 3 were stoned, and the day following an altar in the Franciscan convent was destroyed by the students. The arrest of the offenders was the occasion of a worse riot on December 12, when the mob went to the town officers and demanded their release.

The agitation spread. The monks at Erfurt left the cloister tumultuously. A plan was hatched to stop all masses, not only at Wittenberg, but throughout the surrounding country, on January 1, 1522. At Eilenberg a rectory was plundered. On All Saints' Day (November 1) the citizens of Wittenberg demonstrated in force against the Elector's relics in the Castle church.

Much disturbed by the progress of innovation, Luther made a secret visit to his city early in December, lodging with Melanchthon and privately interviewing other friends, among them Lucas Cranach, who painted his picture. He was rather reassured than otherwise by this visit, deciding not to take too tragically a disturbance in the monastery and a few student riots. He accordingly contented himself with remaining a few days, leaving behind him a *Warning to all Christians to Keep from Uproar and Sedition.* This manuscript he also sent to Spalatin, who, however, prudently refused to have it printed until three months later.

> In this year [says Luther] by God's grace the holy light of Christian truth, formerly suppressed by the Pope and his followers, has been rekindled, by which their manifold and noxious corruption and tyranny has been laid bare and scotched. So that it looks as if tumults would arise, and parsons, monks, bishops, and the whole spiritual estate hunted out and smitten unless they apply themselves earnestly to their improvement. For the common man, agitated and disgusted with the harm done to his property, body and soul, means to do something, and vows that he will never suffer such things more, and has reasons at his tongue's end and threatens to smite with flail and cudgel.

The author adds that though the intimidation of the clergy is a good thing, nevertheless tumult is the work of the devil, and all Christians should keep aloof from it and labour only by word of mouth. It may be doubted whether this pamphlet was expressed in really prudent terms, and whether it would not be more likely to excite discontent than to allay it. Nevertheless things might have quieted down had it not been for the powerful reinforcement received by the party of revolution on December 27 in the advent of the Zwickau prophets.

Among the cloth-weavers of this little Saxon town Thomas Münzer, a fanatic, had formed a sect animated with the desire to renovate both state and church by the readiest and roughest means. When the civil authorities, fearing the openly threatened revolt, imprisoned some of the agitators, Münzer escaped to Bohemia, and three of his followers, Nicholas Storch, Mark Thomas Stübner, and Thomas Drechsel, went to Wittenberg. They proclaimed themselves prophets who talked familiarly with God and foresaw the future, revelation coming to them directly from the Spirit. Their mystic quietism was strangely mingled with an anarchist programme for overturning the civil government and extirpating the priests. The most harmless of the dogmas of the new sect, and the one from which they were to derive the name of Anabaptists, was opposition to infant baptism and institence on rebaptising their proselytes.

At Wittenberg the prophets, or 'ranters' as they were also called, found a soil prepared for the seed of their doctrine. According to their suggestions learning was discouraged, dreams were cultivated, and a systematic propaganda of anarchy organised.

The Wittenberg leaders either succumbed to the ascendancy of the prophets or actively joined them. Carlstadt met them more than halfway: he married, retired to a farm, affected to dress like a labourer, and courted popularity by extolling the revelation vouchsafed to babes and sucklings while disparaging the wisdom of the wise. Other Lutherans, like Amsdorf, though they heartily disapproved of the course things were taking, were powerless to stem the tide.

The most responsible and gifted of all the professors left at Wittenberg was Philip Melanchthon. Luther's admiration for this pious and precociously learned young man was so great that he felt perfectly safe in leaving the guidance of the new cause in the latter's hands. 'They will not need me, dear brother,' he said on departing for Worms, 'while you still live.' When he first heard of the new prophets he modestly opined that Melanchthon would be better able to deal with them than he would be. In this he was destined to disappointment. With much delicacy and refinement, Melanchthon possessed the defects of his qualities in a certain want of robustness. Both now, and still more later, at the crises when he was deprived of the other's strong influence, his life was made miserable and his fame tarnished by the exigencies of a situation too large for his powers. In the present instance he wavered, was inclined to believe the argument against infant baptism, was impressed by the pretensions of the prophets, and hoped his friend Storch might meet his friend Luther. The latter's directions to him how to act are interesting not only for their connection with the prophets, but also as a revelation of the writer's inner life:

TO PHILIP MELANCHTHON AT WITTENBERG
January 13, 1522

Greetings. Had the letter of the Archbishop of Mainz come alone it would have satisfied me, but now that Capito's letter is added it is evident that there is some plot. I am greatly disappointed in Capito. I wished to put a stop to that impious trade, but he pleads for it like an attorney, and by teaching the archbishop to confess his private sins thinks to impose on Luther beautifully. I shall restrain myself and not treat the man as he deserves, yet I shall show him that I am alive.

Coming now to the 'prophets', let me first say that I do not approve your irresolution, especially as you are more richly endowed with the Spirit and with learning than I am. In the first place, those who bear witness of themselves are not to be believed, but spirits must be proved. You act on Gamaliel's contrary advice. Hitherto I have heard of nothing said or done by them which Satan could not emulate. Do you, in my place, search out whether they approve their calling. For God never sent anyone who was not either called by men or attested by miracles, not even his own Son. . . . Do not receive them if they assert that they come by mere revelation. . . .

Pray search their innermost spirit and see whether they have experienced those spiritual strengthenings, that divine birth, death and infernal torture. If you find their experiences have been smooth, bland, devout (as they say) and ceremonious, do not approve them, though they claim to have been snatched up to the third heaven. . . . Divine Majesty does not speak directly; rather no man shall see him and live. Nature bears no small stars and no insignificant words of God. . . . Try not to see even Jesus in glory until you have seen him crucified. [Here follows a long argument in favour of infant baptism.]

Keep my book against the Archbishop of Mainz to come out and rebuke others when they go mad. Prepare me a lodging because my translation of the Bible will require me to return to you, and pray the Lord that I may do so in accordance with his will. I wish to keep hidden as long as may be; in the meantime I shall proceed with what I have begun. Farewell.

Yours,
Martin Luther

But Melanchthon was not the man to cope with the situation. Feeling his own weakness he besought the Elector to allow his friend to return and quiet the disturbances, but the cautious prince, fearing openly to acknowledge the outlaw, positively refused to do so.

The tumults continued. On January 11 the Augustinians solemnly burned all their pictures. On January 24 Carlstadt forced the town council against their will to pass the ordinance mentioned above. They disapproved of two things about it: first, the illegal appropriation of the endowments of masses, and secondly, the abolition of all images in the churches, though the innovators described the making of images as worse than theft, murder, and adultery, because it was forbidden in the first commandment, while the other sins were relegated to the following ones.

The disorders attracted the attention of neighbouring princes. Duke George of Albertine Saxony made representations to his cousin and also laid a complaint before the Imperial Executive Council (*Reichsregiment*) at Nuremberg, on January 20. For a moment it looked as if not only sedition but civil war threatened Germany.

On February 1 there was another riot. The government at last took action. Carlstadt was politely requested not to preach and Zwilling judged it best to leave town. The situation was still extremely delicate, however, and, fearing another outbreak, on February 20 the town council, without consulting the Elector, sent an urgent request directly to Luther imploring him to return to his place at Wittenberg.

This letter was probably the earliest intimation the Reformer had had of the continuation of rioting. His first idea was to send another warning to the people, but the more he thought about it the more certain he became that his presence was necessary. He intimated his intention of returning in a letter to his sovereign, ironically referring to the doings at Wittenberg as a cross which would be a valuable addition to Frederick's famous collection of relics. The mild and pious prince answered at once in a letter to John Oswald, one of his officers at Eisenach, bidding him have a personal interview with the Reformer and communicate the contents of the missive. This relates the course of events at Wittenberg, but also emphasises the complaints already made against them by Duke George and the danger of a new process against Luther, whom he advises to have patience and wait at least until after the next diet, to be called about the middle of Lent. The cross Frederick says he is willing to bear.

This letter arrived on February 28 and its contents were

communicated to the refugee just as he had made all preparations to depart. Unhindered by it, he did so the next day, making the dangerous journey alone on horseback. Reaching Jena on March 3, he chanced to meet two Swiss students, John Kessler and Spengler, on their way to Wittenberg to study. One of them has left us, in an account of the evening at the Great Bear inn, a vivid picture of the Reformer and a little drama as well. The scene is the public room of the hostel, heated with the large German tile stove and lighted by candles. At a table sits a stalwart man, no longer thin and not yet stout; his beard, red cap, jerkin and hose, and a long sword, proclaim him a knight. Before him is a glass of beer; one hand rests on the hilt of his weapon, in the other he holds an open book. Enter the two youths, who on account of their muddy boots sit down near the door.

Luther—Good evening, friends. Draw near and have a drink to warm you up. I see you are Swiss; from what part do you come and whither are you going?

Kessler—We come from St Gall, sir, and we are going to Wittenberg.

Luther—To Wittenberg? Well, you will find good compatriots of yours there, the brothers Jerome and Augustine Schurf.

Kessler—We have letters to them. Can you tell us, sir, whether Luther is now at Wittenberg, or where he may be?

Luther—I have authentic information that he is not at Wittenberg, but that he will soon return. But Philip Melanchthon is there to teach Greek, and Aurogallas to teach you Hebrew, both of which languages you should study if you wish to understand the Bible.

Kessler—Thank God that Luther will soon be back; if God grant us life we will not rest until we see and hear that man. For it is on account of him that we are going there. We have heard that he wishes to overturn the priesthood and the mass, and as our parents have brought us up to be priests, we want to hear what he can tell us and on what authority he acts.

Luther—Where have you studied formerly?

Kessler—At Basel.

Luther—How goes it at Basel? Is Erasmus there and what is he doing?

Kessler—Erasmus is there, sir, but what he does no man knows, for he keeps it a secret. (Aside to his companion as Luther takes a drink) I never knew a knight before who used so much Latin, nor one who understood Greek and Hebrew as this one seems to.

Luther—Friends, what do they think of Luther in Switzerland?

Kessler—There are various opinions of him, sir, as everywhere. Some cannot extol him enough, and thank God for having revealed truth and discovered error by him; others, especially the clergy, condemn him as an intolerable heretic.

Luther—One might expect as much from the preachers.

Spengler—(Raising book which he sees is a Hebrew Psalter) I would give a finger to understand this tongue.

Luther—You must work hard to learn it. I also am learning it, and practise some every day.

(It is getting dark. Host bustles up, lights more candles, stops before table.)

Host—I overheard you, gentlemen, talking of Luther. Pity you were not all here two days ago; he was here then at this table, sitting right there (points).

Spengler—If this cursed weather had not hindered us we should have been here and should have seen him. Is it not a pity?

Kessler—At least we ought to be thankful that we are in the same house that he was and at the very table where he sat. (Host laughs, goes towards door; when out of sight of Luther turns and beckons Kessler, who rises anxiously, thinking that he has done something amiss, and goes to host.)

Host (aside to Kessler)—Now that I see that you really want to hear and see Luther, I may tell you that the man at your table is he.

Kessler—You're just telling me because you think I want to see Luther.

Host—No, it is positively he, but don't let on that you know him. (Kessler returns to table, where Luther had begun to read again.)

Kessler (whispering to his companion)—The host tells me this man is Luther.

Spengler—What on earth? Perhaps he said 'Hutten'; the two names sound alike, and he certainly looks more like a knight than a monk.

(Enter two merchants, who take off their cloaks. One of them lays a book on the table.)

Luther—May I ask, friend, what you are reading?

Merchant—Doctor Luther's sermons, just out; have you not seen them?

Luther—I shall soon, at any rate.

Host—Sit down, gentlemen, sit down; it is supper-time now.

Luther—Come here, gentlemen; I will stand treat. (The merchants sit down and supper is served.) These are bad times, gentlemen. I heard only recently of the princes and lords assembling at Nuremberg to settle the religious question and remedy the grievances of the German nation. What do they do? Nothing but waste their time in tournaments and all kinds of wicked diversions. They ought to pray earnestly to God. Fine princes they are! Let us hope that our children and posterity will be less poisoned by papal errors and more given to the truth than their parents, in whom error is so firmly implanted that it is hard to root out.

First Merchant—I am a plain, blunt man, look you, who understand little of this business, but I say to myself, as far as I can see, Luther must be either an angel from heaven or a devil from hell. I would give ten gulden to have the chance to confess to him; I believe he could give me good counsel for my conscience. (The merchants get up and go out to feed their horses.)

Host (to students)—You owe me nothing; Luther has paid it all.

Kessler—Thank you, sir, shall I say Hutten?

Luther—No, I am not he; (to host) I am made a noble tonight, for these Switzers take me for Ulrich von Hutten.

Host—You are not Hutten, but Martin Luther.

Luther (laughing)—They think I am Hutten; you that I am Luther; soon I'll be Prester John. (Raising his glass) Friends, I drink your health (putting down his glass), but wait a moment; host, bring us a measure of wine; the beer is not so good for me, as I am more accustomed to wine. (They drink.)

Luther (rising to say good-night and offering them his hand)—When you get to Wittenberg, remember me to Jerome Schurf.

Kessler—Whom shall we remember, sir?

Luther—Say only that he that will soon come sends his greetings. (Exit.)

The next morning Luther departed early. At Borna, where he arrived on March 5, he wrote his sovereign to apologise for his reference to the latter's hobby of relic-collecting, and to point out why he must go to Wittenberg even if Frederick could no longer protect him there:

TO FREDERICK, ELECTOR OF SAXONY, AT LOCHAU

Borna, March 5, 1522

Favour and peace from God our Father and from the Lord Jesus Christ, and my humble greetings.

Most serene, highborn Prince, most gracious Lord! Your Grace's kind letter reached me Friday evening as I was about to depart the next day. I need not say that I know your Grace meant the best for me, for I am certain

of it as far as a man can be of anything. Indeed my conviction of it is almost superhuman, but that makes no
difference.

I take the liberty of supposing from your Grace's tone
that my letter hurt you a little, but your Grace is wise
enough to understand how I write. I have confidence
that your Grace knows my heart better than to suppose
I would insult your Grace's famous wisdom by unseemly
words. I assure you with all my heart that I have always
had a perfect and unaffected love for your Grace above
all other princes and rulers. What I wrote was from anxiety to reassure your Grace, not for my own sake (of that
I had no thought), but for the sake of the untoward
movement at Wittenberg carried on by our friends to
the detriment of the Evangelical cause. I feared that
your Grace would suffer great inconvenience from it.
The calamity also bore hard on me, so that, had I not
been certain we had the pure gospel, I should have
despaired. To my sorrow the movement has made a
mockery of all the good that has been done and has
brought it to naught. I would willingly buy the good
cause with my life could I do so. Things are now done
for which we can answer neither to God nor to man.
They hang around my neck and offend the gospel and
sadden my heart. My letter, most gracious Lord, was for
those men, and not for myself, that your Grace might
see the devil in the drama now enacting at Wittenberg.
Although the admonition was unnecessary to your
Grace, yet it was needful for me to write. As for myself,
most gracious Lord, I answer thus: Your Grace knows
(or, if you do not, I now inform you of the fact) that I
have received my gospel not from men but from heaven
only, by our Lord Jesus Christ, so that I might well be
able to boast and call myself a minister and evangelist, as
I shall do in future. I offered to be tried and judged, not
because I had doubts myself, but to convince others and
from sheer humility. But now I see that my too great

humility abuses the gospel, and that if I yield a span the devil will take all. So I am conscientiously compelled to resist. I have obeyed your Grace this year [by staying at Wittenberg] to please you. The devil knows I did not hide from cowardice, for he saw my heart when I entered Worms. Had I then believed that there were as many devils as tiles on the roof, I would have leaped into their midst with joy. Now Duke George is still far from being the equal of one devil. Since the Father of infinite mercy has given us rich confidence to call him dearest Father, your Grace can see for yourself that we are lords even of Duke George's wrath. I am fully persuaded that had I been called to Leipzig instead of Wittenberg, I should have gone there, even if (your Grace will excuse my foolish words) it had rained Duke Georges nine days and every duke nine times as furious as his one. He esteems my Lord Christ a man of straw, but my Lord and I can suffer that for a while. I will not conceal from your Grace that I have more than once wept and prayed for Duke George that God might enlighten him. I will pray and weep once more and then cease for ever. Will your Grace please pray, and have prayers said by others, that we may turn from him the judgement that (God knows) is always in wait for him. I could slay him with a single word.

I have written this to your Grace to inform you that I am going to Wittenberg under a far higher protection than that of the Elector. I do not intend to ask your Grace's protection. Indeed I think I shall protect you rather than you me. If I thought your Grace could and would defend me by force, I would not come. The sword ought not and cannot decide a matter of this kind. God alone must rule it without human care and co-operation. He who believes the most can protect the most, and as I see your Grace is yet weak in faith, I can by no means regard you as the man to protect and save me.

As your Grace desires to know what to do in this

matter, and thinks you have done too little, I humbly answer that you have done too much and should do nothing. God will not and cannot suffer your interference nor mine. He wishes it left to himself; I say no more, your Grace can decide. If your Grace believes, you will be safe and have peace; if you do not believe, *I* do, and must leave your Grace's unbelief to its own torturing anxiety such as all unbelievers have to suffer. As I do not follow your advice and remain hidden, your Grace is excused before God if I am captured or put to death. Before men your Grace should act as a prince of the empire and be obedient to your sovereign, and let his Imperial Majesty rule in your cities over both life and property, as is his right by the Imperial Constitution, and you should not offer any resistance in case he captures and puts me to death. No one should oppose authority save he who ordained it, otherwise it is rebellion and displeasing to God. But I hope they will have the good sense to recognise your Grace's lofty position and so not become my executioners themselves. If your Grace leaves them an open door and free passes, when they come you will have done enough for obedience. They can ask nothing more of your Grace than to inquire if Luther be with you, which will not put your Grace in peril or trouble. Christ has not taught me to be a Christian to injure others. If they are so unreasonable as to ask your Grace to lay hands upon me, I shall then tell your Grace what to do, always keeping your Grace safe from injury and peril in body, soul, or estate, as far as in me is—your Grace may then act as I advise or not as you please. . . .

Your Grace's most humble subject,
Martin Luther

Frederick answered this letter on March 7 with one to the Wittenberg jurist Schurf, bidding him request Luther to draw up a statement that he had only returned to quiet the tumults. The Reformer did as requested on March 9; the Elector was not quite satisfied and a new memorial was accordingly drawn up by Luther on March 12, which the Prince might submit to the Diet soon to assemble in Nuremberg. The reasons here given, and above all the immediate subsidence of tumult, completely satisfied that august body and prevented any measures being taken against the banned heretic or his protector.

10

The Peasants' Revolt, 1525

Peasant risings were not uncommon in Europe for more than a millennium. Such an insurrection had taken place in Gaul in Roman times. Such were the Jacquerie in France in 1358 and the gigantic strike of English labourers in 1381. The struggle for Swiss freedom may also be viewed as a social as well as a national conflict. The fifteenth and early sixteenth centuries saw many local revolts. To the old standing grievances of the lords' tyranny, the heavy taxes and tithes, the game laws, the forced labour and serfdom, common cause of all these risings alike, new motives were added to make this last the most terrible, among them the prevalent intellectual unrest and the powerful leaven of the new religious teaching.

Luther, indeed, could honestly say that he had consistently preached the duty of obedience and the wickedness of sedition, nevertheless his democratic message of the brotherhood of man and the excellence of the humblest Christian worked in many ways undreamed of by himself. Moreover, he had mightily championed the cause of the oppressed commoner against his masters. 'The people neither can nor will endure your tyranny any longer,' he said to the nobles; 'God will not endure it; the world is not what it once was when you drove and hunted men like wild beasts.' Other preachers, among whom Carlstadt and

Münzer were two conspicuous examples, took up the word and carried it to the wildest conclusions of communism and anarchy.

Beginning in the autumn of 1524, in the highlands between the sources of the Rhine and the Danube, the rebellion swept north through Franconia and Swabia. The demands of the insurgents were embodied in the *Twelve Articles,* drawn up not later than February 1525, by a Swabian, Sebastian Lotzer, and tacitly adopted as the official programme by most of the bands of rustics. The fundamental principle of this document is the entire assimilation of civil and divine law; all claims are supported by an appeal to the gospel, under which rule the insurgents declare their intention to live. The articles propose the free election by each parish of its pastor, the reduction of taxes and tithes, the abolition of serfdom, freedom to hunt, fish, and cut wood in the forests, less forced labour, reopening of commons to the public, substitution of the old (German) for the new (Roman) law, and abolition of feudal service.

Continuing to spread, the insurrection reached Thuringia and Saxony about April 1525. In this region all eyes were turned to Luther, the man of the people. In one pamphlet, dated March 7, the peasants requested him, together with Melanchthon, Bugenhagen, and the Elector Frederick to act as arbitrators between them and the lords. As yet Luther had not heard of the atrocities committed by some of the rebels. But there was danger in the air. At the invitation of his old lord, Count Albert of Mansfeld, he journeyed to Eisleben to investigate the situation. Here, while the guest of Chancellor Dürr, on April 19 and 20, he composed *An Exhortation to Peace on the Twelve Articles of the Swabian Peasants.* By this warning, which he states is written in answer to the request of the insurgents for instruction, he hoped to bring both sides to reason and prevent the effusion of blood. He addresses each party by turns, the lords and the commoners. To the former he says:

We need thank no one on earth for this foolish rebellion but you, my lords, and especially you blind bishops, parsons and monks, for you, even yet hardened, cease not to rage against the holy gospel, although you know that our cause is right and you cannot controvert it. Besides this, in civil government you do nothing but oppress and tax to maintain your pomp and pride, until the poor common man neither can nor will bear it any longer. The sword is at your throat, and yet you still think you sit so firm in the saddle that no one can hoist you out. You will find out that by such hardened presumption you will break your necks. . . . If these peasants don't do it, others will; God will appoint others, for he intends to smite you and will smite you.

Some say the rebellion has been caused by Luther's doctrine, but he avers that he has always taught obedience to the powers that be. 'But the prophets of murder are hostile to you as to me, and they have gone among the people these three years and no one has withstood them but I.'

Some of the peasants' articles are right, as the demand to choose their own pastors and the repudiation of the feudal service.

To the peasantry he says: 'It is my friendly and fraternal prayer, dearest brothers, to be very careful what you do. Believe not all spirits and preachers.' Those who take the sword shall perish by the sword and every soul should be subject to the powers that be, in fear and honour. 'If the government is bad and intolerable, that is no excuse for riot and insurrection, for to punish evil belongs not to everyone, but to the civil authority which bears the sword.' Suffering tyranny is a cross given by God. Luther will pray for them.

Coming to a consideration of the *Twelve Articles* he says that even if they were all just, the peasants would have no right to put them through by force. The first article, for the right to elect pastors, is right. The second demand, that the tithes be divided between the priest and the poor, is simply robbery, for the tithes belong to the government. The third, for the abolition of serfdom on the ground that Christ has freed all, makes Christian freedom a carnal thing and is therefore unjustified. The other articles (that on feudal service having been already approved) are referred to the lawyers.

The pamphlet closes with a solemn charge to each side to strive not for its own gain, but for the right, and a warning to keep the peace.

Excellent as were Luther's intentions, his exhortation was imprudently expressed. In any case, however, interference came too late. Already on April 16, the rebel bands had stormed Weinsberg and massacred the inhabitants; within the next two weeks cloisters and castles were burned to the ground, while violence, anarchy, and pillage followed with all the ferocity characteristic of class warfare. The nobles made what terms they could; the towns either capitulated or joined the rising in full force. At Mühlhausen, Münzer, thinking the hour of triumph had come, urged the divine duty of ruthless slaughter.

The princes were entirely unprepared. Old Frederick was lying mortally ill at his castle of Lochau. Without troops and unnerved by disease, he wrote to his brother John that if it was God's will that the common man should rule he would not resist it. John, too, was without hope: 'There are thirty-five thousand men in the field against us,' he wrote; 'we are but lost princes.'

For one awful moment it looked as if the insurgents would carry all before them. Luther saw the whole of Germany threatened with anarchy, and the Evangelical cause with extinction. Never found wanting in the hour of danger, he continued his journey through the disaffected districts, preaching against the rising. According to the somewhat unreliable table-talk, he met with a hostile reception at some places; at any rate his intervention did no good. He found himself, on May 4, at Seeburg, in

Mansfeld. Not a single blow had yet been struck in the cause of order. Luther saw that the only means left to restore peace was force, and accordingly wrote the following stern letter to one of the advisers of the Count of Mansfeld:

TO JOHN RÜHEL AT MANSFELD
Seeburg, May 4, 1525

Grace and peace in Christ. Honoured and dear doctor and friend! I have been intending to answer your last tidings, recently shown me, here on my journey. First of all I beg you not to make our gracious lord, Count Albert, weak in this matter, but let him go on as he has begun, though it will only make the devil still angrier, so that he will rage more than ever through those limbs of Satan he has possessed. We have God's word, which lies not but says, 'He beareth not the sword in vain, etc.,' so there is no doubt that his lordship has been ordained and commanded of God. His Grace will need the sword to punish the wicked as long as there are such sores in the body politic as now exist. Should the sword be struck out of his Grace's hand by force, we must suffer it, and give it back to God, who first gave it and can take it back how and when he will.

May his Grace also have a good conscience in case he should have to die for God's word, for God has so ordered it, if he permits it; no one should leave off the good work until he is prevented by force, just as in battle no one should forgo an advantage or leave off fighting until he is overcome.

If there were thousands more peasants than there are they would all be robbers and murderers, who take the sword with criminal intent to drive out lords, princes, and all else, and make a new order in the world for which they have from God neither command, right, power, nor injunction, as the lords now have to suppress them. They are faithless and perjured, and still worse they bring the divine word and gospel to shame and dishonour, a most horrible sin. If God in his wrath really lets them accomplish their purpose, for which he has given them no command or right, we must suffer it as we do other wickedness, but not acquiesce in it as if they did right.

I hope they will have no success nor staying power, although God at times plagues the world with desperate men as he has done and yet does with the Turks. It is the devil's mockery that the peasants give out that they will hurt no one and do no harm. No harm to drive out and kill their masters? If they mean no harm, why do they gather in hordes and demand that others surrender to them? To do no harm and yet to take all—that is what the devil, too, knows how to do. If we let him do what he likes, forsooth he harms no one.

Their only reason for driving out their lords is pure wickedness. Look at the government they have set up, the worst that ever was, without order or discipline in it but only pillage. If God wishes to chastise us in his wrath, he can find no fitter instrument than these enemies of his, criminals, robbers, murderers, faithless, perjured peasants. If it be God's will, let us suffer it and call them lords as the scripture calls the devil prince and lord. May God keep all good Christians from honouring and worshipping them as the devil tried to make Christ worship him. Let us withstand them by word and deed as long as ever we can, and then die for it in God's name.

They purpose to hurt no one if only we yield to them; and so we should yield to them, should we? Must we indeed acknowledge as our rulers these faithless, perjured, blasphemous robbers, who have no right from God, but only the support of the prince of this world, as he boasts in Matthew, chapter four, that he has dominion and honour over all the world to give it to whom he will? That is true enough when God punishes and does not protect.

This matter concerns me deeply, for the devil wishes to kill me. I see that he is angry that hitherto he has been able to accomplish nothing either by fraud or force; he thinks that if he were only free of me he could do as he liked and confound the whole world together, so I almost believe that I am the cause that the devil can do such things in the world, whereby God punishes it. Well, if I ever get home I will meet my death with God's aid, and await my new masters, the murderers and robbers who tell me they will harm no one. Highway robbers always say the same: 'I will do you no harm, but give me all your have or you shall die.' Beautiful innocence! How fairly the devil decks himself and his murderers! Before I would yield and say what they want, I would lose my head a hundred times, God granting me his grace. If I can do it before I die, I will yet take my Katie to wife to spite the devil, when I hear that they are after me. I hope they will not take away my joy and good spirits.

Some say the insurgents are not followers of Münzer —that let their own god believe, for no one else will.

I write to strengthen you to strengthen others, especially my gracious lord Count Albert. Encourage his Grace to go forth with good spirit, and may God grant him success, and let him fulfil the divine injunction to bear the sword as long as ever he can; conscience at least is safe in case he fall. If God permit the peasants to extirpate the princes to fulfil his wrath, he will give them hell fire for it as a reward. The just judge will come shortly to judge both them and us—us with grace, as we have suffered by their crimes of violence, them with wrath, for they who take the sword must perish by the sword as Christ said. Their work and success cannot long stand.

Greet your dear wife for me.

Dr Martin Luther

Very soon after writing this letter, Luther published a short tract *Against the Thievish, Murderous Hordes of Peasants,* expressed in much the same tone:

> In my former book [*Exhortation to Peace*] I dared not
> judge the peasants, since they asked to be instructed,
> and Christ says Judge not. But before I could look
> around they forgot their request and betook themselves
> to violence—rob, rage, and act like mad dogs, whereby
> one may see what they had in their false minds, and that
> their pretence to speak in the name of the gospel in the
> *Twelve Articles* was a simple lie. They do mere devil's
> work, especially that Satan of Mühlhausen does nothing
> but rob, murder, and pour out blood.

> The peasants have deserved death for three reasons:
> (1) because they have broken their oath of fealty; (2) for
> rioting and plundering; and (3) for having covered their
> terrible sins with the name of the gospel.

> Wherefore, my lords, free, save, help, and pity the poor
> people; stab, smite, and slay all whom you can. If you die
> in battle you could never have a more blessed end, for
> you die obedient to God's word in Romans 13, and in the
> service of love to free your neighbour from the bands of
> hell and the devil. I implore everyone who can to avoid
> the peasants as he would the devil himself. I pray God
> will enlighten them and turn their hearts.

Almost as Luther was writing, steps were taken to suppress the insurgents. On May 5 the Count of Mansfeld,
with a few personal retainers, scattered a small band near
Osterhausen, a success insignificant in itself but important
as the first blow struck for order in central Germany.

The decisive battle followed not long after. Philip of
Hesse, the ablest of the Evangelical princes after Frederick
the Wise, having come to terms with his own peasants by
negotiation, gathered an army and marched, in co-operation with other lords, against eight thousand rebels at
Frankenhausen. Hoping to come to a peaceful agreement,
Philip found the peasants ready to negotiate until on May

12 Münzer arrived with reinforcements from Mühlhausen and roused the poor men by his baleful eloquence to such a pitch of fanaticism, that, in reliance on divine help, they refused all terms. When the troops attacked them on May 15, the raw countrymen fled in the wildest panic, more than half of them perishing on the field. Münzer was captured and put to death.

Rühel sent the tidings to Luther on May 21, and received the following answer:

TO JOHN RÜHEL AT MANSFELD
Wittenberg, May 23, 1525

God's grace and peace. I thank you, honoured and dear sir, for your news. I am especially pleased at the fall of Thomas Münzer. Please let me have further details of his capture and of how he acted, for it is important to know how that proud spirit bore itself.

It is pitiful that we have to be so cruel to the poor people, but what can we do? It is necessary and God wills it that fear may be wrought on the people. Otherwise Satan brings forth mischief. God said: Who hath taken the sword shall perish by the sword. It is gratifying that their spirit be at least so plainly revealed, so that henceforth the peasants will know how wrong they were and perhaps leave off rioting, or at least do it less. Do not be troubled about the severity of their suppression, for it will profit many souls. . . .

After the lords had the upper hand the insurrection was put down with the utmost cruelty. At Frankenhausen and elsewhere the soldiers far outdid the peasants in acts of violence and blood. It is estimated that one hundred thousand of the poor rustics perished, and the rest sank back into a more wretched state than before.

The danger past and the pity of the public aroused, Luther's enemies raised a great outcry against him, accusing him of betraying his allies and the men whom his teaching had misguided, and most of all for the cruelty of his pamphlet. Whatever foundation these charges may have, there is absolutely none in the accusation that he sided with the insurgents while they seemed likely to win and then turned to curry favour with the princes when *they* had triumphed. The direct opposite was the truth, and Luther, excited by these widespread charges, defends himself with spirit in a letter to an old colleague.

TO NICHOLAS AMSDORF AT MAGDEBURG
Wittenberg, May 30, 1525

Grace and peace. You write of a new honour for me, dear Amsdorf, namely that I am called the toady of the princes; Satan has conferred many such honours upon me during the past years. . . .

My opinion is that it is better that all the peasants be killed than that the princes and magistrates perish, because the rustics took the sword without divine authority. The only possible consequence of their satanic wickedness would be the diabolic devastation of the kingdom of God. Even if the princes abuse their power, yet they have it of God, and under their rule the kingdom of God at least has a chance to exist. Wherefore no pity, no tolerance should be shown to the peasants, but the fury and wrath of God should be visited upon those men who did not heed warning nor yield when just terms were offered them, but continued with satanic fury to confound everything. . . . To justify, pity, or favour them is to deny, blaspheme, and try to pull God from heaven. . . .

Thus also, in a note inviting John Rühel to his wedding feast, the Reformer says (June 15, 1526):

What an outcry at Harrow has been caused by my pamphlet against the peasants! All is now forgotten that God has done for the world through me. Now lords, priests, and peasants are all against me and threaten my death.

Rühel accepted the invitation and brought with him a letter from the Chancellor Caspar Müller suggesting that the Reformer should defend himself against the attacks made upon him. In answer to this Luther published in July an open letter to Müller, under the title: *On the Hard Pamphlet Against the Peasants.* In this he has nothing to retract. 'One cannot answer a rebel with reason,' he argues, 'but the best answer is to hit him with the fist until blood flows from his nose.' He never meant to order slaughter after battle, 'but neither did I undertake to instruct those mad, raging, insane tyrants, who even after combat cannot satiate their thirst for blood and never in their whole life ask after Christ, for it is all the same to such bloodhounds whether they are guilty or innocent, or whether they please God or the devil. They use the sword to satisfy their passions, so I leave them to their master the devil.

That Luther really pitied the poor people after their defeat is shown by an intercessory letter:

TO ALBERT,
ARCHBISHOP AND ELECTOR OF MAINZ
Wittenberg, July 21, 1515

Grace and peace in Jesus Christ. Most venerable Father in God, most serene, highborn Prince, most gracious Lord. I am informed that one Asmus Günthel, the son of a citizen of Eisleben, has been arrested by your Grace on the charge of having stormed a barricade. His father is sore distressed and tells me he did not take part in the storming, but only ate and drank there at the time, and as he begged me piteously to intercede for his life I could not refuse him. I humbly pray your Grace to consider that this insurrection has been put down not by the hand of man but by the grace of God who pities us all, and especially those in authority, and that accordingly you treat the poor people graciously and mercifully as becomes a spiritual lord even more than a temporal one. . . .

Alas! there are too many who treat the people horribly

and so act unthankfully to God as if they would recklessly awaken the wrath of heaven and of the people again and provoke a new and worse rebellion. God has decreed that those who show no mercy should also perish without mercy.

It is not good for a lord to raise displeasure, ill-will and hostility among his subjects, and it is likewise foolish to do so. It is right to show sternness when the commonalty are seditious and stubborn, but now that they are beaten down they are a different people, worthy that mercy be shown to them in judgement. Putting too much in a bag bursts it. Moderation is good in all things, and, as St James says, mercy rejoiceth against judgement. I hope your Grace will act as a Christian in this matter. God bless you. Amen.

Your Grace's obedient servant,
Martin Luther

The Peasants' War was the hardest storm weathered by the new church. Had not an iron hand been at the helm it might well have foundered the ship of reform and scattered all that was hopeful and good in it in a thousand fragments. As it was, the cause suffered heavily, and the reputation of its leader suffered still more. In steering too far from the dread whirlpool which would have engulfed all his cause, he sailed too close to the Scylla on the other side and lost men thereby. From his own day to the present he has been reproached with cruelty to the poor people who were partly misguided by what they believed to be his voice. And yet, much as the admirers of Luther must and do regret his terrible violence of expression, the impartial historian can hardly doubt that in substance he was right. No government in the world could have allowed rebellion to go unpunished; no sane man could believe that any argument but arms would have availed. Luther first tried the way of peace, he then risked his life preaching against the rising; finally he urged the use of the sword as the *ultima ratio.* He was right to do so, though he put himself in the wrong by his immoderate zeal. It would have been more becoming for Luther, the peasant and the hero of the peasants, had he shown greater sympathy with their cause and more mercy. Had he done so his name would have escaped the charge of cruelty with which it is now stained.

11

Catharine von Bora

From the fierce war Luther's thoughts were turned to faithful, if unromantic love. Although convinced while still at the Wartburg of the nullity of vows of celibacy, it was a long time, as Erasmus sneered, before he made use of the liberty he preached to others. After all the brothers save one, Brisger, had departed to take up a worldly career, he continued to reside at the Black Cloister, as the Augustinian monastery was called, not from its own colour, a brick red, but from the popular designation of its dark-robed inmates as black monks. Having laid aside their cowls and assumed the simple garb of laymen, the two like-minded men dwelt here with one servant, a student of theology named Sieberger. The building was large, but as the revenues had been dissipated by the custom of giving a handsome present to each departing brother, the two remaining inhabitants dwelt in poverty, for the professor had a salary of but one hundred gulden. One of his reminiscences of this period paints a graphic picture of his manner of life:

> Before I was married, the bed was not made up for a whole year and became foul with sweat. But I worked all day and was so tired at night that I fell into bed without knowing that anything was amiss.

When at last he decided to marry, it was something of an accident that his choice fell upon Catharine von Bora. She had been born, on January 29, 1499, at Lippendorf, a hamlet some twenty miles south of Leipzig. The name Bora (cognate in form and meaning with our word *fir*) is, like that of Staupitz and other aristocratic families of the region, of Wendish or Slavonic origin, but the family, deriving its name from the village of Bora, was Teutonic. Catharine's father, Hans von Bora, held modest estates, a portion of which, the farm of Zulsdorf, later passed by purchase to his famous son-in-law. The mother, Catharine von Haugwitz, died shortly after the birth of her little girl, and Hans, marrying again, sent his five-year-old daughter to the convent school of the Benedictine nuns near Brehna. About four year later he transferred her to a Cistercian cloister at Nimbschen near Grimma, intending that in due time she should become a nun. Nimbschen was a wealthy foundation in which the education of the girls and their taking of the veil were gratuitous; it was therefore largely patronised by gentlemen like Bora of more influence than means. At the time of her entrance, one of her relatives was abbess, and another, Auntie Lena, as she afterwards came to be known at Wittenberg, was a sister.

The quiet years at Nimbschen, hardly broken by Catharine's consecration as a nun at the age of sixteen (October 8, 1515), were spent in the round of devotion, learning and teaching, prayer and charity, which form the routine of monastic life. The girl was well educated; besides the elementary accomplishments of reading and writing her own tongue, she knew some Latin. The cloister had large estates, tilled under the direct supervision of the nuns, so that she may have here gained that knowledge of practical farming which she later turned to good account.

In almost any other age and country, Catharine would have finished her life in the convent as quietly as she had begun it. But she lived in stirring times. Luther's proclamation of monastic emancipation was promptly followed by a general evacuation of the cloisters, especially of those of his own order, one of which was situated at Grimma. Inspired by the example of these monks, several of the sisters at Nimbschen tried to follow it. One who was caught writing to Luther was severely disciplined. This did not prevent the others from doing the same, and it was at his advice that, after vainly applying to their relatives to receive them, twelve of the younger nuns secured the aid of Leonard Coppe, a wealthy and honourable burger of Torgau who had long stood in business relations with Nimbschen. Though the attempt was not without danger, for the abduction of a nun was a capital offence, he, with the assistance of his nephew and another young man, helped them to escape on the night of April 4–5, 1523. Three of them went to their own homes, the other nine were conveyed by Coppe first to Torgau and then to Wittenberg.

The Reformer, who at once took up their cause, defending them in a publication, announces their arrival in these words:

TO GEORGE SPALATIN AT ALTENBERG
Wittenberg, April 10, 1523

Grace and peace. Nine fugitive nuns, a wretched crowd, have been brought to me by honest citizens of Torgua. I mean Leonard Coppe and his nephew Wolf Tomitzsch; there is therefore no cause for suspicion. I pity them much, but most of all the others who are dying everywhere in such numbers in their cursed and impure celibacy. This sex so very, very weak, joined by nature or rather by God to the other, perishes when cruelly separated. O tyrants! O cruel parents and kinsmen in Germany! O Pope and bishops, who can curse you enough? Who can sufficiently execrate the blind fury which has taught and enforced such things? But this is not the place to do it.

You ask what I shall do with them? First I shall inform

their relatives and ask them to support the girls; if they will not I shall have the girls otherwise provided for. Some of the families have already promised me to take them; for some I shall get husbands if I can. Their names are: Magdalene von Staupitz, Elsa von Canitz, Ave Gross, Ave von Schönfeld and her sister Margaret, Laneta von Goltz, Margaret and Catharine Zeschau and Catharine von Bora. Here are they, who serve Christ, in need of true pity. They have escaped from the cloister in miserable condition. I pray you also to do the work of charity and beg some money for me from your rich courtiers, by which I can support the girls a week or two until their kinsmen or others provide for them. For my Capernaäns have no wealth but that of the word, so that I myself could not find the loan of ten guldens for a poor citizen the other day. The poor, who would willingly give, have nothing; the rich either refuse or give so reluctantly that they lose the credit of the gift with God and take up my time begging from them. Nothing is too much for the world and its way. Of my annual salary I have only ten or fifteen gulden left, besides which not a penny has been given me by my brothers or by the city. But I ask them for nothing, to emulate the boast of Paul, despoiling other churches to serve my Corinthians free. . . .

Farewell and pray for me.

Martin Luther

Luther was as good as his word in providing for the fugitives. For Staupitz's sister he interceded so effectually with the clergy of Grimma that a little house was presented her in that town in remembrance of her brother. For another nun the Reformer secured the position of teacher, while most of the rest returned to their relatives or married. The three who remained longest at Wittenberg were Ave and Margaret von Schönfeld and Catharine von Bora. For Ave, Luther felt a certain attraction, even love, but she, too, as well as her sister, married, and of all the Nimbschen runaways, Catharine, whose father was now dead, was left alone. She had been taken into the house of the rich and honourable Reichenbach, who at times held the office of burgomaster at Wittenberg. Here the girl lived about two years, during which time she learned housekeeping, and a marvellously apt pupil she was, to judge by her later ménage.

What a contrast was Wittenberg to Nimbschen! A good deal of the world could be seen in this little town, with its students from all parts of Germany and from foreign lands, too. Here Catharine learned to know many a great man, Lucas Cranach, the artist, and Philip Melanchthon, the preceptor of the fatherland. In October 1523, she was presented to King Christian II of Denmark, on his visit to Wittenberg, and was given a gold ring by the lavish monarch. In all her new experiences the girl's piety and modesty, or perhaps something in her looks, won her the nickname of St Catharine of Siena.

Then she had an unhappy love-affair. Jerome Baumgärtner, a promising youth who had graduated from the university in 1521, in the autumn of 1523 made a long visit to Melanchthon. When he returned to his native Nuremberg there was an understanding, though not a formal engagement, that he should come back and marry Katie. The young man, though his later career was highly honourable, was unable in this case to fulfil his intentions, and his failure to return was so taken to heart by the poor girl that she actually became ill over it. About a year after Baumgärtner's departure, Luther wrote to him: 'If you want your Katie you had best act quickly before she is given to someone else who wants her. She has not yet conquered her love for you and I would willingly see you married to each other' (October 12, 1524).

Jerome, however, stayed away, and in January his betrothal to a rich girl was announced.

The suitor who wanted Katie was a certain Dr Glatz. The Reformer himself had no intention of marriage: 'Not that

I lack the feelings of a man,' as he wrote to Spalatin on November 30, 'for I am neither wood nor stone, but my mind is averse to matrimony because I daily expect the death decreed to the heretic.'

But a little more than a month after this, Luther preached and published his sermon on marriage, highly extolling that estate as the one honoured by all the patriarchs and prophets, and pointing out the duties both of those who wished to marry and of husbands and wives. A little later he issued a regular manifesto in the form of an open letter to a friend who was considering wedlock. One can easily see that the arguments here given apply equally well to the writer's position:

TO WOLFGANG REISSENBUSCH
AT LICHTENBERG
Wittenberg, March 27, 1525

God's grace and peace in Christ. Honoured Sir! I am moved by good friends and by the esteem I bear you to write you this epistle on the estate of matrimony, as I have noticed you would like to marry, or rather are forced to do so by God himself, who gave you a nature requiring it.

O do not think you should be hindered by the rule of the Order or by a vow, for no vow can bind or be valid except under two conditions. First, a vow must be possible of performance, for who would vow an impossible thing, or who would demand it? . . . Now chastity is not in our power, as little as God's other wonders and graces, but we are made for marriage as the scripture says: It is not good for man to be alone: I will make an help meet for him.

Who, therefore, considers himself a man, should hear what God decrees for him. . . . This is the word of God, through whose power seed is created in man's body and the burning desire for the woman kindled and kept alight which cannot be restrained by vows nor laws. . . .

Secondly, that a vow may be valid it must not be against God and the Christian faith, and everything is against that which relies on works and not on God's grace. . . .

It would be a fine, noble example if you married, that would help many feeble ones and give them more scope, so that they might escape the dangers of the flesh. What harm is it if people say: 'So the Lichtenberg professor has taken a wife, has he?' Is it not a great glory that you should thereby become an example to others to do the same? Christ was an example to us all how to bear reproach for conscience' sake. Do I say reproach? Only fools and fanatics think marriage a reproach, men who do not mind fornication but forbid what God has commanded. If it is a shame to take a wife, why is it not a shame to eat and drink, for we have equal need of both and God wills both? . . .

Friend, let us not fly higher nor try to be better than Abraham, David, Isaiah, Peter, Paul, and all the patriarchs, prophets, and apostles, as well as many holy martyrs and bishops, who knew that God had made them men and were not ashamed to be and to be thought so and therefore considered that they should not remain alone. . . .

Luther was evidently intending to marry. In casting about for an eligible wife, his first choice did not fall upon Katie but one of the other nuns. In 1538 he spoke of this inclination in rather a tasteless and rather a heartless way:

Had I wished to marry fourteen years ago, I should have chosen Ave von Schönfeld, now wife of Basil Axt. I never loved my wife but suspected her of being proud (as she is), but God willed me to take pity on the poor abandoned girl and he has made my marriage turn out most happily.

For another girl, perhaps Ave Alemann of Magdeburg,

Luther also had a certain liking, but this yielded to circum-stances and Katie became the sole object of his attentions. When he had tried to marry her to Dr Glatz, Baumgärt-ner's rival, she absolutely refused, saying that she would take Amsdorf or Luther himself but Glatz never. This naturally brought her to the Reformer's attention. He speaks of his various love-affairs in a jocose letter to his confidant:

TO GEORGE SPALATIN AT LOCHAU
Wittenberg, April 16, 1525

I have commended everything to friend Cranach and have asked him to be sure to send a hundred copies of my letter to Reissenbusch. . . .

You write to me about my marriage. Do not be sur-prised if I, so famous a lover, do not wed, though it is really wonderful that I who write so much about mar-riage and have so much to do with women should not turn into a woman, let alone marry one. If you wish for my example you already have it. For I have had three wives at once and loved them so hard that I drove two away to get other husbands. On the third I have a pre-carious hold, but she, too, may soon be torn from me. It is really you who are the timid lover, not daring to marry even one. But take care, lest I, the old bachelor, should get ahead of lusty young bridegrooms like you, for God is accustomed to do what we least expect. I say this seri-ously to encourage you. Farewell, dear Spalatin.

Martin Luther

On the same day on which he wrote this letter Luther started on his trip to Mansfeld to preach against the peas-ants' rising. His already half-formed purpose of taking the frank nun at her word was increased by his father, whom he saw at this time and who urged him to marry. His first announcement of his intention is in the letter to Rühel of May 4, where he says he will take 'his Katie' to wife 'to spite the devil'. The formal betrothal followed soon after, and the wedding, hastened on by malicious gossip about the pair, took place very privately at the Black Cloister on the evening of June 13. Owing to its suddenness, the customary festivities had to be put off until two weeks later, on June 27. Among the invitations sent far and wide, the following have an especial interest:

TO JOHN RÜHEL, JOHN THUR AND CASPAR MÜLLER AT MANSFELD

Wittenberg, June 15, 1525

Grace and peace in Christ. What an outcry at Harrow, my dear sirs, has been caused by my pamphlet against the peasants! All is now forgotten that God has done for the world through me. Now lords, priests, and peasants are all against me and threaten my death.

Well, since they are so silly and foolish, I shall take care that at my end I shall be found in the state for which God created me with nothing of my previous papal life about me. I will do my part even if they act still more foolishly up to the last farewell.

So now, according to the wish of my dear father, I have married. I did it quickly lest those praters should stop it. On Thursday week, June 27, it is my intention to have a little celebration and house-warming, to which I beg that you will come and give your blessings. The land is in such a state that I hardly dare ask you to undertake the journey; however, if you can do so, pray come, along with my dear father and mother, for it would be a special pleasure to me. Bring any friends. If possible let me know beforehand, though I do not ask this if inconvenient.

I would have written my gracious lords Counts Gebbard and Albert of Mansfeld, but did not risk it, knowing that their Graces have other things to attend to. Please let me know if you think I ought to invite them. God bless you. Amen.

Martin Luther

TO GEORGE SPALATIN

Wittenberg, June 16, 1525

Grace and peace. Dear Spalatin, I have stopped the mouths of my calumniators with Catharine von Bora. If we have a banquet to celebrate the wedding we wish you not only to be present but to help us in case we need game. Meantime give us your blessing and pray for us.

I have made myself so cheap and despised by this marriage that I expect the angels laugh and the devils weep thereat. The world and its wise men have not yet seen how pious and sacred is marriage, but they consider it impious and devilish in me. It pleases me, however, to have my marriage condemned by those who are ignorant of God. Farewell and pray for me.

Martin Luther

To Katie's old acquaintance and rescuer he wrote on June 21:

God has suddenly and unexpectedly caught me in the bond of holy matrimony. I intend to celebrate with a wedding breakfast on Thursday. That my parents and all good friends may be merry, my Catharine and I kindly beg you to send us, at my cost and as quickly as possible, a barrel of the best Torgau beer.

To Amsdorf the bridegroom confides that 'I married to gratify my father, who asked me to marry and leave him descendants. . . . I was not carried away by passion, for I do not love my wife that way, but esteem her as a friend. (*Non amo sed diligo*).'

The proudest of the many guests on the great day were assuredly old Hans and Margaret Luther. Among the wedding presents the most prized came from the town, the university, the Elector, and Cranach. Rühel brought a surprise in the way of twenty gulden from Albert of Mainz, who was thinking of becoming Lutheran in order to turn his electorate into a temporal fief as his cousin Albert had done with Prussia. The bridegroom wanted to return this gift, but the thrifty bride managed to keep it.

At this time Martin and Katie sat for their pictures for the celebrated Lucas Cranach. The bridegroom is forty-two, well built and very pale. His face is at once good-humoured and strong. And yet who can be satisfied with this picture? Dürer's criticism that the Wittenberg artist could depict the features but not the soul is extremely just.

The portrait of Katie does not bear out the conjecture of Erasmus that the monk had been led astray by a wonderfully charming girl (*mire venusta*). She was of a type not uncommon among Germans, in whose features shrewdness, good sense, and kindliness often give a pleasant expression to homely persons—though even this can hardly be seen in Cranach's picture. Her scant reddish hair is combed back over a high forehead; the brows over her dark blue eyes slant up from a rather flat nose; her ears and cheek-bones are prominent.

Katie was sometimes reproached with pride and avarice. But that an orphan, without friends, money, or beauty should have any pride left is rather subject for praise than blame, and what is sometimes called her greed of money was only the necessary parsimony of a housewife in narrow circumstances whose husband was uncommonly generous. Without marked spirituality, she was a Martha busied with many things rather than a Mary sitting in devotion at her master's feet. If there was little passion and no romance in the courtship, there was deep devotion and friendship in the twenty years following marriage. Of his own thoughts, and his wife's affection during their first year together, the Reformer once spoke thus:

In the first year of marriage one has strange thoughts. At table he thinks: 'Formerly I was alone, now I am with someone. In bed when he wakes, he sees beside him a pair of pigtails which he did not see before. The first year of our marriage Katie sat beside me when I studied, and once, when she could think of nothing else to say, asked me: "Doctor, is the Grand Master of Prussia the Margrave's brother?"'

A still more intimate view of the relations of man and wife is given in the next letter to Spalatin. Luther lived in a time when it was considered not at all indelicate to speak of what few refined men, not to say pious preachers, would mention in these days. Spalatin had now retired from his position at court, married, and taken the incumbency of the first church at Altenberg. Here he remained the trusted counsellor of Frederick's succcessor, John the Steadfast. Though the new elector was an open convert to the Evangelical faith, as his brother had not been, nevertheless there was a party at court so hostile to Luther, whom they regarded as the real author of the peasants' rising, that when Spalatin invited the Wittenberg professor to attend his wedding, the latter felt unable to do it.

TO GEORGE SPALATIN AT ALTENBERG
Wittenberg, December 6, 1525

I wish you grace and peace in the Lord, and also joy with your sweetest little wife, also in the Lord. Your marriage is as pleasing to me as it is displeasing to those priests of Baal. Indeed God has given me no greater happiness, except the gospel, than to see you married, though this, too, is a gift of the gospel, and no small fruit of our Evangelical teaching. Why I am absent, and wherefore I could not come to your most pleasing wedding, Brisger will tell you. All things are changed under the new elector, who right nobly confesses the Evangelical faith. I am less safe on the road than I was under an elector who dissimulated his faith, but now where one hopes for citadels of refuge one is forced to fear dens of robbers and traitors. I wish you great happiness and children, with Christ's blessing. Believe me, my mind exults in your marriage no less than yours did in mine. Poor as I am I would have sent you that Portuguese gold

piece which you gave my wife, did I not fear that it
would offend you. So I am sending you what is left over
from my wedding, not knowing whether it will also be
left over from yours or not. . . . Greet your wife kindly
from me. When you have your Catharine in bed, sweetly
embracing and kissing her, think: Lo this being, the best
little creation of God, has been given me by Christ, to
whom be glory and honour. I will guess the day on
which you will receive this letter and that night my wife
and I will particularly think of you. My rib and I send
greetings to you and your rib. Grace be with you. Amen.

Yours,
Martin Luther

Luther's marriage excited the interest of all Europe.
Henry VIII of England and many other enemies taunted
him with it as if it were a crime. Erasmus sneered that what
he had taken to be a tragedy had turned out a comedy. The
marriage did indeed turn out happily. After his hard experiences in the monastery, Luther's whole nature blos-
somed out in response to the warm sun of domestic life. A
true instinct for the best side of the man has made artists love
to portray him surrounded by wife and children.

Katie was a woman of enormous energy—the morning
star of Wittenberg as her husband called her with reference
to her early rising. Her superintendence of a large household and growing estate was masterly. She faithfully cared
for her husband on the numerous occasions when he was ill,
and of course much of her time was taken up with the children whom she nursed and tended in the unabashed publicity of her crowded home. She took a lively interest in her
husband's affairs and was confided in by him. Her piety is
more a matter of inference than record; Martin probably
appealed to her weaker side when he offered her a large
sum to read the Bible through. That her studies in this book
were successful may be inferred from her husband's
remark that 'Katie understands the Bible better than any

papists did twenty years ago.' Her picture, like that of her husband, comes to life in the table-talk. Among many other sayings taken down during the last fifteen years of Luther's life (1531–1546), the following gives a charming picture of his happy marriage:

> I would not change my Katie for France and Venice, because God has given her to me, and other women have much worse faults, and she is true to me and a good mother to my children. If a husband always kept such things in mind he would easily conquer the temptation to discord which Satan sows between married people.

> The greatest happiness is to have a wife to whom you can trust your business and who is a good mother to your children. Katie, you have a husband who loves you; many an empress is not so well off.

> I am rich, God has given me my nun and three children; what care I if I am in debt, Katie pays the bills.

Luther loved to poke good-natured fun at his wife, but she was usually able to hold her own:

> *Luther*—We shall yet see the day when a man will take several wives.
> *Katie*—The devil thinks so.
> *Luther*—The reason, dear Katie, is that a woman can have only one child a year, whereas a man can beget several.
> *Katie*—Paul says, 'Let each man have his own wife.'
> *Luther*—Aye, his own wife, but not only one; that is not in Paul. Thus the doctor joked a long time until Katie said: 'Before I would stand that I would go back to the convent and leave you and your children.'

> Something struck Katie in the side and she cried out, '*Ave Maria!*' The doctor said: 'Why don't you finish your prayer? Would it not be a comfort to say 'Jesus Christ' too?'

> Speaking jocosely of Katie's loquacity he said: 'Will you not preface your long sermons with a prayer? If you do,

your prayer will doubtless be long enough to prevent your preaching at all.'

While he was talking in an inspired way during dinner, his wife said: 'Why do you keep talking all the time instead of eating?' He replied: 'I must again wish that women would pray before they preach. Say the Lord's prayer before you speak.

'Women's sermons only make one tired. They are so tedious that one forgets what they are saying before they finish.' By this name he called the long speeches of his wife with which she was always interrupting his best sayings.

On November 4 [1538] a learned Englishman who did not know German came to table. Luther said: 'I will let my wife be your teacher. She knows the tongue so thoroughly that she completely beats me. But eloquence is not to be praised in women; it becomes them better to stammer and lisp.'

While Luther gladly devolved upon Katie the care of his household and property—tasks for which he had neither time, aptitude, nor inclination—he had no intention of letting himself be ruled by her—indulgence to wives he once described as 'the vice of the age'. At other times he said:

My wife can persuade me anything she pleases, for she has the government of the house in her hands alone. I willingly yield the direction of domestic affairs, but wish my rights to be respected. Women's rule never did any good.

The inferior ought not to glory over the superior, but the superior over the inferior. Katie can rule the servants but not me. David gloried in his own righteousness before men, not before God.

George Karg has taken a rich wife and sold his freedom. I am luckier, for when Katie gets saucy she gets nothing but a box on the ear.

This is the only time corporal chastisement of the wife is ever mentioned in respect to Katie, though the practice was not unknown to the best society of the day. In spite of a little blustering, it is probable that Luther gave in as often as not:

> As we were sitting in the garden, Jonas remarked that the women were becoming our masters, to which the town-councillor of Torgau added that it was indeed, alas! true. Luther said: 'But we have to give in, otherwise we would have no peace.'
>
> A priest came to Luther complaining of misery and want. Melanchthon, who was present, said: 'You have vowed poverty, obedience, and chastity, now practise them'; and Luther added: 'I, too, have to be obedient to my wife and all kinds of desperate fools and knaves and ingrates.
>
> 'I must have patience with the Pope, ranters, insolent nobles, my household and Katie von Bora, so that my whole life is nothing but mere patience.'

In general Katie seems to have enjoyed good health. In the winter of 1539–1540, however, she had a terrible illness resulting from a misacrriage. For weeks she was prostrate. When the crisis was past her energy returned faster than her strength, and one of the most realistic accounts of her tells how she crawled around the house with the aid of her hands before she was able to walk upright. Her excellent constitution stood her in good stead, however, and she recovered rapidly and thoroughly. Her husband's piety attributed this to the prayer he offered for her.

12

Erasmus

Before Luther's fame had eclipsed that of all his contemporaries, the great figure in the republic of letters was Desiderius Erasmus of Rotterdam, who had attained to an acknowledged sovereignty like that later accorded to Voltaire. He combined great learning with a wonderful mastery of style, especially of the lighter kind, sparkling with wit. He was, moreover, inspired with a serious purpose of reform, in the service of which he used all his great and various talents. In his *Praise of Folly* (1511) he had written a cutting satire on the least admirable aspects of the mediaeval church, and by his edition of the Greek Testament (1516) he had given an immense stimulus along with the necessary means to a fruitful study of the Bible. He was the deadly enemy of superstition and obscurantism, and the bold champion of sound learning and free thought. His true greatness would be proved, if by nothing else, by the fact that two such opposite and such large men as Martin Luther and François Rabelais derived much of their inspiration from him.

Erasmus' idea of a reformation differed from that of Luther partly in aim but more in method. The humanist had a strong love of peace and a sincere horror of the 'tumult'. He judged that strong measures were *always* inexpedient, and, had he judged otherwise, he would not, by

167

his own confession, have had the courage to adopt them.

The Wittenberg professor, who keenly sought the best and most recent books on divinity, learned to know many of Erasmus' commentaries and used them freely, along with the new edition of the Greek Testament, in preparing his lectures. With his usual independence of judgement he did not acquiesce in all the conclusions of the great scholar. On October 19, 1516, he wrote to Spalatin that he had detected an unsound exegesis in the humanist's commentary on Romans, and begged his friend to communicate the objection to the author. Spalatin complied but received no answer. Luther continued to read Erasmus, and in the *Commentary on Galatians* referred with appreciation to his predecessor's work in this field. Indeed the first of the Ninety-five Theses may have been suggested by Erasmus' translation of Mark 1:15. That the monk also read the lighter works of the man of letters is proved by his reference in an epistle of November 1517, to the *Dialogue* between Peter and Julius II: 'It is written', said he, 'so merrily, so learnedly and so ingeniously—that is, so Erasmianly—that it makes one laugh at the vices and miseries of the church, at which every Christian ought to weep.' Nevertheless he at one time had the intention of translating it into German, but gave it up, fearing that he could not do it justice.

That the young reformer expected to find an ally in the elder was perfectly natural. It was probably the influence of Melanchthon that first induced his friend to approach the great scholar definitely with this end. The first letter, somewhat condensed, is as follows:

TO DESIDERIUS ERASMUS AT LOUVAIN
Wittenberg, March 28, 1519

Greetings. I chat much with you and you with me, O Erasmus, our glory and hope!—but yet we are not acquainted. Is not that monstrous? No, it is not monstrous, but a thing we see daily. For who is there whose innermost parts Erasmus has not penetrated, whom Erasmus does not teach and in whom he does not reign? I mean of those who love letters, for among the other gifts of Christ to you, this also must be mentioned, that you displease many, by which criterion I am wont to know what God gives in mercy from what he gives in wrath. I therefore congratulate you, that while you please good men to the last degree, you no less displease those who wish only to be highest and to please most. . . .

Now that I have learned from Fabritius Capito that my name is known to you on account of my little treatise on indulgences, and as I also learn from your preface to the new edition of your *Handbook of the Christian Knight,* that my ideas are not only known to you but approved by you, I am compelled to acknowledge my debt to you as the enricher of my mind, even if I should have to do so in a barbarous style. . . .

And so, dear Erasmus, if it please you, learn to know this little brother in Christ also: he is assuredly your very zealous friend, but otherwise deserves, on account of his ignorance, only to be buried in a corner, unknown even to your climate and sun. . . .

Erasmus, who had already praised the Theses (though he denied the reference to them in the preface to the *Handbook*), replied to this letter in a friendly way, assuring his correspondent that he had many friends in the Netherlands and in England, commending his *Commentaries on the Psalms,* but warning him to guard against violence (May 30, 1519). About the same time the humanist wrote to Frederick the Wise and to Melanchthon, testifying his high esteem for the Saxon monk.

The letter of May 30, which the author had intended to be private, was shortly printed at Leipzig. Partly to guard against misapprehension, and partly to help the cause of reform, Erasmus wrote in November to Albert of Mainz, praising Luther's character and urging that he be not condemned unheard, adding: 'He wrote me a right Christian letter, to my own mind, which I answered by warning him not to write anything seditious or irreverent to the Pope or arrogantly or in anger. . . . I said that thus could he conciliate the opinion of those who favour him, which some have foolishly interpreted to mean that I favour him. This letter, entrusted to the impetuous Ulrich von Hutten, was by him forthwith published, with "Luther" changed into "our Luther".'

This indiscretion, to call it by its mildest name, was intended to make Erasmus declare for the reform at once, but it had rather the opposite effect. The humanist was already at swords' points with the Dominicans, and now an enormous buzz arose from this quarter that he of Rotterdam was in straight alliance with him of Wittenberg and helped him to compose his works. The theologians of Louvain, where Erasmus then lived, published a condemnation of the heretic's doctrine; the man attacked struck back (1520), saying, 'They have condemned not only me, but Occam, Mirandola, Valla, Reuchlin, Wesel, Lefèvre d'Étaples, and Erasmus, that ram caught by the thorns in the bushes.' The humanist wrote in March to Melanchthon, saying that the *Answer to the Condemnation of Louvain* pleased him wonderfully, but at the same time wrote to the author a letter (now lost), probably asking him not to mention his name any more, to which Luther replied (if we may conjecture from other indications, for his letter, too, is lost) that he would not do so.

Throughout the year 1520 Erasmus did his best to secure the accused heretic a fair hearing. 'They find it easier to burn his books than to refute them,' he said, and set about writing and speaking, to Frederick the Wise, to Henry VIII of England, to Albert of Mainz, even to the Pope and cardinals, urging them not to proceed by force. When Aleander came to Louvain, on October 8, 1520, published the bull and burned Luther's books, Erasmus, who was attacked by him, replied in an anonymous polemic, *The Acts of Louvain,* discrediting the legate and declaring his belief that the bull was forged. His interview with the Elector of Saxony at Cologne on November 5, in which he urged him to insist that his subject have an impartial trial, has already been mentioned, as has his *Council of One Desiring the Peace of the Church,* a memorial at this time pressed upon the Emperor's advisers, and the plan of arbitration composed by Erasmus and presented by Faber at the Diet of Worms.

Although these efforts immensely helped the Reformer, they did not accomplish all that the humanist hoped. Moreover he began, about 1521, to be alienated by the other's violence. The *Babylonian Captivity* he thought prevented the possibility of reconciliation, and he was especially incensed by the charge that this work, first published anonymously, was written by him.

When the news spread abroad of Luther's disappearance after the Diet of Worms, many expected that the humanist would take up the banner of reform. Albrecht Dürer, then travelling in the Netherlands where he had learned to know the great scholar, wrote in his diary: 'O Erasmus of Rotterdam, where wilt thou abide? . . . O thou knight of Christ, seize the martyr's crown! . . .' But this was an honour the great scholar did not aspire to. A few days later he wrote to Pace that the Germans were alienating him by trying to force him to declare for Luther, but that he feared, were a tumult to arise, that he would follow the example of Peter and deny his Lord.

Nevertheless he sought to remain neutral, although by so doing he brought on himself the suspicion of favouring the heretic. In numerous letters to his patrons and friends he excused himself from this charge. Some of these letters were published, and so Luther was kept posted on his quondam ally's change of attitude. In June 1523, he wrote to Œcolampadius:

I note the pricks that Erasmus gives me now and then,

but as he does it without openly declaring himself my foe, I act as though I were unaware of his sly attacks, although I understand him better than he thinks. He has done what he was called to do; he has brought us from godless studies to a knowledge of the tongues; perhaps he will die in the land of Moab, for to enter the promised land he is unable.

That Erasmus finally came out as the opponent of the man he had once supported was due not only to the urging of his friends and patrons but also to the provocation given by the reformers. In the letter to Œcolampadius, Luther spoke slightingly of the humanist's theology, and this letter was shown Erasmus, who had, since 1521, removed from Louvain to Basel.

The fiery Hutten, who could bear no indecision, precipitated hostilities by publishing in June, 1523, an *Expostulation with Erasmus,* roundly attacking him for duplicity and cowardice. Erasmus defended himself in the *Sponge* (August), in which he incidentally blames Luther for disturbing the peace, for scurrility, and especially for his recent unmeasured attack on Henry VIII. In a dedicatory letter to Zwingli he mentions as the chief errors of the Wittenberg professor: (1) Designation of all good works as mortal sin; (2) denial of free will; (3) justification by faith alone. Erasmus may have taken the idea from the letter of Henry VIII to Duke George (January 1523), which mentioned these as the fundamental errors of the heretic. This letter with the Duke's answer was printed, and Erasmus read them both.

The reasons for Erasmus' choice of this subject, the freedom of the will, on which to attack Luther, have been much discussed. It has often been said that he chose the subject with the least practical interest, hoping in the first place not to put an obstacle in the way of reforms of which he really approved, and secondly not to antagonise the Reformer, whose person he spared while criticising his doctrine. This motive probably had its weight with the humanist, but not the decisive weight. The matter was 'in the air'. Lorenzo Valla, always admired by Erasmus, had written a work on the freedom of the will in 1440, which had recently been edited by Vadin, in 1518. The English Bishop Fisher had chosen this subject in his attack on Luther, the *Refutation of Luther's Assertion,* being a rebuttal of the *Assertion of All the Articles Wrongly Condemned by the Last Bull of Leo X,* in which, as we have seen, Luther argues at length, in the thirty-sixth article, for his opinion that free will is but a name. The Reformer himself had selected this as the foundation of all his theology, being, in fact, no more than another form of the famous doctrine of justification by faith alone. His position was emphasised and clarified in Melanchthon's *Common-Places of Theology,* appearing in December 1521.

The Diatribe on the Free Will was first mentioned by its author in a letter to Henry VIII of September 4, 1523, and it is possible that a first draft of it followed in this year. Finding that the printers at Basel were unwilling to publish anything against the popular hero of Germany, Erasmus had some thoughts of going to Rome to publish it.

The news of the impending attack soon spread. Luther himself, judging that the best way to prevent it was to threaten reprisals, wrote the following letter:

TO DESIDERIUS ERASMUS AT BASEL
Wittenberg (about April 15), 1524

Grace and peace from our Lord Jesus Christ. I have been silent long enough, excellent Erasmus, having waited for you, as the greater and elder man, to speak first; but as you refuse to do so, I think that charity itself now compels me to begin. I say nothing about your estrangement from us, by which you were made safer against my enemies the papists. Nor do I especially resent your action, intended to gain their favour or mitigate their hostility, in censuring and attacking us in various books. For since we see that the Lord has not given you courage or sense to assail those monsters openly and confidently with us, we are not the men to exact what is beyond our power and measure. Rather we have tolerated and even respected the mediocrity of God's gift in you. The whole world knows your services to letters and how you made them flourish and thus prepared a path for the direct study of the Bible. For this glorious and splendid gift in you we ought to thank God. I for one have never wished you to leave your little sphere to join our camp, for although you might have profited the cause much by your ability, genius, and eloquence, yet as you had not the courage it was safer for you to work at home. We only fear that you might be induced by our enemies to fall upon our doctrine with some publication, in which case we should be obliged to resist you to your face. We have restrained some who would have drawn you into the arena, and have even suppressed books already written against you. We should have preferred that Hutten's *Expostulation* had not been written, and still more that your *Sponge* had not seen the light. Incidentally I may remark, that, unless I mistake, when you wrote that book you felt how easy it is to write about moderation and blame Luther's excesses, but how hard or rather impossible it is to practise what you preach except by a special gift of the Spirit. Believe it or not as you like, but Christ is witness that I heartily regret that such zeal and hatred should be roused against you. I cannot believe that you remain unmoved by it, for your fortitude is human and unequal to such trials. Perhaps a righteous zeal moved them and they thought that you had provoked them in various ways. Since they are admittedly too weak to bear your caustic but dissembled sarcasm (which you would have pass for prudent moderation), they surely have a just cause for indignation, whereas if they were stronger they would have no reason to be indignant. I, too, am irritable, and quite frequently am moved to write caustically, though I have only done so against hardened men proof against milder forms of admonition. Otherwise I think my gentleness and clemency towards sinners, no matter how far they are gone in iniquity, is witnessed not only by my own conscience but by the experience of many. Hitherto, accordingly, I have controlled my pen as often as you prick me, and have written in letters to friends which you have seen that I would control it until you publish something openly. For although you will not side with us and although you injure or make sceptical many pious persons by your impiety and hypocrisy, yet I cannot and do not accuse you of wilful obstinacy. What can I do? Each side is greatly exasperated. Could my good offices prevail, I would wish my friends to cease attacking you with so much animus and to allow your old age a peaceful death in the Lord. I think they would do so if they were reasonable and considered your weakness and the greatness of the cause which has long since outgrown your littleness, especially as the cause has now progressed so far that it has little to fear from the might—or rather the sting and bite—of Erasmus. You on your side, Erasmus, ought to consider their infirmity and abstain from making them the butt of your witty rhetoric. Even if you cannot and dare not declare for us, yet at least you might leave us alone and mind your own business. If they suffer from your bites, *you* certainly will confess that human weakness has cause to fear the name and fame of Erasmus and that it is a very much graver matter to be snapped at by you than to be ground to pieces by all the papists together. I say this, excellent Erasmus, as an evidence of my *candid moderation*, wishing that the Lord might give you a spirit worthy of your reputation, but if he delays doing so I beg that meanwhile if you can do nothing else you will remain a spectator of the conflict and not join our enemies, and especially that you publish no book against me, as I shall write none against you. Remember that the men who are called Lutherans are human beings like ourselves, whom you ought to spare and forgive as Paul says: 'Bear one another's burdens.' We have fought long enough, we must take care not to eat each other up. This would be a terrible catastrophe, as neither one of us really wishes harm to religion, and without judging each other both may do good. Pardon my poor style and farewell in the Lord. . . .

Martin Luther

Erasmus' answer, dated May 8, asserts that he is not less zealous for the cause of religion than others who arrogate to themselves the name 'evangelical', and that he has as yet written nothing against Luther, though had he done so he would have won the applause of the great ones of the world.

Very soon after this he finished the *Diatribe on the Free Will*. On account of its pure Latinity, its moderation, wit, and brevity, this work is still very readable. It is also distinguished by the absence of scurrility; indeed it hardly makes the impression of a polemic at all, but rather of a conversation on the intellectual movement of the times, addressed to a wide audience.

The author expresses his perfect readiness to appeal only to reason and to scripture, as these are the only grounds recognised by Luther. He defines free will as the power to apply one's self to the things leading to salvation, and appeals to the universal opinion of mankind that each one has such a power. His strongest argument is that it would be unjust for God to damn a man for doing what he could not help. He devotes long sections to explanations of scriptural passages, such as 'God hardened Pharaoh's heart', which would seem to militate against free will, and he refutes point by point Luther's arguments in the *Assertion of All the Articles Condemned by the Bull*—a part of the work in which he borrows much without acknowledgement from Bishop Fisher. Finally he sums up: 'Those please me who attribute something to free will but much to grace.' Both must co-operate to save a man, one may assign as small a part as one likes to the former factor, only it must be *some* part.

The *Diatribe* was published in September 1524, and promptly sent to the author's patrons and friends, most of whom it had the good fortune to please. Even Melanchthon liked the moderation of tone and the reasonableness of the argument. Luther himself confessed that of all his opponents only Erasmus had gone to the root of the matter and instead of threatening him with ban and stake had undertaken to refute him with arguments. He once said that of all the books written against him, the *Diatribe* was the only one he read through, but even this made him feel like throwing it under the bench and heartily disgusted him. He did not answer it for more than a year, a delay partly accounted for by his preoccupation with the 'heavenly prophets', the Peasants' War, and his marriage, and partly by the unusual care with which he prepared his reply. His book on the *Unfree Will* (*De servo arbitrio*) at last appeared in December 1525.

This bulky volume has been acclaimed by most Protestant biographers of Luther as his ablest polemic and a work of extraordinary power. It is needless to remark that much of this ability is wasted on a generation for which the question, then so passionately disputed, has sunk almost into oblivion. In point of earnestness he is a striking contrast to Erasmus. What for the latter is the subject of an interesting discussion is to him a matter of life and death. It is in this sense that he attributes eloquence and mastery of speech to his opponent, but to himself substance and real understanding of the issue.

Luther takes his former stand for extreme predestinarianism. His determination is not founded, as that of a modern philosopher might be, on any conception of the immutability of natural law, but is simply and solely the logical deduction from his doctrine of justification by faith alone, or, as it is technically called, of the monergism of grace. Man is a simple instrument in God's hands, and the Almighty arbitrarily saves whom he wills and damns whom he wills. The extreme form in which Luther put this doctrine, which is certainly revolting to our ideas, can only be realised by a few quotations of his own words:

> The human will is like a beast of burden. If God mounts it, it wishes and goes as God wills; if Satan mounts it, it wishes and goes as Satan wills. Nor can it choose the rider it would prefer, nor betake itself to him, but it is the riders who contend for its possession. . . .

> This is the acme of faith, to believe that God who saves so few and condemns so many is merciful; that he is just who at his own pleasure has made us necessarily doomed to damnation, so that, as Erasmus says, he seems to delight in the tortures of the wretched, and to be more deserving of hatred than of love. If by effort of reason I could conceive how God, who shows so much anger and iniquity, could be merciful and just, there would be no need of faith. . . .

> God foreknows nothing subject to contingencies, but he foresees, foreordains, and accomplishes all things by an unchanging, eternal, and efficacious will. By this thunderbolt free will sinks shattered in the dust.

Besides defending his main thesis, Luther here puts forward his doctrine of the infallibility of scripture. He is enraged at the assertion of his opponent that there seem to be contradictions in the Bible. According to Luther every text must be taken literally, and yet all must be made to agree, for as the whole is plenarily inspired by divine wisdom there can be no diversity of doctrine. Moreover, he apologises for his whole theology, especially replying to the charge that tumult followed it by asserting that uproar always follows the preaching of God's word.

He sent a copy of the work, with a letter asserting his

conviction of its truth, to his opponent, but the messenger was delayed and Erasmus did not receive it until April. In the meantime a friend in Leipzig (Duke George?) had sent him a copy, which he received on February 10. He commenced his reply at once, spending only twelve days in answering it so as to have the reply ready to be sold at the Frankfurt Fair. He was astonished by the violence of Luther's invective, of which he complained to the Elector of Saxony. To Luther himself he wrote as follows:

ERASMUS TO MARTIN LUTHER
AT WITTENBERG

Basel, April 11, 1526

Your letter was delivered to me too late and had it come in time it would not have moved me. . . . The whole world knows your nature, according to which you have guided your pen against no one more bitterly and, what is more detestable, more maliciously than against me. . . . The same admirable ferocity which you formerly used against Fisher and against Cochlaeus, who provoked it by reviling you, you now use against my book in spite of its courtesy. How do your scurrilous charges that I am an atheist, an Epicurean, and a sceptic, help the argument? . . . It terribly pains me, as it must all good men, that your arrogant, insolent, rebellious nature has set the world in arms. . . . You treat the Evangelical cause so as to confound together all things sacred and profane, as if it were your chief aim to prevent the tempest from ever becoming calm, while it is my greatest desire that it should die down. . . .

The *Hyperaspistes*, Part I, is a work three times as large as the *Diatribe*, of which it is a defence, and is moreover a general attack on all points of Luther's doctrine. In it the question of free will recedes behind the other question of the excellence of the Lutheran movement. Erasmus cannot convince himself that the Reformer is really inspired with the spirit of the gospel, as he has not learned to avoid giving offence. He attacks Luther's person and the results of his doctrine, among which are included the Peasants' War. As the book is written in such haste, he promises a continuation of it later with fuller consideration of the main argument.

After his first heat had cooled down, Erasmus put off this promised work for eighteen months. That he wrote it at all was again the work of Henry VIII. This monarch's answer to Luther, published in the early part of 1527, contains some references to free will which made the Reformer suspect Erasmus' hand in its composition. This charge, coupled with the violence of the Wittenberg reformer, which alienated many persons besides Erasmus, induced him to reply. This he did in a book six times the size of the *Diatribe*, which appeared about September 1, 1527, and was called *Hyperaspistes*, Part II.

Now at last the fundamental difference between Erasmus and Luther is revealed, the opposite trend of the two natures. The humanist reacts against Luther's absolutism; he cannot abide hard-and-fast rules admitting no exception. Of himself he said, 'I am prone to those things like nature; I abhor portents'; of his antagonist, 'He never recoils from extremes.' For the dogmatic reformer there is one absolute right and one absolute wrong; for the classical scholar men and things cannot be divided into such uncompromising categories; there are shades and degrees. Luther is a logician; from premises impeccable, because directly revealed in the Bible, he draws conclusions of mathematical precision; Erasmus is an evolutionist and a rationalist, to whom all truth does not come through the Bible, but much from reason. He believes, moreover, that men have a natural trend to the good. At the close of this comprehensive work he tries to hedge and make peace again. After all, the strife is mainly one of words, and man should remember that salvation is God's work, but damnation that of sin. Just as the *Hyperaspistes*, Part II, appeared, its author wrote to Duke George that Luther's spirit was neither a wholly good nor an entirely bad one.

The work was received by the Evangelical party as might have been expected. Justus Jonas, a quondam Erasmian, now at Wittenberg, referred to his former beloved master as a toad. Melanchthon, indeed, who resembled Erasmus in many ways, was half-convinced that determinism would be bad for the morals of the common man, for who would try to be good if he was convinced it was no use? Luther himself punned on the double meaning of *aspis*, which in Greek means both shield and viper (*Hyperaspistes*, a soldier), calling the work 'super-viperian'. He never deigned to answer it for reasons explained to Montanus in a letter of May 28, 1529:

> Erasmus writes nothing in which he does not show the impotence of his mind or rather the pain of the wounds he has received. I despise him, nor shall I honour the fellow by arguing with him any more. . . . In future I shall only refer to him as some alien, rather condemning than refuting his ideas. He is a light-minded man, mocking all religion as his dear Lucian does, and serious about nothing but calumny and slander.

But the last word was not yet said. In 1533 George Witzel, a liberal Catholic and an admirer of Erasmus, begged 'that Solon' to draw up a plan for pacifying the church. The old scholar, who, in the meantime, had been forced to withdraw from Basel, now too Protestant for him, to Freiburg, flattered by the request, published a reasonable and irenic pamphlet, *On Mending the Peace of the Church*, advising that each side tolerate the other in non-essential matters, that all controversial writings be forbidden, and that a general council take measures with the civil authorities for restoring unity and healing the schism.

The anger of the reformers was roused afresh by this apparently inoffensive essay towards compromise. Corvinus answered it in full, Luther writing a preface for his work, proving that there could be no peace between Christ and Belial. At the same time he expressed himself more fully in a long printed letter to Amsdorf, written about March 11, 1534, calling Erasmus by the somewhat contradictory names of heretic, atheist, blasphemer, and Arian, and worst of all, one who makes jokes of serious things and serious business of jokes.

Erasmus answered with *A Justification Against the Intemperate Letter of Luther,* denying all the accusations point by point. Two years later he died, in the opinion of his adversary, 'without light, without the cross, and without God'.

The table-talk (1531–1546) is full of the most rancorous expressions about the great scholar:

> In writing his *Folly,* Erasmus begot a daughter worthy of himself. He turns, twists, and bites like an awl, but yet shows himself a true fool.
>
> On my death-bed I shall forbid my sons to read his *Colloquies.* . . . He is much worse than Lucian, mocking all things under the guise of holiness.
>
> He goes so far as to compare our Lord to the god Priapus. . . .
>
> In his New Testament he is ambiguous and cavilling . . . trying to perplex the reader and make him think the doctrine doubtful. He reviles all Chrsitians, making no exception of Paul or any pious man.

The battle between Luther and Erasmus was a real tragedy. The humanist had set himself, as his life's task, a peaceful reformation of the church; abuses, he thought, would fade away before gentle sarcasm and the cultivation of good letters and the sacred texts. The boisterous attack of the Wittenberg monk, said he sadly, destroyed all hope of this. He lived to see his ideal of peace shattered in war, the followers trained to carry on his work reft from him by one side or the other, and his own name spat upon by almost all.

For Luther the loss was hardly less. He saw the man in whom he had confidently expected the most valuable of all

allies gradually draw back from his side and become not
only a neutral but an enemy, to the great scandal of his
own followers and to the hurt of the Evangelical church.
In his anger and disappointment he more and more
expressed himself in unmeasured terms, and more and
more forgot the good in Erasmus and the services he had
done the world. But those who regret his one-sidedness
and especially his violence should not blame him too hastily. Every great leader of a new and struggling movement
must feel that he who is not with him is against him and
that he who gathereth not scattereth. The citizen who
refuses to take arms in wartime is a public enemy. His
scruples may be honourable, but one can hardly blame the
general for expelling him from the ranks. In the American
civil war no character was so much detested as the 'Cop-
perhead', the northern man who refused to fight for the
Union.

The Reformation is still a living issue. A reflecting mind
must have an opinion on its merits. Some judge it as a
great step forward, others as a blow to human progress. A
few are still Erasmians; approving the principle of the
Reformation, they think it might have been better
accomplished without rending the peace of the world. But
the mass of mankind are not led in that way. To reform
any institution it is not sufficient to secure the intellectual
adherence of a few choice spirits, the whole soul of a
people must be aroused. One may estimate the Reformation as one pleases, but to think of it without Luther is as
unhistorical as the fancy that Christianity might have
grown up without its great Founder, or that Islam could
have been born in the deserts of Arabia without the
Prophet.

13

Ulrich Zwingli

The tendency of Protestantism to split up into manifold sects has often been noticed and explained. When once individual judgement is set up against authority, all the followers of the leaders of the revolt will claim the same privilege against him. Even before the church which rebelled had made its position secure against Rome, it divided into many sects. Most of these were small, and, though holding the most diverse and even opposite opinions, were classed together under the name of Anabaptist; but besides the Lutheran community there was one other of great importance. Its leader was Ulrich Zwingli; the doctrinal difference of the two churches was on the eucharist.

The theory of the Roman Catholic church, at least for several centuries, had been that the bread and wine in the Lord's Supper were actually turned into the body and blood of Jesus, though without a corresponding change in the accidents of taste, appearance, and so forth; this is transubstantiation. Luther's theory, known as consubstantiation, is nearly allied to it, namely, that though there was no actual change, yet the body of the saviour was present with the natural bread and wine as fire is in red-hot iron, or a sword in a sheath, and that it was so truly present that it was 'bitten by the teeth' of the communicant. The belief adopted by Zwingli and most of the other reformed churches was that the rite was merely commemorative and that the body and blood of Christ were partaken of in a purely figurative and spiritual sense.

This doctrine came to Luther's attention soon after his return from the Wartburg (if not before) in the writings of a certain Honius, in those of the Bohemian Brethren, and in the pamphlets of Carlstadt, who taught it, along with his other advanced tenets, while Luther was away. The Reformer speaks of it in his letter to the Christians of Strasbourg, of December 14, 1524, as follows:

I freely confess that if Carlstadt or any other could have convinced me five years ago that there was nothing in the sacrament but mere bread and wine, he would have done me a great service. I was sorely tempted on this point and wrestled with myself and tried to believe that it was so, for I saw that I could thereby give the hardest rap to the papacy. I read treatises by two men who wrote more ably in defence of the theory than has Dr Carlstadt and who did not so torture the word to their own imaginations. But I am bound; I cannot believe as they do; the text is too powerful for me and will not let itself be wrenched from the plain sense by argument.

And if anyone could prove today that the sacrament were mere bread and wine, he would not much anger me if he was only reasonable. (Alas I am too much inclined that way myself when I feel the old Adam!) But Dr Carlstadt's ranting only confirms me in the opposite opinion.

The second half of Luther's work *Against the Heavenly Prophets of Images and the Sacrament* appeared in January 1525, and was entirely on the subject of the sacrament. This work was not particularly successful; in fact it seemed rather to alienate some men who were hesitating between the two dogmas.

The controversy might have fallen into oblivion, especially after the disgrace of Carlstadt and Münzer in the

Peasants' Revolt, had it not been taken up by one of the ablest men of the generation, Ulrich Zwingli.

Born at Wildhaus, Switzerland, on January 1, 1484, he had received a humanistic education and entered the church in 1506. After varied experiences as an army chaplain and parish priest, he was called to Zurich in December 1519, and here, quite independently of the Wittenberg movement, he began a similar reformation. He at once protested against the sale of indulgences on lines suggested by the writings of Erasmus, whose ardent admirer he was. He soon rose to the leading position in the city, and, carrying his reform farther than had Luther, was able, in April 1525, to abolish the mass and substitute for it a simple communion service.

The wide difference between the personal experiences and careers of the two reformers is chiefly accountable for the divergence of their opinions. The German had gone through a rebirth of spiritual anguish which made the forgiveness of sin the central point of his theology as of his life; the Swiss had never felt this need so strongly; the central idea of *his* theology was that of Christian fellowship fostered by the analogy of the republican freedom of the canton. Again, Luther was at bottom a monk, reasoning with the depth, and also with something of the limitations, of scholastic philosophy; Zwingli was a humanist, anxious only to get at the exact meaning of the Greek Testament.

It is possible that the two men might have agreed on this point, at least better than they did, had it not been for the unfortunate manner in which Zwingli first crossed Luther's horizon, as a supporter of Carlstadt and 'the ranters'. When the division of the two became recognised, it was deepened by the proud consciousness, on the part of each leader, of the independence of his own movement. How bitterly Luther felt against men whom he regarded as rebels and traitors may be seen in a letter:

TO NICHOLAS HAUSMANN AT ZWICKAU
Wittenberg, January 20, 1526

Grace and peace in the Lord. I wrote to Duke George with good hope, but am deceived. I have lost my humility and shall not write him another word. Indeed I am not moved by his lies and his curses. Why should I not bear with him who am compelled to bear with these sons of my body, my Absaloms, who withstand me so furiously? They are scourges of the sacrament compared with whose madness the papists are mild. I never understood before how evil a spirit is Satan, nor did I comprehend Paul's words about spiritual wickedness. But Christ lives. Now Theobald Billican, pastor at Nördlingen, writes against Zwingli, Carlstadt, and Œcolampadius. God raises up the faithful remnant against the new heretics; we greatly hope that Christ will bless the undertaking. I would write against them if I had time, but first I wish to see what Billican does.

I am glad that my book on the *Unfree Will* pleased you, but I expect the same or worse from Erasmus as from Duke George. That reptile will feel himself taken by the throat and will not be moved by my moderation. God grant that I be mistaken, but I know the man's nature; he is an instrument of Satan unless God change him. I have no other news. Farewell and pray for me.

Martin Luther

In a similar strain the Reformer says in his *Answer to the King of England's Libel* (1527): 'Hitherto I have suffered in all ways. But not until now did my Absalom, my dear son, hunt and shame his father David. My Judas [Zwingli] had not yet shamed the disciples and betrayed his master; but now he has done his worst on me.'

The new 'Judas' had simply published, in February 1526, a pamphlet entitled *True and False Religion,* and followed it up soon after with *A Clear Explanation of Christ's Supper.* Along with cogent argument in support of his

position that the elements were mere bread and wine, the
author alleges that the truth of his opinion has been
revealed to him in a dream. This method of proof unfortunately impressed Luther still more deeply with the idea
that Zwingli's 'spirit' was akin to that of Münzer and the
prophets who had cultivated dreams with such disastrous
results. His works had considerable success, however; so
many of the South German pastors came over to the Swiss
opinion that the leader was able to prophesy that within
three years all Christendom would be converted.

Luther replied in a comprehensive treatise, entitled *That
the Words of Christ, 'This is my Body,' Still Stand Against the
Ranting Spirits* (March 1527). The greater part of this book
is a proof from scripture that the words quoted in the title
are to be taken literally. The theory of the opposite party,
that Christ's body cannot be in the bread because it is in
heaven, is rebutted by showing, from mediaeval
philosophy, that it may be extended through space, and is,
in fact, omnipresent. Again, a careful exegesis of John
6:63, 'the flesh counts for nothing', is devoted to proving
that Christ's flesh is not meant, as supposed by the Swiss.
Further proofs are adduced from other passages of scripture and from the Fathers. The last part of the book is
devoted to a practical exposition of the use, necessity, and
significance of the sacrament, which last, in Luther's opinion, would be entirely destroyed if the consecrating words
were not taken literally.

While Luther was writing this, Zwingli had composed two
treatises, *A Friendly Exegesis of Christ's Words,* and *A Friendly
Appeasement and Rebuttal,* the former in Latin, the latter in
the vernacular, both of which he sent to his opponent with a
letter of April 1. His tone was pastoral, not to say pedagog-
ical; he seemed to instruct Luther in calm superiority;
though perhaps he intended to be conciliatory, he was in
fact extremely irritating to the older man, to whom he said:
'You have produced nothing on this subject worthy either
of yourself or of the Christian religion, and yet your ferocity

daily increases.' Luther wrote on May 4 to Wenzel Link: 'Zwingli has sent me his foolish book and a letter written in his own hand worthy of his haughty spirit. So gentle was he, raging, foaming, and threatening, that he seems to me incurable and condemned by manifest truth.—And my comprehensive book has profited many.'

In the meantime the Swiss had received the last-named work of the Wittenberg professor. They were greatly exasperated by its violent tone; Zwingli writing to Vadian on May 4 'that its whole contents were nothing but lies, slander, sycophancy, and suspicion'.

A reply, composed by Zwingli and Œcolampadius, was published in June under the title *That these Words of Christ, 'This is my Body,' still have the same old Sense.* It was dedicated to John, Elector of Saxony.

Luther was too ill to read it at once. His answer, a huge *Confession on Christ's Supper,* appeared in February 1528. He is glad, he declares, that his words have so greatly angered Satan, by which sign he knows that they have done much good. He goes over the old arguments with more thoroughness than before, refuting first Zwingli's philosophy and then his exegesis of scripture, showing that he contradicts the Bible, the Fathers, and himself.

The book only increased the rage without shaking the convictions of the sacramentarians. Capito wrote that Luther had hurt himself by it; Zwingli judged that it was 'a denial of what Luther had said before, and a fog through which Christ's mystery could not be discerned'. He, and Œcolampadius, published in one book *Two Answers to Martin Luther's Book.* It was dedicated, in a letter dated July 1, 1528, to the Elector John and the Landgrave Philip of Hesse, whom Zwingli refused to salute with the customary titles 'highborn' and 'serene', 'because', as he explained to them, 'you are only highborn in comparison to the world and the flesh, but before God you are mean; and serene [German *Durchlaut,* literally transparent] is a word which is only applicable to glass windows'.

That one, at least, of the princes thus addressed did not take the letter ill, is shown by the attempt of Philip of Hesse to reconcile the opposing sections of the reformed church. His main motive was political, for he saw that in union was strength and he wished to make an alliance between the German Protestant states and the Swiss cantons. He was, however, something of a theologian himself; he had a clearer comprehension of Zwingli's opinion than had Luther, and was, perhaps, inclined to adopt it himself. Hoping to bring about an understanding that would enable both parties to present a united front to the common enemy, he invited the reformers and other distinguished theologians to a conference at his capital, Marburg. After some negotiation the consent of all concerned was secured and during the last days of September 1529 the famous divines gathered in the pretty Hessian town on the banks of the Lahn. All were received right royally by the host, of whom Luther many years afterwards related the following characteristic bit:

At Marburg Philip went around like a stable-boy, concealing his deep thoughts with small talk as great men do. He said to Melanchthon: 'Shall I suffer the Archbishop of Mainz to take away my clergy by force?' To which the latter replied: 'Yes, if they are under the jurisdiction of that see.' Then the Landgrave said: 'I have asked your advice on this, but I won't take it.'

The public discussion was preceded by private conferences of the leaders. At these, or perhaps at the main discussion, Luther was annoyed by the display of humanistic learning made by his opponent. Long afterwards he spoke of him in these terms:

People always want to seem more learned than they are. When we were at Marburg, Zwingli wanted to speak Greek. Once, when he was absent, I said: 'Why isn't he ashamed to speak Greek in the presence of so many learned classicists — Œcolampadius, Melanchthon,

Osiander, and Brent? *They* know Greek.' These words
were carried to him, wherefore the next day he excused
himself in the presence of the Landgrave by saying: 'Illustrious Lord, I speak Greek because I have read the New
Testament for thirteen years.' No indeed! It is more than
reading the New Testament, it is vainglory that blinds
people. When Zwingli spoke German he wanted everyone to adopt the Swiss dialect. Oh, how I hate people who
use so many languages as did Zwingli: at Marburg he
spoke Greek and Hebrew from the pulpit.

The great colloquy took place on October 2, in the large,
darkly wainscotted hall of a noble castle, the battlements of
which, crowning the steep hill in the centre of the town,
seem rather to protect them than to overawe the smiling
region round about. Here, before an audience of some fifty
or sixty notables, Luther debated, for some hours, that
autumn day, with Zwingli and Œcolampadius. The speaking was temperate, the arguments in the main the old familiar ones. Though it can hardly be denied that the German
showed himself the better debater, the result was indecisive,
all persons retaining their former opinions.

Although nothing, or next to nothing had been
accomplished, the Landgrave was anxious to have some
tangible result to draw up for all his trouble. He therefore
induced his guests to draw up a statement of their common
beliefs, known as the *Marburg Articles*. Fourteen of these
articles were on points agreed to by both sides; the fifteenth
defined the eucharist and stated that the subscribers were
unable to agree 'on the bodily presence of the body and
blood' in the elements, with a prayer for enlightenment.
The principal divines present signed this confession, but
when Philip requested them to give each other the right
hand of fellowship, Luther refused with the remark, especially unfortunate on account of its previous connotations,
that the Swiss had a different spirit from his own. His idea
of what had been accomplished is given in this next letter. It

is especially interesting as it is his first known letter to Katie. It shows that he confided his deepest interests to her.

TO CATHARINE LUTHER AT WITTENBERG
Marburg, October 4, 1529

Grace and peace in Christ. Dear Katie, know that our friendly conference at Marburg is now at an end and that we are in perfect union on all points except that our opponents insist that there is simply bread and wine in the Lord's Supper, and that Christ is only in it in a spiritual sense. Today the Landgrave did his best to make us united, hoping that even though we disagreed yet we should hold each other as brothers and members of Christ. He worked hard for it, but we would not call them brothers or members of Christ, although we wish them well and desire to go and see the Elector at Schleitz in Vogtland, whither he has summoned us.

Tell Bugenhagen that Zwingli's best argument was that a body could not exist without occupying space and therefore Christ's body was not in the bread, and that Œcolampadius' best argument was that the sacrament is only the sign of Christ's body. I think God blinded them that they could not get beyond these points. I have much to do and the messenger is in a hurry. Say good-night to all and pray for me. We are all sound and well and live like princes. Kiss little Lena and Hans for me.

Your humble servant,
Martin Luther

14

Feste Coburg and the Diet of Augsburg, 1530

That the Edict of Worms remained a dead letter was due to the excessive decentralisation of the empire. Since Charles had left Germany after the memorable visit of 1520–1521, three important diets, one held at Nuremberg (1524) and two at Spires (1526 and 1529) had dealt with the religious question without being able to enforce any consistent policy. The Emperor himself had been too busy in his other dominions and with his French and Turkish wars even to attempt to suppress the German heresy. Towards the end of 1529, however, the success of his arms in other quarters enabled him to turn his attention north-ward. Fully bent on settling the religious dispute for his subjects, he summoned a diet to meet at Augsburg in 1530, announcing his intention of being present himself.

Early in April of this year Luther, Melanchthon, and other theologians set out from Wittenberg with the inten-tion of appearing at the Diet. At Coburg, the most south-ern town of Ernestine Saxony, they met the Elector, and waited for an imperial safe-conduct before proceeding further. About the middle of the month an urgent sum-mons from Charles V to the Elector John arrived, together with safe-conducts for himself and others of his party, but none for Luther, who was still, be it remembered, under the ban of both the church and the empire. In these circumstances it was impossible for the outlaw to attend the meetings of the Estates, and accordingly when John set out with the other theologians on April 22, he was consigned to the castle near the town where he spent nearly six months.

Feste Coburg, as the fortress is called, crowns a small eminence, the only one in the region, and, like a little city built on a hill, dominates the whole surrounding country. Within its ample walls, picturesque towers, and rambling battlements, a garrison might well be maintained. Without the austere grandeur of the Wartburg, with less of the romantic attraction of Marburg, Feste Coburg surpasses both these castles in size and situation.

With Luther were his amanuensis Veit Dietrich, his nephew Cyriac Kaufmann, and some thirty retainers of the Elector. From his retreat the Reformer kept up a lively correspondence with his friends at Augsburg as well as with those left at Wittenberg; there are extant almost as many letters written from the castle as days he spent there. Among these epistles are many of the finest he ever penned; in some the depths of his religious faith are sounded, in others the chinks and crannies of his deep love are searched. Whatever he wrote is full of humour, of fancy, of an idyllic love of nature and a childlike trust in God.

On the very day on which he moved into his new quarters the Reformer tells of them thus:

TO PHILIP MELANCHTHON (AT NUREMBERG?)
The Realm of the Birds at three p.m. (April 23, 1530)
Grace and peace in the Lord Jesus. I have come to my Sinai, dearest Philip, but I shall soon make it a Zion and build three tabernacles, one for the Psalter, one for the Prophets, and one for Æsop—I speak after the manner of men. It is indeed a very pleasant place and convenient for study, save that your absence saddens it.

I am beginning to be stirred up against the Turk and

Muhammad, even passionately when I see the intolerable fury of Satan waxing proud against body and soul. I shall therefore pray and weep nor cease until I know that my clamour has been heard in heaven. *You* are more affected by the home-bred monsters of the Empire. We are those to whom these last woes were predestined, to feel and suffer the furious impetus of the final assault. But the attack itself is a witness and prophecy of its own end and of our redemption.

I pray Christ to give you sleep and to free your heart from the cares which are the fiery arrows of Satan. Amen. I write this at leisure, not yet having received my books and papers. Neither have I yet seen either of the castle wardens. I lack nothing; this huge building crowning the hill is all mine; the keys of all the rooms are given to me. Thirty men are said to take their meals here, among them twelve night guards and two scouts who keep watch from the towers. Why should I write all this? Because I have nothing else to do. By evening I hope the post will arrive and then I shall have some news. The grace of God be with you. Amen. Give my remembrances to Dr Caspar Lindemann and Spalatin. I shall ask Jonas to greet Agricola and Adler for me.

Martin Luther

To Wittenberg Luther also wrote of his new life. His large household had not been entirely depleted. The guests who remained wrote him a common letter giving the domestic news, and he promptly answered them in this delightful epistle:

TO HIS TABLE COMPANIONS
At the Diet of the Grain Turks, April 28, 1530

Grace and peace in Christ. Dear gentlemen and friends, I have received the letter which you all sent me and so have learned how everything is. And that you may also learn how things are with us, I would have you know that we, namely, Veit Dietrich, Cyriac Kaufmann, and I, did not press on to the Diet of Augsburg, but stopped to attend another diet here. There is a coppice directly under our windows, like a little forest, where the daws and crows are holding a diet; they fly to and fro at such a rate and make such a racket day and night that they all seem drunk, soused and silly. I wonder how their breath holds out to bicker so. Pray tell me have you sent any delegates to these noble estates? For I think they must have assembled from all the world. I have not yet seen their emperor, but nobles and soldier lads fly and gad about, inexpensively clothed in one colour; all alike black, all alike grey-eyed, all alike with the same song, sung in different tones of big and little, old and young. They care not for a large place to meet in, for their hall is roofed with the vault of the sky, its floor is the carpet of green grass, and its walls are as far as the ends of the world. They do not ask for horses and trappings, having winged chariots to escape puissant lords, but I have not yet learned what they have decided upon. As far as I can gather from an interpreter, however, they are for a vigorous campaign against wheat, barley, oats, and all kinds of corn and grain, a war in which many a knight will do great deeds. So we sit here in the diet and spend time agreeably seeing and hearing how the estates of the realm make merry and sing. It is pleasant to see how soldierly they discourse and wipe their bills and arm themselves for victory against the grain. I wish them good luck—to be all spitted on a skewer together. I believe they are in no wise different from the sophists and papists who go for me with their sermons and books all at once; I see by the example of the harsh-voiced daws what a profitable people they are, devouring everything on earth and chattering loud and long in return.

Today we heard the first nightingale, who could hardly believe that it was April. The weather has been splendid, with no rain except a little yesterday. Perhaps you are not so fortunate in this respect. God bless you all. Keep house well.

Martin Luther

With his dear wife, too, he kept up regular correspondence. Just after his father's death she sent him a picture of their year-old baby Magdalene, a pair of needed spectacles, and a box of home comforts, for which he thanks her:

TO CATHARINE LUTHER AT WITTENBERG
Feste Coburg, June 5, 1530

Grace and peace in Christ. Dear Katie, I believe I have received all your letters. This is my fourth to you since John left me for Wittenberg. I have Lena's picture and the box you sent. At first I did not know the little hussy, she seemed so dark. I think it would be a first rate thing if you weaned her; do it little by little as Argula von Grumbach who has been here tells me she did with her son George. John Reinecke of Mansfeld has also been to see me and so has George Römer; in fact I shall soon have to go elsewhere if the pilgrimage hither continues.

Tell Christian Döring that I have never in my life had worse spectacles than those that came with his letter; I could not see a line through them. I did not receive the note sent in care of Conrad Vater, as I am not at Coburg, but I shall try to get it. You can send your letters care of the superintendent, who will forward them to me.

Our friends at Nuremberg and Augsburg are beginning to doubt whether anything will happen at the Diet, for the Emperor still tarries at Innsbruck. The prelates have some infernal plot, God grant the devil foul them. Amen. Let Bugenhagen read the copy of my letter to Link. I must hurry, as the messenger will not wait. Greet, kiss, hug, and be kind to each according to his degree.

Martin Luther

Katie was not entirely dependent for information on the

letters of her husband. One to her from Veit Dietrich is too characteristic of that interesting person and too good of its kind to omit. The writer, now twenty-three years old, had come to Wittenberg to study medicine, but abandoned that vocation for theology when he came under the influence of Luther. He became the professor's amanuensis in 1527 and was taken into his house in 1529. His unbounded idolatry of the great man led him to treasure all he wrote and all he said; much of the table-talk he noted down, as well as the letter given below, is worthy of Boswell.

VEIT DIETRICH TO MISTRESS CATHARINE LUTHER AT WITTENBERG

Feste Coburg, June 19, 1530

Grace and peace in God. Kind, gracious, dear lady! Know that your husband and we are hale and hearty by God's grace. May God also bless you and the children. You did a mighty good stroke of work in sending the doctor the picture, for it makes him entirely forget his cares. He has hung it on the wall opposite the table in the Elector's apartment where we eat. When he first saw it he did not recognise it for a long time. 'Dear me,' said he, 'Lena is so dark!' But now it pleases him well, and the more he looks at it the better he sees it is Lena. She looks extraordinarily like Hans in the mouth, eyes, and nose, in fact in the whole face, and she will grow more like him. I just had to write you this!

Dear lady, pray don't worry about the doctor; he is, thank God, hale and hearty, and, although his father's death was very bitter to him, he ceased mourning for it after two days. When he read Reinach's letter he said to me, 'My father is dead.' And then he took his Psalter and went to his room and wept so much that for two days he couldn't work. Since then he has not given way to grief any more. On Saturday, June 3, the town clerk was our guest for the evening, and the doctor told us, among other things, how he had dreamed the night before that he lost a tooth so large that it astonished him beyond measure, and the next day came the news of his father's death! I thought you ought to know this, so pray take it with my service. May God bless Hans and Lena and the whole houseful. My friend George will give you three gulden, which please accept until I can get more.

Veit Dietrich of Nuremberg

What a picture of the man these chatty letters give! As at the Wartburg, he dressed in laymen's clothes and grew a thick beard. He had grown stouter and aged a little since then, more with toil and illness than with his forty-seven years. Sometimes he rambled about the wide-flung battlements, gazing with a smile at the busy birds in the tree-tops, or lost in thought and wonder at the mysteries of nature, the clouds, the rainbow, and the stars.

Most of the time he spent in his little wooden room with the narrow window, poring over the Hebrew prophets and the Psalter, or adapting an old German translation of Æsop to the needs of his own day, or writing letters. His first task was the composition of *A Warning to the Prelates at Augsburg* which was printed in May and sent to the Diet in June. He solemnly begs the clergy there assembled not to make the session vain and not to induce 'the noble blooded Charles' to damn him and his doctrine. He insists that he is not responsible for the tumults which have shaken Germany; rather he alone withstood the turbulent spirits 'so that I might truly say I was your protector'. He reminds them of his moderation at Worms and recounts the history of his attacks on indulgences, confession, penance, private masses, and monastic vows. If they ask what good has come of the new teaching, he replies rather what good has remained with his opponents? Have they not perverted all God's laws? Have they not abused the ban, the sacrament, which ought to be administered in both kinds, and vows of celibacy which ought to be left free? But they talk only of these and similar indifferent things, whereas they should first concern themselves with the primary things, the law, the gospel, sin, grace, the gifts of the Spirit, right repentance, Christian fredom, faith, free will, and love, and next to these practical reforms such as the erection of schools, hospitals, and the regulation of poor-relief.

Just after he had finished this, he had one of his old nervous breakdowns, partly due to the unaccustomed richness of the fare. Thus he writes:

TO PHILIP MELANCHTHON AT AUGSBURG
Feste Coburg, May 12, 1530

Grace and peace in the Lord. Dear Philip, I began to answer your letter from Nuremberg on May 8, but business interfered to prevent me finishing my reply. I have completed my *Warning to the Prelates* and sent it off to the Wittenberg press. I have also translated the two chapters of Ezekiel about Gog and have written a preface to them, so that they be printed at the same time. Then I took the Prophets in hand and attacked the labour with such ardour that I hope to finish it before Pentecost and after that turn to Æsop and other things. But the old outer man cannot keep up with the ardour of the new inner man; my head has begun to suffer from ringing or rather thundering, and this has forced me to stop work. Yesterday and the day before when I tried to work, I narrowly escaped fainting, and this is the third day on which I am unable even to look at a letter of the alphabet. I get worse as the years go by. My head (*caput*) is now a mere heading (*capitulum*) or chapter, soon it will be a paragraph, and then a bare sentence. I can do nothing but idle ... so now you know why I am slow in answering your letter. On the day that it came Satan was busy occupying my attention with an embassy. I was alone, Dietrich and Cyriac were away, and Satan conquered me so far that he forced me to leave my room and seek the society of men. I hardly expected to see the day when that spirit would have so much power and simply divine majesty.

Such is our domestic news; other news comes from abroad, such as that you mention about the strife between Eck and Billican. What is happening at the Diet? What do those blockish asses think of the cause of the church and how are they disposed? But let them be.

Camerarius has sent me some dainties consisting of fine grapes and sack and has written me two Greek letters. When I feel better I shall write him in Turkish, that he too may have to read what he does not understand. Why should he write to me in Greek?

I must stop now lest my head, still sensitive, go bad again. I pray; do you pray also. I would most willingly write, as you suggest, to the Landgrave of Hesse and to the Elector and to all of you, but I must take my own time. The Lord be with you. Give heed to my example and be sure not to lose your head as I have done. I command you and all my friends to keep regular habits for the sake of your health. Do not kill yourself and then pretend you did it in God's service. For God is just as well served, if not better, by resting, wherefore he commanded the Sabbath to be rigidly kept. Do not despise this warning, for it is the word of God.

Martin Luther

When the Elector heard of Luther's sufferings he sent him a kind message not to worry about his enforced idleness, and at the same time expressing some anxiety on his own part at the dark outlook of the Protestants in the present crisis. The answer encourages him in turn:

TO JOHN, ELECTOR OF SAXONY, AT AUGSBURG
Feste Coburg, May 20, 1530

Grace and peace in Christ our Lord and saviour. Amen. Most Serene, Highborn Prince, most Gracious Lord! I have delayed answering your Grace's first letter from Augsburg, kindly written to tell me the news and express your hope that time was not hanging heavy on my hands. Truly your Grace need not worry about me in the kindness of your heart, although I am anxious about you and pray God for you. The time does not seem heavy to me; I live like a lord and the weeks scarcely seem three days to me. It is your Grace who is really in the tedious place. . . .

Consider that God shows himself merciful to you in making the word fruitful in your Grace's land. Verily Electoral Saxony has the greatest number and best ministers and preachers of all the world, men who teach pure, true, and peaceable doctrine. Now the tender youth of both sexes are growing up so well instructed in the Catechism and in the Bible that it does my heart good to see how the boys and girls can pray and believe and speak more of God and Christ than formerly any religious foundation, cloister, or school could or yet can. Such young people in your Grace's land are a fair paradise, the like of which is not to be found in all the rest of the world. It is planted by God in your Grace's land as a true sign of favour to you, just as if he should say: 'Well, dear Prince John, I commend to you my most precious treasure, my pleasant paradise; you shall be father in it, for I put it under your protection and rule and give you the honour of being my gardener and caretaker.' . . . It is just as if God himself were your daily guest and ward, as he makes his gospel and his children your guests and wards. On the other hand, consider what terrible harm the other princes have done, and yet do to their youth, making the paradise of God a sinful, worthless, foul slough of Satan, destroying all and inviting the genuine old devil to be their guest. . . .

May your Grace be pleased with my letter; God knows I speak the truth and do not flatter, for it is a sorrow to me that Satan can still trouble and disturb your heart. I know him somewhat myself, for he is accustomed to play with me. He is a gloomy, sour spirit who cannot suffer a heart to be glad or have peace, and especially the heart of your Grace, for he knows how much depends on you, not only for us but for the world, and I can truly say for heaven itself. . . . Wherefore we are bound loyally to pray for and encourage your Grace, for if you are happy we live, if you are in trouble we sicken. . . .

Your Grace's subject,

Martin Luther

The Diet, though summoned to meet on April 8, did not really open until June 20, a few days after the arrival of the Emperor. It decided to take up the religious question first. Melanchthon, as the active leader of the Protestants, had drawn up an official statement of their doctrine to be presented to the Estates, the so-called *Augsburg Confession*. This document had been submitted to Luther and approved by him, but after this Melanchthon had somewhat altered it, hoping to make its wording more acceptable to the Catholics and to show that the Protestants were the real defenders of the old faith against novel abuses. For example, the article on the sacrament was put into language which good Catholics could have subscribed to, had they not known that declarations on transubstantiation and on the mass as an offering had been intentionally omitted. Again, private masses were gently deprecated instead of being described as a horror in the style of the previous confession. In spite of these concessions Melanchthon was fearful that they might not satisfy his opponents.

The *Confession* was read before the Diet, though only in a secret session. Luther regarded this as a great triumph for the cause, for which he alone had stood nine years before, as he writes to a friend and ardent supporter:

TO CONRAD CORDATUS AT ZWICKAU

The Wilderness, July 6, 1530

. . . Jonas writes to me that he was present during the session when the *Confession* was read before the Diet and supported in a two-hour oration by Dr Brier, and that he will tell me later what he gathered from the faces of the audience. . . . Our enemies certainly did their best to prevent the Emperor allowing it to be read, and they did succeed in preventing its being read in the public hall before all the people. But the Emperor heard it before the princes and estates of the Empire. I am overjoyed to be living at this hour, when Christ is openly confessed by so many in a great public assembly and with so good a confession. . . . Do not cease to pray for the good young Emperor, worthy of the love of God and of men and for the not less excellent Elector who bears the cross and for Melanchthon who tortures himself with care. . . .

The reading of the *Confession* was only the beginning of negotiations, which, dragging along week after week, sorely tried the patience and firmness of the Protestant minority. In these dark days, when the sun was hidden and the way seemed lost, Luther, though absent, the heart and spirit of his party, encouraged and revived their fainting spirits. One of the most wonderful letters he ever wrote is the following to the chancellor, or, as we might say, prime minister of Electoral Saxony.

TO DR GREGORY BRÜCK AT AUGSBURG
The Wilderness, August 5, 1530

. . . I have recently seen two miracles. The first was, that, as I looked out of my window, I saw the stars and the sky and the whole vault of heaven, with no vault to support it; and yet the sky did not fall and the vault remained fast. But there are some who want to see the pillars and would like to clasp and feel them. And when they are unable to do so they fidget and tremble as if the sky would certainly fall in, simply because they cannot feel and see the pillars under it. If they could only do this, they would be satisfied that the sky would remain fast.

Again I saw great, thick clouds roll above us, so heavy that they looked like great seas, and I saw no ground on which they could rest nor any barrels to hold them and yet they fell not on us, but threatened us and floated on. When they had passed by, the rainbow shone forth, the rainbow which was the floor that held them up. It is such a weak think little floor and roof that it was almost lost in the clouds and looked more like a ray coming through a stained glass window than like a strong floor, so that it was as marvellous as the weight of the clouds. For it actually happened that this seemingly frail shadow held up the weight of water and protected us. But some people look at the thickness of the clouds and the thinness of the ray and they fear and worry. They would like to feel how strong the rainbow is, and when they cannot do so they think the clouds will bring on another deluge.

I permit myself such pleasantries with your Honour, although I write with earnest purpose. . . . I hope we can keep the peace politically, but God's thoughts are above our thoughts. . . . If he should hear our prayers now and grant us peace, perhaps it would turn out worse than we hoped, and God would get less glory than the Emperor. . . . I do not mean to despise the Emperor, and only hope and pray that he may do nothing against God and the imperial constitution. If, however, he does this, we as faithful subjects are bound to believe that it is not the Emperor himself who is so doing, but tyrannical advisers usurping his authority, and we should make a distinction between the acts of our sovereign and those of his wicked counsellors. . . .

While Luther was writing these lines bad news was on the way. *A Refutation of the Confession,* prepared by his old enemy Eck and others, was read before the Diet on August 3. Charles refused to allow the Protestants a copy of this, which they desired in order to frame a reply. Thereupon Philip of Hesse, thinking all was over, suddenly and secretly left Augsburg, on August 6. Just a week before he had, in spite of Luther's warning to beware of the sacramentarians, entered into an alliance with Zurich and Constance. The Wittenberg professor did not hear of this for some time, and when he did judged the ambitious chief severely for a step likely to bring on a war between Lutherans and Swiss.

But negotiations were still continued by the Protestants who stood fast and by a Catholic peace party headed by Albert of Mainz. Crafty Eck had appointed a committee of six consisting of himself, four other Catholics, and Melanchthon. The one reformer in this body had not the stamina to withstand a hostile majority and made such concessions on all points save marriage of the clergy, the dispensation of the sacrament in both kinds and the abolition of private masses, that an agreement was almost reached. It must be remembered, however, that when articles of faith were expressed in purposely ambiguous terms acceptable to both parties, the interpretation of these words was diametrically opposite. In return for the Protestant agreement to call the mass an offering, if the word were qualified with the term commemorative, the Catholics conceded that communion might be administered in both kinds if it were taught that this was a matter of convenience and not of principle. One of the most dangerous points yielded by Melanchthon was that the bishops should be restored to their ancient jurisdictions, a measure justified by him as a blow to turbulent sectaries.

Negotiations continued, to the increasing prejudice of the Protestants, throughout most of August and September. Melanchthon, whose humanistic training gave him a broader outlook than that of many of his contemporaries, animated by a sincere love of peace, yielded on matters which to him were indifferent, but to his co-religionists vital. Justas Jonas, also a humanist by education, sided with him, but most of the other Protestant leaders raised an outcry that he was a greater enemy to the faith than any Catholic and appealed over his head to Luther. The numerous letters written by him to his friends at

Augsburg, though they sometimes show perplexity as to what was actually being done, are consistently and energetically opposed to all compromise. To Melanchthon he wrote on August 26 that he was even sorry that Eck had told such a lie as to say that he believed in justification by faith; communion in both kinds must be insisted on as necessary in all cases, and there was great danger of civil war in restoring the bishops to their old power. 'In short, all treaty about harmonising our doctrines displeases me, for I know it is impossible unless the Pope will simply abolish the papacy.' On September 20 he wrote: 'If we yield a single one of their conditions, be it that on the Canon or on private masses, we deny our whole doctrine and confirm theirs. . . . I would not yield an inch to those proud men, seeing how far they play upon our weakness. . . . I am almost bursting with anger and indignation. Pray break off all transactions at once and return hither. They have our *Confession* and they have the gospel; if they wish let them hear those witnesses, if not let them depart to their own place. If war follows it will follow; we have prayed and done enough.'

Luther has often been blamed for his uncompromising spirit and for his narrowness on this occasion. An age which has ceased to regard many points then hotly disputed as vital or even as interesting can hardly appreciate the opinion of a man who made so much of them. Nevertheless, while Melanchthon's conciliatory breadth is far more congenial to our modern spirit, I believe that in this case Luther was right. The problem before a statesman is not what is the best possible policy in perfect conditions, but what is the best practical course to pursue under given limitations. The question for the Protestants of 1530 was not what line might be safely followed in an enlightened, tolerant age, but what measures were necessary, in the face of an exigent and perilous situation. It was a plain fact that however much they might juggle with words their differences were far too fundamental to be resolved by any treaty. Luther saw this, Melanchthon did not.

The Catholics also saw it. Notwithstanding the immense concessions wrung from their opponents, they voted, on September 22, that the *Confession* had been refuted and rejected, and that consequently the Protestants were bound to recant. The Diet, in this Recess, gave the heretics until April 15, while the Emperor was to use his influence with the Pope to call a general council for the decision of still doubtful points; after that respite they were to be coerced.

Luther was deeply disappointed at this result. 'I think the Recess is worldly wisdom,' he wrote on October 1, 'but let us believe that Christ is yet strong enough to rule all fools and babblers who condemn him.' A day or two later the whole Saxon delegation returned to Coburg, which the Reformer left on the fourth, arriving home on the thirteenth.

15

The German Bible

Luther's greatest monument is the German Bible. The old error of supposing that his was the first German version and that before his time the book had been much neglected has been often exposed; yet it remains true that his translation, by its superior scholarship and wonderful style, marks a new era in both religion and literature.

Begun at the Wartburg in the latter part of 1521, the work was prosecuted with such energy that the New Testament was completed by the time that Luther returned to Wittenberg in March, 1522. It was published the following September in a handsome quarto with woodcuts from Cranach's workshop—some of them after Dürer's famous Apocalypse series—a description of the Holy Land by Melanchthon, marginal explanatory notes and introductions to the whole and to the separate books by Luther.

Work on the Old Testament was begun at once with the help of Melanchthon, Aurogallas, and Rörer. The first part appeared in the summer of 1523 and the second in December of that year. Of the work taken up next, Luther writes, on February 23, 1524, to Spalatin:

> We have so much trouble translating Job, on account of the grandeur of his sublime style, that he seems to be much more impatient of our efforts to turn him into

German than he was of the consolations of his friends. Either he always wishes to sit upon his dunghill, or else he is jealous of the translator who would share with him the credit of writing his book.

The third part of the Old Testament, however, containing this difficult book, appeared in September or October, 1524. There still remained the Prophets, and labour on them had to be postponed for some years by the controversies with Erasmus, the Heavenly Prophets, and Zwingli. When they were taken up again, in 1528, the Reformer wrote to Wenzel Link, on June 14:

I am now at work translating the Prophets. Good heavens! how hard it is to make the Hebrew writers speak German! They withstand our efforts, not wishing to give up their native tongue for a barbarous idiom, just as the nightingale would not change her sweet song to imitate the cuckoo whose monotonous note she abhors.

In the same year Isaiah was finished, after which some portions of the Apocrypha were taken up. At Feste Coburg the Prophets were almost completed, though it was not until March 16, 1532, that the last portion of the Old Testament came out. This was shortly followed by the Apocrypha. In 1539 a careful revision was undertaken by a 'Sanhedrin' as Mathesius calls it, consisting of Melanchthon the Greek scholar, Cruciger with the Chaldean paraphrase, Bugenhagen skilful in the Latin version, Jonas the rhetorician, Aurogallas professor of Hebrew, Rörer the proof-reader, and Luther the president and inspiring the spirit of the whole. He took a legitimate pride in his own work, of which he said:

I do not wish to praise myself, but the work speaks for itself. The German Bible is so good and precious that it surpasses all the Greek and Latin versions, and more is found in it than in all the commentaries, for we clear the sticks and stones out of the way that others may read without hindrance.

In point of scholarship Luther's version was far superior to all that had preceded it. They had been made from the Latin Vulgate, adding to the errors of their original others of their own. The basis of Luther's translation was the original tongues: the Hebrew Massoretic text of the Old Testament published by Gerson Ben Mosheh at Brescia in 1494 and the Greek New Testament of Erasmus in the edition of 1519. Modern critics have been able to improve on the work of Erasmus, nevertheless his text was better than anything which had preceded it and was in some points, as for example in omitting 1 John 5:7, superior to that from which our King James version was made.

Other helps were of course much scantier than they are today. For example a diligent search failed to secure a map of the Holy Land. Luther undoubtedly used the Latin and even the older German versions as aids, though in no sense did he copy them. The work was indeed done with astounding rapidity, and the success of the work testifies to its excellence.

Luther's principles, indeed, were not strictly scientific, but rather apologetic. The protocols laid down for the revision of 1539 indicate this, and so does the following saying of 1540:

Dr Forster and Ziegler conferred with us about our version and gave us much help. I gave them three rules: 1. The Bible speaks and teaches of God's works, of this there is no doubt. But these works are divided into three classes: the home, the state, and the church. If a saying does not fit the church, let us place it in whichever of the other classes it best suits. 2. When there is doubt about the words or construction, we must choose the sense—saving the grammar—which agrees with the New Testament. 3. If a sentence is repugnant to the whole of scripture, we must simply throw it away, for the rabbis have corrupted the whole text with their notes, trying to make it appear that the Messiah will come to give us meat and drink and afterward will die. That is a horror and we must simply throw it away. I took many a questionable sentence to Forster; if he said, 'But the rabbis understand it so and so,' I replied, 'But could you not write the vowel points differently and construe so as to agree with the New Testament?' If his reply was affirmative I would say that it should then be so construed. That sometimes surprised them, and they said that they would not have thought of that sense their whole life long.

Such a saying gives a rather unfavourable idea of the probable accuracy of the version; nevertheless as a matter of fact Luther's scholarship was far sounder than that of his predecessors. But it was less remarkable for this excellence than for the superiority of its style. The English Bible has also become a classic, but hardly attains the exalted position of the German in this respect. Luther's influence, exerted chiefly through this work, has been so enormous on the literature of his people that it is sometimes said that he created the modern written language. Other scholars are inclined to see in him rather the culmination of a literary activity which began some centuries before. It is certain that there existed before him a common German apart from the numerous local dialects, spoken at the court first of the Luxembourg and then of the Hapsburg emperors. Luther himself recognises this:

I talk a common, standard German rather than a particular dialect, and thus I can be understood in both Upper and Lower Germany. I speak according to the usage of the Saxon chancery, the form used by the German princes in addressing one another. Maximilian and Frederick the Wise brought the whole empire to a sort of common speech by combining all the dialects in one.

Whatever may be thought of Luther's speech, whether he merely gave currency to 'the ugly dialect of the Luxembourg emperors', or created a strong and flexible literary language, it is certain that his writings were for a long time the standard of good form and that they gave an immense impetus to German thought.

His own principles, which conduced to great freedom of treatment, are well set forth by himself:

It is not possible to reproduce a foreign idiom in one's native tongue. The proper method of translation is to seek a vocabulary neither too free nor too literal, but to select the most fitting terms according to the usage of the language adopted.

To translate properly is to render the spirit of a foreign language into our own idiom. I do this with such care in translating Moses that the Jews accuse me of rendering only the sense and not the precise words. For example when the Hebrew says, 'the mouth of the sword' I translate 'the edge of the sword', though in this case it might be objected that the word 'mouth' is a figurative allusion to preachers who destroy by word of mouth.

I try to speak as men do in the market-place. Didactic, philosophic, and sententious books are, therefore, hard to translate, but narrative easy. In rendering Moses I make him so German that no one would know that he was a Jew.

No Englishing of Luther's German can give any conception of the peculiar flavour of his version, which, to be appreciated, must be read in the original. One or two examples, however, may serve to point out the extreme freedom of the rendering. The word 'church' (*Kirche*) is never used, but for it 'congregation' (*Gemeinde*), as more consistent with the original idea. Again, 'Repent' (Matthew 3:2 and 4:17; Mark 1:15) is not *'tut Busse'*, as in the older versions, but *'bessert euch'*, 'improve yourselves'. In Romans

3:28, 'For we maintain that a man is justified by faith apart from observing the law,' Luther added 'alone' after 'faith', to bring out what he believed to be the meaning of the apostle. He was violently attacked for this alteration by his enemies, and defended himself in an angry *Letter on Translation* in 1530:

> It is my testament and my translation [he bursts out] and if I have made any mistakes (though I never falsified intentionally) I will not let the papists judge me. . . . As to Romans 3:28, if the word 'alone' is not found in the Latin or Greek texts, yet the passage has that meaning and must be rendered so in order to make it clear and strong in German.

Luther's attitude to the Bible contains one striking contradiction. He insisted that it should be taken as a whole and literally as God's inerrant word; and at the same time he was himself the freest of 'higher critics'. In his works against the Heavenly Prophets (1524) and against Erasmus (1525) he introduced long arguments to show that the Bible is consistent and binding in the literal interpretation of each text. In a work of 1530 he says: 'Let no one think he can master the articles of faith by reason. . . . What Christ says must be so whether I or any other man can understand it.' In his book *Against the Papacy at Rome* (1545) he says: 'This writer would have done better to leave his reason at home or to ground it on texts of scripture, rather than ridiculously and crazily to found faith and the divine law on mere reason.' These and many another saying lend substance to the charge, often brought against Luther, of having merely substituted an infallible book for an infallible church, or as a recent writer has expressed it, 'of having set up bibliolatry in place of ecclesiolatry'.

But Luther was not the man to be bound by his own rule; few of his followers have ever interpreted, commented on, and criticised the Bible with the freedom habitual to him. The books he judged according to his spiritual needs. He often exercised his reason in determining the respective worth of the several books of the Bible, and in a way which has been confirmed to a surprising degree by subsequent researches. He denied the Mosaic authorship of part of the Pentateuch; he declared Job to be an allegory; Jonah was so childish that he was almost inclined to laugh at it; the books of Kings were 'a thousand paces ahead of Chronicles and more to be believed'. 'Ecclesiastes has neither boots nor spurs, but rides in socks, as I did when I was in the cloister.'

The Psalter was prized highly: 'It should be dear to us,' he said in his preface to it, 'if only because it so clearly promises Christ's death and resurrection and prefigures his kingdom with the estate and nature of all Christendom, so that it may well be called a small Bible wherein all that stands in scripture is most fairly and briefly comprehended.'

But we must not make Luther more in advance of his time than he really was. He naïvely accepted all the miracles of the Bible, as illustrated by the following:

> I would give the world to have the stories of the antediluvian patriarchs also, that we might see how they lived, preached, and suffered. . . . I have taught and suffered, too, but only fifteen, twenty, or thirty years; they lived seven or eight hundred and how they must have suffered!

Similar freedom was used in judging the books of the New Testament. In the preface of 1545 he says: 'St John's gospel and his first epistle, St Paul's epistles, and especially Romans, Galatians, and Ephesians, and St Peter's first epistle are the books which teach all that is necessary for salvation, even if you read no other books. In comparison with them, James is a right straw epistle, for it has no evangelical manner about it.'

In the introduction to Romans (1522), he says: 'This

epistle is the kernel of the New Testament and the clearest of all gospels, worthy and worth that a Christian man should not only know the words by heart, but should converse with them continually as the daily bread of the soul. It can never be too much read nor considered, but the more it is used the more precious it becomes.' Then, by way of explaining the apostolic use of such words as law, sin, grace, faith, justification, flesh, and spirit, he gives an excellent summary of his own doctrine.

Revelation he holds neither apostolic nor prophetic, for Christ is neither taught nor recognised in it.

Again, when he was asked what were the best books of the Bible, he said the Psalms, St John's and St Paul's epistles for those who had to fight heretics, but for the common man and young people the first three gospels.

The often quoted condemnation of James as an epistle of straw is far better known than the more drastic things he said about it to his table companions:

Many sweat to reconcile St Paul and St James, as does Melanchthon in his *Apology,* but in vain. 'Faith justifies' and 'faith does not justify' contradict each other flatly. If anyone can harmonise them I will give him my doctor's hood and let him call me a fool.

Let us banish this epistle from the university, for it is worthless. It has no syllable about Christ, not even naming him except once at the beginning. I think it was written by some Jew who had heard of the Christians but not joined them. James had learned that the Christians insisted strongly on faith in Christ and so he said to himself: 'Well, you must take issue with them and speak only of works,' and so he does. He says not a word of the passion and resurrection of Christ, the text of all the other apostles. Moreover, he has no order nor method. He speaks now of clothes, now of wrath, jumping from one topic to another. He has this simile: 'For as the body without the spirit is dead, so faith without works is dead also.' Mary, mother of God! He compares faith to the body when it should rather be compared to the soul! The ancients saw all this and did not consider the epistle canonical.

Luther's marginal notes in one of his own Bibles are equally trenchant. To James 1:6 ('When he asks, he must believe and not doubt'), he remarks: 'That is the only good place in the whole epistle'; to 1:21 ('Accept the word planted in you, which can save you'), 'Others engrafted it, not this James'; to 2:12ff., 'What a chaos!' and to 2:24 ('You see that a person is justified by what he does and not by faith alone'), 'That is false.'

16

The Wittenberg Agreement, 1536

To the Diet of Augsburg in the 1530 Zwingli sent a confession of faith in which he designated the Lutherans as men who longed after the fleshpots of the old Egypt. Still another confession, more irenic in tone, was brought by the German Zwinglians. Their representative, Martin Bucer of Strasbourg, since 1518 a friend and admirer of the Wittenberg reformer, visited Feste Coburg in hopes of bringing about a union. He succeeded in convincing Luther of the good intentions of the South German cities, and, wishing to push his advantage, sent to him, not long after the close of the Diet, a very conciliatory creed, for which he received the following acknowledgement:

TO MARTIN BUCER AT STRASBOURG
Wittenberg, January 22, 1531

Grace and peace in Christ. I have received the confession sent by you, dear Bucer; I approve it and thank God that we are united in confessing, as you write, that the body and blood of the Lord is truly in the supper, and is dispensed by the consecrating words as food for the soul. I am surprised that you say that Zwingli and Œcolampadius believe this too, but I speak not to them but to you. [Here follows an exposition of the minute differences in the belief of Luther and of Bucer.]

I cannot, therefore, admit a full, solid peace with you without violating my conscience, for did I make peace on these terms I should only sow the seeds of far greater theological disagreement and more atrocious discord between us in future. . . . Let us rather bear a little discord with an imperfect peace, than, by trying to cure this, create a more tragic schism and tumult. Please believe what I told you at Coburg, that I would like to heal this breach between us at the cost of my life three times over, for I see how needful is your fellowship to us and what damage our disunion has done the gospel. I am certain that, were we but united, all the gates of hell and all the papacy and all the Turks and all the world and all the flesh and whatever evil there is could not hurt us. Please impute it not to obstinacy but to conscience that I decline the union you propose. After our conference at Coburg I had high hopes, but as yet they have not proved well founded. May the Lord Jesus illumine us and make us more perfectly at one. . . .

How insistent Luther was that all with whom he claimed Christian fellowship should believe exactly as he did, and how sensitive he was lest it be thought that he had changed an iota of his opinion, is set forth in a letter to John Frosch, a minister of Augsburg, dated March 28, 1531:

I have heard of the boasting of you Zwinglians that peace is made between us and that we have gone over entirely to your opinion. But, my dear Frosch, you must know that we have yielded nothing. Martin Bucer, indeed, seems to be thoroughly convinced that we believe and teach the same doctrine, and of him personally I therefore entertain some hopes. Of the others I know nothing certain, but if they desire peace I should wish to indulge them little by little, tolerating their opinion for a time while holding fast to our own as heretofore. This much charity demands.

Luther not only condemned the Swiss theology, but he entertained a deep, and as it proved, a well-founded distrust of the political aspirations of their leader. From the alliance of Hesse, Zurich, and Constance he predicted disaster.

His gloomy prognostications were strikingly confirmed by the battle of Cappel, October 11, 1531, in which Protestant cantons were defeated by the Catholic, Zwingli lost his life, and the Swiss allies of Hesse were rendered powerless. As in the destruction of Münzer and the prophets six years before, the radical wing of the Protestant party was cut off and the leadership left to the conservative Lutheran branch. The Reformer regarded both events as providential judgements on error. Far from being moved by the heroic death of his rival, he was, if possible, more confirmed than ever in his unfavourable estimate of his opinions and character. When he first heard of Cappel, he exclaimed:

> God knows the counsels of the heart, and it is therefore a good thing that Zwingli, Carlstadt, and Pellican lie prostrate, for otherwise we could not have withstood them and Strasbourg and Hesse altogether. What a triumph for us it is that they have thus stultified themselves!

Again, when he learned of the death of Œcolampadius, which followed a few weeks later, he said:

> Erasmus, Œcolampadius, Zwingli, and Carlstadt all relied on their own wisdom and were therefore confounded. But I know that God knows more than I do and I thank him for it. . . . Who would have believed ten years ago that we should have been so successful?

Regarding the heresy of Zwingli as so poisonous, Luther naturally continued to combat it vigorously.

TO DUKE ALBERT OF PRUSSIA
Wittenberg, February or beginning of March, 1532

Grace and peace in Christ our Lord and saviour. Serene, highborn Prince. . . . Although neither Münzerites nor Zwinglians will admit that they are punished by God, but give out that they are martyrs, nevertheless we, who know that they have gravely erred in the sacrament and other articles, recognise God's punishment and beware of it ourselves. Not that we rejoice in their misfortune, which is and always has been a sorrow to our hearts, but we cannot let the witness of God pass unnoticed. We hope from the bottom of our hearts that they are saved, as it is not impossible for God to convert a man in a moment at his death; but to call them martyrs implies that they died for a certain divine faith, which they did not. . . .

Your Grace must think that if you tolerate such ranters in your dominions when you can prevent it, you will terribly burden your conscience, so that perhaps you can never quiet it again; you would be troubled not only for the sake of your soul, which would be damned thereby, but for the sake of the whole Christian church, for if you allow any to teach against the long and unanimously held doctrine of the church when you can prevent it, it may well be called an unbearable burden to conscience. I should rather have not only all ranters, but all powerful, wise emperors, kings, and princes testify against me than let one jot of the holy Christian church hear or see anything against me. For we must not trifle with the articles of faith so long and unanimously held by Christendom, as we can with papal or imperial law or the human traditions of the fathers and the councils.

This is my brief, humble, and Christian answer to your Grace. May Christ our saviour richly enlighten and strengthen you to believe and act according to his holy word. Amen.

Your Grace's devoted
Martin Luther

The blow to Protestantism in Switzerland made it all the more advisable that German Lutherans and Zwinglians should unite, and the danger of sacramentarian leadership being averted removed the obstacle to doing so on the part of Wittenberg. Philip of Hesse was again the mediator. Judging that better results would follow from a conference at which Luther was not present, he invited Melanchthon to meet Bucer at Cassel in December 1534, to discuss terms of agreement. Fearing that his friend would yield too much, Luther sent with him a written statement of his opinion in the strongest form, namely, that the body of the Lord was bitten by the teeth of the communicant. The meeting was, however, successful; Bucer admitted the absent reformer's contentions in such a way as to convince the latter that the church of Upper Germany, at least, was on the right road. Thus he wrote to Philip of Hesse on January 30, 1535:

> I have now arrived at the point, thank God, where I can confidently hope that the ministers of Upper Germany heartily and earnestly believe what they say. But inasmuch as neither side has completely ascertained the opinion of the other, it seems to me that we have done enough for the present until God helps us to a real, thorough union. A long standing and deep difference cannot come to an end suddenly.

Nevertheless he wrote to Gerbel on November 27, 1535:

> How could I be more joyful, now that I have discharged the duties of life, than that before my death I should see an unexpected peace? . . . I say this that you may not doubt that I am heartily desirous of an agreement, whatever may seem to interfere with one. If you will mediate I am willing to do and suffer all. I wish to be found a faithful servant of Christ in the church even if I am not a very wise one.

With such a spirit of eagerness on one side and of

willingness on the other, it was natural that a still closer approach to unity should be made. Free correspondence between the leaders of both parties impressed on them the belief that all that was needed for perfect mutual understanding was a personal interview. The Upper Germans appealed to Luther to fix the time and place for such an assembly and he in turn consulted the Elector in a letter of January 25, 1536:

> The ministers of Strasbourg and Augsburg are anxious for a meeting, for having thoroughly canvassed the subject, we are convinced that nothing remains but to draw up an agreement. There is no need, as they themselves acknowledge, of a great concourse, among whom some might be restless and recalcitrant and thus spoil our peaceful intentions. I therefore humbly beg your Grace to state what city would be best.

The Elector at first selected Eisenach as the meeting-place, but this was later changed, on account of Luther's health, to Wittenberg. A small number of the leading clergy of Upper Germany arrived on May 21, and the next day the conference was finally convinced that the men present believed and taught the orthodox doctrine of the sacrament, namely, that the body and blood are really present in the elements of the eucharist. When Luther announced that he regarded them all as brothers tears sprang to the eyes of many. The conference was closed on Saturday, May 27. The day following, one of the visiting divines, Alber, preached in the morning, Bucer at noon, and Luther in the afternoon. The same evening Bucer and others were guests at the Black Cloister; of their conversation on that occasion the following interesting fragment has been recorded:

> *Luther*—I liked your sermon right well, friend Bucer, and yet I think mine was better.
> *Bucer*—I gladly admit your superiority, doctor.

Luther—I don't mean to boast; I know my weakness and that I am not so acute and learned as you in my sermons. But when I enter the pulpit, I consider my audience, mostly poor laymen and Wends, and preach to them. Like a mother I try to give my children milk, and not some fine syrup from the apothecary. You preach over their heads, floating around in the clouds and in the 'spirit'.

In the meantime Melanchthon had drawn up a formula embodying the results of the conference, the *Wittenberg Concord,* as it was called, which was signed by all present, save one, on Monday, May 29.

Although the Wittenberg Agreement had reunited the Lutherans with the German followers of Zwingli, the breach with the Swiss still remained. Bucer, cheered by the success of his last venture, hoped to heal this schism also, and, finding the Swiss divines ready to meet him halfway, approached Luther. His letter reached the Reformer while he was lying at Schmalkalden very ill, and was therefore not answered until December 6, 1537. This noncommittal reply left matters as they had been.

In 1538 the Swiss again addressed themselves to Wittenberg. On April 15 one of their ministers, Simon Sulzer, visited Saxony and was received with friendliness at the Black Cloister. A little later Zwingli's successor at Zurich, Henry Bullinger, wrote to Luther with the same end in view. The Reformer replied on May 14:

Of Zwingli I will freely say that when I saw and heard him at Marburg I judged him an excellent man, as I did Œcolampadius. Their fate deeply shocked me, being, as I am forced to believe, a retribution on their obstinately held errors.

After this no further efforts at unification were made.

17

Character and Habits

There is no good portrait of Luther after his forty-third year, but from the numerous inferior portraits painted by Lucas Cranach's sons and apprentices and from a number of descriptions it is possible to get a fairly good idea of his personal appearance. The accounts are somewhat contradictory in details, as, for example, his eyes are variously reported to have been black, brown, and dark with yellow rings around the pupils. Almost all, however, were impressed by the restless fire that flashed upon them, and by the lion-like mien of the man. In later life his form became portly, but in spite of illness he retained a look of uncommon youth and vigour. His hair turned grey but did not become sparse. In his last years traces of suffering and irritability appeared.

In dress Luther's tastes were of the simplest. His ordinary habit was the layman's jerkin and hose, which were sometimes poor and patched. He occasionally mended his clothes himself; in the first half of 1539 Lauterbach heard Katie complain that her husband had cut a piece out of his son's trousers to supply his own. He defended himself thus:

> The hole was so large that I had to have a large patch for it. Trousers seldom fit me well, so I have to make them

last long. If the Electors Frederick and John had not better tailors than I have they would mend their own breeches. The Italian tailors are the best. They divide the labour, some making coats, some cloaks, and some trousers. But in Germany they do it hit or miss, making all trousers according to one pattern. Think what an eyesore it is to see a man with trousers like a pigeon and a coat so short that one can see his back between it and the trousers. There is a proverb that 'short-coated Saxons jump like magpies'.

On festive occasions and when preaching, Luther wore a gown and on gala days a gold chain around his neck. At all times a silver ring graced one finger. Luther's standards of cleanliness were relatively high. He had a bathroom with tubs in his house; after using it one day he remarked, at dinner:

Why is the water so dirty after bathing? Ah! I forgot that the body is dirt, as the Bible says, 'Thou art dust and ashes.'

The day began early, the time of rising varying according to the season. The morning was devoted to lecturing and preaching, though Luther frequently felt headaches and dizziness which prevented him from doing much work. The principal meal of the day came at ten o'clock, after which the long afternoon was spent in writing and other business. After supper at five o'clock the evening was spent in conversation, reading, or work until nine, the regular bedtime. Of his evening devotions he once said:

I have to hurry all day to get time to pray. It must suffice me if I can say the Ten Commandments, the Lord's Prayer, and one or two petitions besides, thinking of which I fall asleep.

Luther's enemies called him a glutton and a wine-bibber. But in the monastery he had fasted until he became emaciated, and in later life his ill-health often made it difficult for him to eat. In general he tried to eat, thinking it good for his health and spirits, as when he said:

> This morning the devil had a dispute with me about Zwingli and I found a full head better able to withstand the fiend than one weakened with fasting.

And again:

> We ought to do our part and take care of our bodies; when we are tempted, abstinence is a hundred times worse than eating and drinking. Had I followed my appetite I should have taken nothing for three days, but I do eat though without pleasure. The world sees it and calls it drunkenness, but God will judge it rightly. . . . Sleep is also a good thing; when I lie awake the devil comes at once to dispute with me until I say: 'Devil, go hang, God is not angry with me as you say.'

Of good drink Luther was undoubtedly fond, but his practice in this respect must be judged by the standard of his age. No one advocated total abstinence, and the greatest licence was allowed not only to moderate indulgence but to intemperance. Charles V is reported to have taken habitually three quarts of wine at dinner—some authorities say more—and he was never charged with excess in this respect, as was the Elector John Frederick. Luther had special reasons for his drinking habits. It is now believed that alcohol is little better than poison to one suffering as he did from diseases of the nerves or of the kidneys, but four centuries ago drink was actually prescribed for these ailments, and moreover he took a 'strong little potation' at bedtime to make himself sleep. Other motives are more questionable, as, for example, when he tells Weller that he often drinks freely to 'spite the devil'.

Nevertheless, Luther certainly stopped short of intemperance. No one who did the enormous amount of work that he did could have been a habitual drunkard. In a sermon to the courtiers he tells them that, though constant intemperance is not to be borne, an occasional carouse may be overlooked. Did he allow himself these occasional carouses? The argument from silence is in this case decisive in the negative; knowing almost every act of his private life for fifteen years, we never once hear of such an outburst. At times, however, his conviviality bordered on the extreme, and he was always appreciative of the merits of good liquor.

The most damaging evidence has been found in an autograph of the Vatican archives:

TO CASPAR MÜLLER,
CHANCELLOR OF MANSFELD, AT EISLEBEN
Wittenberg, March 1, 1536

... Pray tell his Grace of Mansfeld from me to be merry, as in the story of the two students and the cook. People begin to say, or murmur, that a great deal depends on cheerfulness, and I half believe them. I haven't written to his Grace myself for fear that the Buck of Lübeck would make a fool of me. Yet as I now and then cast an inquisitive eye on his Grace, please tell him my opinion. What harm does a little jollity do? The beer is good, the maid fair, the boys young. The students are so merry that I am sorry that my health prevents me being oftener with them. Understand me like the poor, simple sheep you are said to be. I would willingly be good but I fear that I can never be as simple as you are. God bless you and greet all good friends. Amen.

Dr Martin
Dr Luther
Dr Johannes

P.S. My Katie sends her greetings and so does your god-son Hans.

The three signatures are for the three persons who send greetings to Müller, Dr Martin, 'my Katie' as Dr Luther, and nine-year-old Hans (Dr Johannes).

Luther has been charged by his enemies, from his own day to the present, with being a profligate as well as a drunkard—the two usually going together. This accusation may be summarily denied. In the age of Henry VIII, Francis I, and Philip of Hesse, the example of the monk of Wittenberg was a striking contrast to the prevalent immorality. So light indeed was the condemnation visited upon sexual offences in that licentious age that one of the great Reformer's guests once asked him if simple fornication was a sin at all. He replied by quoting 1 Corinthians 6:9. At another time he wrote a most uncompromising opinion of houses of ill-fame; the conversion of Freiberg had been accompanied by the abolition of these dens, but it was later proposed to reinstate them on the customary plea that regulated vice was the lesser of two evils. When Weller, now the pastor of that town, wrote to his chief to ascertain the stand he should take in the matter, he received the following injunctions:

TO JEROME WELLER AT FREIBERG
Wittenberg, September 8, 1540

Grace and peace. Dear Jerome, have nothing to do with those who wish to reintroduce houses of ill-fame. It would have been better never to have expelled the devil than to have done so only to bring him back again stronger than ever. Let those who favour this course deny the name of Christ and become as heathen ignorant of God. We who are Christians cannot do so. We have the plain text: 'Whoremongers and adulterers God will judge,' much more, therefore, will he judge those who protect and encourage vice. How can the priests preach against impurity if the magistrates encourage it? They allege the precedent of Nuremberg, but forget that she is the only town that has thus sinned. If the young men cannot contain, let them marry—indeed, what is the use of marriage if we permit vice

unpunished? We have learned by experience that regulated vice does not prevent adultery and worse sins, but
rather encourages them and condones them. . . . Let the
magistrate punish one as well as the other, and if there is
then secret vice, at least he is not to blame for it. We can
neither do nor permit nor tolerate anything against
God's command. We must do right if the world comes to
an end. Farewell in haste.

Dr Martin Luther

If Luther's life was pure, his words certainly were not so
at all times. It strikes the modern reader with no less than
astonishment, almost with horror, to find the great
moralist's private talk with his guests and children, his lectures to the students, even his sermons, thickly interlarded
with words, expressions, and stories, such as today are confined to the frequenters of the lowest bar-rooms. The only
justification for this is to be found in the universal practice
of the day. Not only was the popular literature of the time
unspeakably filthy, but the conversation of the best society
had a liberty exceeding that of the men and women of
Shakespeare's plays. Shocking stories are told of the conversation of England's virgin queen, and Margaret of
Navarre, one of the most devout and refined women of the
sixteenth century, wrote a series of stories that no decent
woman can now read with pleasure. In that day it was
thought strange that anyone should be forbidden to speak
of things which everyone knows.

With all possible excuses allowed in extenuation, it is to
be regretted that Luther's talk did not rise above the level
of his age. If his student Mathesius found nothing shameful in his words his friend Melanchthon did.

His good humour bursts forth on all occasions when not
crushed by ill-health or overwork.

TO PRINCE JOACHIM OF ANHALT AT DESSAU
Wittenberg, June 12, 1534
Grace and peace in Christ. Gracious Prince and Lord!

John Beichling has brought me very good news, namely, that your Grace is very merry. For truly I prayed without ceasing (as did my gracious lord, the cathedral provost), 'O God, make my prince sound and happy,' and I expected he would. And as soon as I have fed the printer a little bit so that I can have rest, I will come to you with Pomeranian Bugenhagen and his little pomeranians and marmots, so that my gracious lady your wife may see how like the old dog the puppies are and how merry. God bless you. Amen. Your Grace must really look out for that marvellous chess-player, Francis Burkhardt, for he is qute sure that he can play the game like a professional. I would give a button to see him play as well as he thinks he can. He can manage the knights, take a castle or two, and fool the peasant-pawns, but the queen beats him on account of his weakness for the fair sex, which he cannot deny.

Your Grace's obedient servant,
Martin Luther

Luther's constant advice to his friends to cultivate the virtue of cheerfulness was made the more emphatic by the fact that he himself was often subject to melancholy and depression. His letters and table-talk are full of counsel to young friends on the subject, the best perhaps being an epistle written to Jerome Weller at Wittenberg while the Reformer was at Feste Coburg in the summer of 1530. He says:

Whenever the temptation comes to you beware not to dispute with the devil nor allow yourself to dwell on these lethal thoughts, for so doing is nothing less than giving place to the devil and so falling. Try as hard as you can to despise these thoughts sent by Satan. In this sort of temptation and battle contempt is the easiest road to victory; laugh your enemy to scorn and ask to whom you are talking. By all means flee solitude, for he lies in wait for those alone. This devil is conquered by despising and mocking him, not by resisting and arguing. Therefore, Jerome, joke and play games with my wife and others, in which way you will drive out your diabolic thoughts and take courage. . . .

Be strong and cheerful and cast out those monstrous thoughts. Whenever the devil harasses you thus, seek the company of men or drink more, or joke and talk nonsense, or do some other merry thing. Sometimes we must drink more, sport, recreate ourselves, aye, and even sin a little to spite the devil, so that we leave him no place for troubling our consciences with trifles. We are conquered if we try too conscientiously not to sin at all. So when the devil says to you: 'Do not drink,' answer him: 'I will drink, and right freely, just because you tell me not to.' One must always do what Satan forbids. What other cause do you think that I have for drinking so much strong drink, talking so freely and making merry so often, except that I wish to mock and harass the devil who is wont to mock and harass me. Would that I could contrive some great sin to spite the devil, that he might understand that I would not even then acknowledge it and that I was conscious of no sin whatever. We, whom the devil thus seeks to annoy, should remove the whole decalogue from our hearts and minds.

No picture of Luther would be complete without making his humour conspicuous; his letters and table-talk are as full of puns as are Shakespeare's plays. Like all puns they can only be appreciated in the original. But of his stories, many of them indeed old in his time, some specimens must be given:

Whatever one does in the world is wrong. It is with me as in the fable of the old man, his son, and the ass; whatever I do is wrong. One physician advises me to bathe my feet at bedtime, another before dinner, a third in the morning, and a fourth at noon; whatever I do displeases some. So it is in other things; if I speak I am turbulent, if I keep silence I spit on the cross. Then Master Wiseacre comes along and hits the poor beast on the rump.

I am the father of a great people, like Abraham, for I am responsible for all the children of the monks and nuns who have renounced their monastic vows.

Women wear veils because of the angels; I wear trousers because of the girls.

When I am dead I shall be a ghost to plague bishops and priests and godless monks, so that they will have more trouble with one dead Luther than with a thousand living.

A liar must be careful. I sinned against this rule when I was a student and said that permission had not been granted to take baths on Sunday. An excellent story illustrating the same point is told about a man who said he had seen some bees as big as sheep. When asked how they could get through the little holes into their hives, he replied, 'Oh, I let them think of that for themselves.'

Luther's constant good spirits and joyousness are remarkable when it is considered that he was a prey to several torturing diseases. Stone, gout, rheumatism, sciatica, ulcers, abscesses in the ears, toothache, and palpitation of the heart gradually added their pains to make his life a constant agony. He always used what means were available for recovery, though, indeed, the medical science of that day was barbarous. Once he said:

Our burgomaster asked me whether it was against God's will to use medicine, for Carlstadt publicly preached that the sick should not use drugs, but should only pray to God that his will be done. In reply I asked the burgomaster if he ate when he was hungry, and when he answered in the affirmative, I said, 'You may then use medicine which is God's creature as much as food, drink, and other bodily necessities.'

It is no wonder that irritability and world-weariness grew upon the afflicted man.

TO CASPAR MÜLLER AT MANSFELD

Wittenberg, January 19, 1536

Grace and peace. My dear Chancellor, I have long been desirous of writing to you but have been laid up with a cold and cough. But my chief illness is that the sun has shone on me too long, a disease, you know, common and fatal to many. It makes some blind, other grey, sallow and wrinkled. Perhaps the trouble with your toe is that you stubbed it on a piece of mud hardened by the sun, albeit it is not the fault of the dear sun that it hardens mud and softens wax, for everything must act according to its nature and find its own place at last.

Of all things I should have liked to take Kegel as a boarder, but as our student eating-club is just back from Jena the table is full and I cannot turn away old friends. But when a place is vacant, as may happen at Easter, I will take him if my Katie is gracious to me. . . .

The Pope's nuncio was here, as you know, but I have not time to relate the answer he took back to Schmalkalden. My cough prevents me hunting for it; if I stop coughing I will look for it. I think my cough would leave off if you would pray for me. . . .

My Katie greets you and asks, although I am already too much in the sun, that you won't outshine yourself without shining on me. Your god-son, master Martin, greets you; he is getting big but not bad, God keep him! God bless you. Don't mind my ways, for you know that I am so hard and cross, gross, grey, and green, so overladen, overcrowded and overstocked with business that once in a while, for the sake of my poor carcass, I have to break out to a friend. A man is no more than a man save that God can make what he will of one if we only let him. Greet all good gentlemen and friends.

Dr Martin Luther

Much the same tone prevails in a letter written two years later to Justus Jonas:

We confess Christ in quietness and confidence, but sometimes without much strength. We are oppressed by business, especially Melanchthon and I, on account of your absence, and I am sick of it, for I am an old veteran who has served his time and would prefer to spend my days in the garden enjoying the senile pleasure of watching God's wonders in the blooming of the trees, flowers, and grass, and in the mating of the birds. I should have merited this pleasure and leisure had I not deserved to be deprived of it on account of my past sins. . . .

18

At Work

After the return from Feste Coburg, Luther continued to occupy the Wittenberg pulpit. His pastoral duties were especially heavy during the frequent absence of Bugenhagen, the parish priest. On December 1, 1530, he wrote to Link:

> I have no time to write to all, as I am not only Luther but Bugenhagen and notary-public and Moses and Jethro and what not, all in all, Jack of all trades and master of none.

As time went on his style became freer. He preached *ex tempore*, no longer writing out his sermons, many of which were taken down by Rörer. He often alluded in his sermons to questions of the day. One thing he especially cultivated was simplicity, for, as he said:

> A preacher should bare his breast and give the simple folk milk, for every day a new need of first principles arises. He should be diligent with the catechism and serve out only milk, leaving the strong wine of high thoughts for private discussion with the wise. In my sermons I do not think of Bugenhagen, Jonas, and Melanchthon, for they know as much as I do, so I reach not to them but to my little Hans and Lena and Elsa. It would

be a foolish gardener who would attend to one flower to the neglect of the great majority.

Luther's professorial work was also continued till his death. Some conception of his methods in the classroom may be formed from this saying:

Some masters berate the proud youngsters to make them understand what they are, but I always praise the arguments of the boys, no matter how crude they are, for Melanchthon's strict manner of overturning the poor fellows so quickly displeases me. Everyone must rise by degrees, for no one can attain to excellence suddenly.

Luther also exercised a certain supervision over the morals of his pupils, warning them against impurity, and endeavouring to see justice done when they got into scrapes. An amusing letter, written during a summer when a light epidemic of the plague swept over Wittenberg, shows how similar the students of the sixteenth were to those of the twentieth century:

TO JOHN FREDERICK, ELECTOR OF SAXONY
Wittenberg, July 9, 1535

Grace and peace in Christ and my poor paternoster. Most serene, highborn Prince, most gracious Lord! Your Grace's chancellor, Dr Brück, has communicated to me the kind invitation to visit you while the plague is here. I humbly thank your Grace for your care, and will show myself ready to comply if there is real need. But your bailiff, John von Metsch, is a reliable weather-cock; he has the nose of a vulture for the plague, and would smell it five yards underground. As long as he stays I cannot believe that there is any plague here. A houses or two may be infected, but the air is not tainted. There has been neither death nor any new case since Tuesday, but as the dog-days are near the boyos are frightened, so I have given them a vacation to quiet them until we see what is going to happen. I observe that the strong youths rather like the outcry about the plague; some of them get ulcers from their school-satchels, others colic from the books, others scurvy from the pens, and others gout from the paper. The ink of the rest has dried up, or else they have devoured long letters from their mothers and so got homesickness and nostalgia; indeed there are more ailments of this kind than I can well recount. If parents and guardians don't speedily cure these maladies it is to be feared that an epidemic of them will wipe out all our future preachers and teachers, so that nothing will be left but swine and dogs, which perchance would please the papists. May Christ our Lord give your Highness his grace and mercy (and to all Christian rulers) to guard against such a plague as this, to the praise and honour of God and to the vexation of Satan, that enemy of all decency and learning. Amen. God bless you. Amen.

Your Grace's obedient
Martin Luther

The most abiding portion of the Reformer's work is of course contained in his writings. These are voluminous; an incomplete edition fills more than one hundred volumes. During his lifetime he was often urged to publish a complete edition of them, but he disliked the idea, writing to Capito that he felt a Saturnian hunger to devour his offspring rather than a wish to give them a new lease of life. To the citizens of Wittenberg and Augsburg who made the same request he replied that he would prefer that all his writings perish, so that only the Bible might be read. He was finally induced, however, to supervise such an edition undertaken by Rörer and Cruciger, of which, however, only two volumes appeared before his death.

A number of Luther's letters were also published during his lifetime, but not in large collections, as were those of Erasmus. Those that saw the light were rather single epistles like pamphlets or newspaper articles of the present day. Nevertheless, Luther's secretaries preserved a large number of letters, and in 1540 someone told him they would be published. He replied:

> Don't believe it! No one will do it, though, to be sure, nothing has given me more thought and trouble. I must often consider my answer so as to say neither too much nor too little. . . . My letters are not Ciceronian and oratorical like those of Grickel, but at least I have substance if not elegant Latin.

Luther was, perhaps, too conscious of his own imperfect Latinity. In 1516, writing to Mutian, he apologises that 'this barbarian Martin, accustomed only to cry out among geese', should venture to address so learned a man, and he rarely fails to make similar excuses whenever he writes to a noted humanist. At these times he took especial pains with his diction, and was capable of a certain refinement. He always wrote, indeed, with correctness, and though he lacks the laboured and often pedantic Ciceronian style, so carefully cultivated by the scholars of the Renaissance, he more than makes up for this deficiency by the freshness and force of his Latin, which he treats as if it were a living language.

In German, Luther was one of the leading authors. His greatest fault, perhaps, is verbosity. His works contain endless repetition. He was conscious of this defect himself, and regretted that he was unable 'to be as concise and perspicuous as Melanchthon and Amsdorf'. 'I am garrulous and rhetorical,' he said at another time, and once confessed, 'Formerly I almost talked the world to death. Then I could say more about a feather than now about a farm, and yet I do not like verbosity.'

Another quality, closely allied to this, very obvious in all Luther's writings, and felt by him as a lack, is the absence of system. The Reformer was no organiser; he had not the gift of ordered presentation. This quality, which he admired so much in Melanchthon and would have admired still more in Calvin, has sometimes been said to be usually lacking in Germans. Among the four hundred and twenty works from Luther's pen, none, therefore, is to be found which gives in succinct form the essentials of his philosophy. All his commentaries are concerned with the text alone; all his tracts are written to meet the exigencies of some particular situation. Moreover, he habitually wrote at great speed, often finishing a work while the first part was in press. Of his rapidity in composition he once observed:

> I bring forth as soon as I conceive. First, I consider all my arguments and words diligently from every point of view, so that I have a perfect idea of my book before I begin to write. . . . But my enemies the papists and others burst forth and bawl whatever comes into their heads first.

Whatever his faults, however, Luther remains one of the greatest of writers. His fury and mirth are alike Titanic; his polemics are informed with matchless vigour, and his musings over the cradle of his baby are in the grand style. It is well known that Goethe and Lessing and many another great German author drank deep of the great river of his inspiration. To foreign writers, too, he has been a mighty influence. Thomas Carlyle, in his suggestive, impressionistic way, thus assesses his qualities:

> In no books have I found a more robust, I will say noble, faculty of a man than in these of Luther. A rugged honest homeliness, simplicity; a rugged sterling sense and strength. He flashes out illumination from him; his smiting idiomatic phrases seem to cleave into the very secret of the matter. Good humour, too, nay tender affection, nobleness, and depth: this man could have been a poet too!

19

Lutheran and Sacramentarian, 1539–1546

It sometimes seems that Luther hated the other branches of the Protestant church more than he did even Rome, and his wrath against them, far from being healed with time, became more and more bitter until his death. In October 1540, he speaks of his first opponents in the doctrine of the sacrament thus:

> Verily Œcolampadius' curse has come true, for he wrote, in his work against Pirkheimer: 'If I act with evil intention, may Jesus Christ smite me!' Good God! how bold these men are! And others are not frightened by Zwingli's fate! Verily it is not good to joke with Christ!

John Calvin, Zwingli's great successor, was born too late (1509) to be well known to Luther. The Wittenberg professor read one of his books in 1539, liked it, and sent the author his greetings. On the other hand, when Calvin wrote to him, in February 1545, Luther never answered, and in the saying next translated he gives a very dubious opinion of the great divine of Geneva:

> (October or November, 1540.) When someone pointed out to Luther that Watt had written against Schwenkfeld, he said, 'I have seen the book but not read it. These

books written to refute others need refutation themselves. Thus Calvin hides his opinions on the sacrament. They are mad and cannot speak out, though the truth is simple. Don't read their books to me!'

(Spring, 1543.) Against the sacramentarians who complain that we sin against the law of charity he said: 'They plague us with their charity in all their books, saying, "You of Wittenberg have no charity." If you say, "What is charity?" they reply, "To agree in doctrine. Let us not strive about religion." Well, what of that? There are two laws, primary and secondary; charity belongs to the second class, although she precedes all works. It is written: "Fear God and obey his word." They don't ask about that. "Whoso has loved father or mother more than me," says Christ, "is not worthy of me." You must have charity to parents and children; love, love, be kind to your father and mother! But, "whoso hath loved them more than me." Where "me" begins charity stops. I am willing to be called obstinate, proud, headstrong, what they will, but not their fellow. God keep me from that!'

The old animosity broke out again in the summer of 1544 on the occasion of the conversion of Cologne from the Catholic to the Protestant faith. Melanchthon and Bucer went to that important city, and drew up for it a *Plan of Reform,* in which, to avoid altercation, they minimised the differences of the several bodies of reformers on the doctrine of the sacrament. This plan was sent to Nicholas von Amsdorf, now Bishop of Naumburg, who forwarded his criticism of it, together with the original document, to Luther. The latter expresses himself on both papers as follows:

TO CHANCELLOR BRÜCK
Wittenberg, end of July or beginning of August, 1544

Honourable, learned Sir, dear Friend. The bishop's articles please me right well. . . . But the Plan of Reform does not please me. It speaks at length about the use, fruit, and honour of the sacrament, but mumbles about the substance, so that one cannot gather what it believes. . . . In short, I am sick and disgusted with the book . . . which, besides other objections, is much, much too long, a great tedious talk, in which I see traces of that chatterbox, Bucer. I will say more at another time.

Your Honour's devoted,
Martin Luther

The above letter did not make things any easier for Luther's friends, and when he announced that he was going to write a book expressly against the sacramentarian heresy, Melanchthon feared the worst. The treatise, *A Short Confession on the Holy Sacrament*, came out towards the end of September. It contains these words: 'As I am about to descend into the grave, I will take this testimony and boast before the judgement seat of my Lord, that I have always damned and shunned the ranters and enemies of the sacrament, Carlstadt, Zwingli, Œcolampadius, Stenkefeld, and their disciples at Zurich and elsewhere, according to the command in Titus 3:10.' ('Warn a divisive person once, and then warn him a second time. After that, have nothing to do with him.') The book did not, however, attack Melanchthon, and caused no further schism in the church; that it was taken ill by the Swiss had been expected.

In the next letter, written a month before his death, Luther expresses his final hatred of the sacramentarians:

TO JAMES PROBST AT BREMEN
Wittenberg, January 17, 1546

Greetings and peace. Dear James, old, decrepit, sluggish, weary, worn out, and now one-eyed, I write to you. Now that I am dead—as I seem to myself—I expect the rest I have deserved to be given to me, but instead I am overwhelmed with writing, speaking, doing, transacting business, just as though I had never done, written, said, or accomplished anything. But Christ is all in all, able to do and doing, blessed world without end. Amen.

I greatly rejoice at what you tell me about the Swiss writing against me so vehemently, condemning me as an unhappy man of unhappy genius. This is what I sought, this is what I wished my book, so offensive to them, to do, namely, to make them publicly testify that they are my enemies; now I have attained this, and, as I have said, rejoice at it. The blessing of the Psalm is sufficient for me, the most unhappy of all men: 'Blessed is the man that walketh not in the way of the Zwinglians, nor sitteth in the seat of the men of Zurich.' You have my opinion. . . .

I have begun to write against Louvain, according as God gives me power; I am more angry at those brutes than is becoming to an old man and a theologian; but we ought to resist the monsters of Satan, even if we expended our last breath in doing so. Farewell. You know that you are most dear to me not only on account of our old and intimate friendship, but on account of Christ, whom you teach as I do. We are sinners, but he, who lives for ever, is our righteousness. Amen. Greet your friends and ours in the name of us all.

Yours,

Dr Martin Luther

Besides the Zwinglians there were the Anabaptists; a sect detested still more, if possible, than the others. It is fair, however, to give Luther credit for standing out against the death penalty for their belief, contrary to the practice not only of Catholics but of Zwingli and Calvin.

Someone asked if the Anabaptists were to be put to death. Luther replied: 'There are two kinds. Those who are openly seditious are rightly punished by the Elector with death; the others who merely have fanatic opinions ought in general to be banished.'

One of the lesser religious leaders of his time, usually

classed as an Anabaptist, though he aspired to found a new sect of his own, the 'Middle Way', was a certain Silesian gentleman named Caspar von Schwenkfeld. He had been known to Luther for a great many years and was detested for his heresy concerning the nature of Christ. Submitting his opinions to the theologians who met in the Congress of Schmalkalden early in 1540, Schwenkfeld was warned of his errors by them, whereupon he had the poor judgement to appeal from them to Luther. The opinion of the latter, together with his terribly rude answer, are recorded by Besold on November 8, 1543:

Schwenkfeld sent the doctor his book on the humanity of Christ, entitled *Dominion*. Luther said: 'He is a poor man, without genius or talents, smitten like all the ranters. He knows not of what he babbles, but his meaning and sense is: "Creatures are not to be adored, as it is written: 'Thou shalt worship the Lord thy God and him only shalt thou serve.'" Then he argues: "Christ is created, therefore we should not pray to the man Christ." He makes two Christs. He says the created Christ, after his resurrection and glorification, was transformed into a deity and is therefore to be adored, and he foully cheats the people with the lordly name of Christ, saying all the while that it is for Christ's glory! Children go to the heart of the doctrine with: "I believe in Jesus Christ our Lord, conceived of the Holy Ghost, etc.," but this fool will make two Christs, one who hung on the cross and the other who ascended into heaven, and says I must not pray to the Christ who hung on the cross and walked on earth. But he let himself be adored when one fell down before him, and he says: "Whoso believeth in me, believeth in him who sent me." This maniac has stolen some words out of my book.' . . .

Katie said: 'Dear husband, you are too rude.' Luther answered: 'They teach me to be rude.'

War with Rome, war with Zurich, war with the innumerable lesser sects! This is apt to be the thought with which one closes the history of Luther's public career. He was, indeed, a born fighter. His amazing strength and courage, animated by the strongest of all motives, devotion to conscience, and fortified by the intolerance of his age, found ample scope in the great load of wrong and superstition to be combated. However much some of the excesses of his passion may be regretted, it must be remembered that they are the defects of his qualities; that, had he not been such a man, he would not have been the leader of the great Revolt.

And the wars, though the most conspicuous, are not the most enduring portion of Luther's work. If Napoleon wished to go down to history with his code in his hand, Luther gave posterity the German Bible and a great volume of poetry and prose which has permanently enriched the world. Luther was, indeed—the point must be repeated—the founder of a new culture. Like other such men, Voltaire for example, he has suffered by the very effectiveness of his own work. Much that he was the first to make valid has become commonplace now; in proportion as he raised the standard he is judged by the severer rule. The new culture, the fresh spirit, the glorious life he imparted to Europe has become as commonplace as the alphabet, whereas the fierce wars he waged are remembered to his discredit, and have made him, especially in recent years, the object of misunderstanding and dislike.

20

Death

Increasing ill-health made Luther's last years sad and bitter. Though he sometimes had cheerful days, they were sufficiently uncommon to be remarked, as for example:

On Sunday, October 3 [1540], he was happy in mind and joked with his friends and with me [Mathesius], and disparaged his own learning. 'I am a fool,' said he; 'you are cunning and wiser than I in economy and politics. For I do not apply myself to such things, but only to the church and to getting the best of the devil. I believe, however, if I did give myself to other business I could master it. But as I attend only to what is plain to my view anyone can overreach me, until, indeed, I see that he is a sharper, and then he can't cheat me. . . . Don't take it ill of me that I am happy and light-hearted, for I heard much bad news today, and since then have read a letter of the Archbishop of Mainz saying that he has released his subjects from prison. The devil makes it go hard with us, but we shall win, for God is with us.

Again, in 1542 he said:

Nothing is more hurtful than sadness. It eats the marrow of the bones, as it is written: 'A broken spirit drieth up the bones.' A young fellow should be merry. There I write for such an one, over the table: 'sadness slayeth many'.

Such a tone was, however, very exceptional. Luther often wished and sometimes thought he was going to die.

He was inclined to look back on his youth as a better period for the world. With increasing frequency and bitterness he judged the immorality of his age. His enemies have often taken his words as proof that the new teaching had a disastrous moral effect. On the other hand, evidence seems to show that in places the religious revival was accompanied by an ethical uplift, notably in the suppression of houses of ill-fame. The basis of Luther's criticisms must be chiefly looked for in subjective conditions.

I [Mathesius] once stood with the doctor in the garden; he said that he was so oppressed and borne down by his own followers that he must get the Elector to build a preachers' tower in which such wild and troublesome people might be imprisoned, for many of them would no longer hear the gospel; all who had entered the cloister for the sake of their bellies and a good time burst out again for the sake of carnal freedom, and only a few of them, as far as he could see, had left their monasticism behind them in the cloister. . . .

Now we have good books and bad scholars, formerly we had bad books and good scholars; then there were golden preachers and wooden images, dark churches and bright hearts; now there are wooden preachers and golden images, bright churches and dark hearts.

Notwithstanding his bodily afflictions, never once did Luther relax his enormous energy. The last year of his life saw the publication of eleven books or pamphlets, besides sermons and lectures at the university. For the same period there are extant more than seventy letters, only a part of his correspondence.

During his last summer, Luther's disgust with life reached a crisis. He had another disagreeable experience with a servant, which reminded him of the detested impostor Rosina. Throughout the town he saw signs of moral corruption, objecting especially to the immodest, low-necked dresses of the women. When he could bear it no longer he left home, intending never to return, taking with him his son Hans and his lodger Ferdinance von Maugis. The party travelled the well-known road to Leipzig, and thence to Zeitz, to share, at Amsdorf's wish, in settling a dispute between two clergymen of the diocese of Naumburg. At Zeitz they found Cruciger on the point of returning to Wittenberg. With him Luther sent this letter:

TO CATHARINE LUTHER AT WITTENBERG
Zeitz, July 28, 1545

Dear Katie, . . . I should like to arrange not to have to go back to Wittenberg. My heart has grown cold so that I do not care to live there, but wish you would sell garden and the farm, house and buildings, except the big house, which I should like to give back to my gracious lord. Your best course would be to go to Zulsdorf; while I am alive you could improve the little estate with my salary, for I hope my gracious lord will let my salary go on, at least during this last year of my life. After my death the four elements will not suffer you to live at Wittenberg, therefore it will be better for you to do during my lifetime what you will have to do after my death. . . . The women and girls have begun to go bare before and behind and there is no one to punish or correct them and God's word is mocked. Away with this Sodom. Our other Rosina and deceiver is Leak's dung, and yet not in prison; do what you can to make the wretch stultify himself. I hear more of these scandals in the country than I did at Wittenberg, and am therefore tired of that city and do not wish to return, God helping me. . . . I can no longer bear its wrath and displeasure. God bless you. Amen.

Martin Luther

When this news reached Wittenberg, consternation followed. Melanchthon said that if Luther left he would leave, too. The university sent him and Bugenhagen, and the town her burgomaster, to persuade Luther to return; the Elector, too, when he heard of it, dispatched his physician to induce the old man to change his plan. They met him at Merseburg and found him so amenable to reason that by August 16 he was home again. Here he continued his usual activities, though feeling that his end was drawing near. On November 10 he celebrated his last birthday with his friends. On the 11th he gave his last lecture at the university, completing his course on the book of Genesis with the words:

> This is dear Genesis; God grant that others do better with it after me; I can do no more, I am weak. Pray God to grant me a good, blessed hour.

When another call to danger came the worn old warrior went out to his last battle—his splendid courage undaunted to the end. It is characteristic of Luther that all his bravest and best acts were done in the simple course of everyday duty. He never seems to have had the thought of achieving fame, which inspired so many others—Loyola, for example, confesses to this motive. He simply saw the duty before him and did it.

When a dispute broke out between the brother counts of Mansfeld, to whom, as a native of their dominions, Luther always felt especially loyal, and when they asked the mediation of the Reformer, without hesitation, with broken health, in the bitterest winter weather, he twice left home to give them his services. The first journey was to the town of Mansfeld, in December 1545. Christmas was celebrated here, but Melanchthon's frail health forced the party to return home with the work half done. Later it was decided to continue the arbitration without Melanchthon's assistance, and the older man again left home for Mansfeld—this time for the town of Eisleben—attended by his three sons, and John Aurifaber. The party set out on January 23, reaching Halle two days later.

TO CATHARINE LUTHER AT WITTENBERG
Halle, January 25, 1546

Grace and peace in the Lord. Dear Katie, we arrived at Halle this morning at eight o'clock, but have not journeyed on to Eisleben because a great lady of the Anabaptist persuasion met us, covering the land with waves of water and blocks of ice and threatening to baptise us. We could not return on account of the Mulda, and so lie here between waters. Not that we venture to drink it, but we take good Torgau beer and Rhenish wine while the Saale is trying to make us angry. All the people, the postillions as well as we ourselves, are timid, and so we do not betake ourselves to the water and tempt God; for the devil is furious against us and lives in the water, and is better guarded against before than repented of after, and it is unnecessary for us to add to the foolish joy of the Pope and his gang. I did not think the Saale could make such a broth, which has flooded the embankments. No more at present. Pray for us and be good. I think had you been here you would have advised me to do as I did, in which case I should have taken your advice for once. God bless you.

Martin Luther

On the 28th the party crossed the Saale, and passed on to Eisleben with a cavalry guard of honour, through the little village of Rixdorf inhabited by the Jews. From Eisleben Luther wrote often to his wife, the most beautiful letters he ever penned, full of affection, trust, and gentle humour.

TO CATHARINE LUTHER AT WITTENBERG

Eisleben, February 1, 1546

I wish you grace and peace in Christ, and send you my poor old, infirm love. Dear Katie, I was weak on the road to Eisleben, but that was my own fault. Had you been with me you would have said it was the fault of the Jews or of their God. For we had to pass through a village hard by Eisleben where many Jews live; perhaps they blew on me too hard. (In the city of Eisleben there are at this hour fifty Jewish residents.) As I drove through the village such a cold wind blew from behind through my cap on my head that it was like to turn my brain to ice. This may have helped my vertigo, but now, thank God, I am so well that I am sore tempted by fair women and care not how gallant I am.

When the chief matters are settled, I must devote myself to driving out the Jews. Count Albert is hostile to them, and has given them their deserts, but no one else has. God willing, I will help Count Albert from the pulpit.

I drink Naumburger beer of just that flavour which you praised so much at Mansfeld. It pleases me well and acts as a laxative.

Your little sons went to Mansfeld the day before yesterday, after they had humbly begged Jackanapes to take them. I don't know what they are doing; if it were cold they might freeze, but as it is warm they may do or suffer what they like. God bless you with all my household and remember me to my table companions.

Your old lover,

M.L.

On the same day Luther wrote to Melanchthon more fully of his ill-health and of the progress of negotiations. The two disputants were the brothers Count Albert and Count Gebhard. Among the several questions at issue, the hardest was that of the legal rights of each brother in

Neustadt Eisleben, recently founded by Count Albert. Luther urged mutual concession and brotherly love; he made much progress and, in his own opinion, would have made more had it not been for the lawyers.

TO PHILIP MELANCHTHON AT WITTENBERG
Eisleben, February 1, 1546

Grace and peace in the Lord. I thank you, dear Philip, for praying for me and I ask you to keep on doing so. You know that I am an old man, and that some of the rough work even of my own calling should be spared me, whereas now I am involved in a quarrel alien to my interests, beyond my power to cope with and distasteful to my age. I should wish that you were with me did not the argument of your health rather force me to think that we did well to leave you at home. . . . A little learning makes lawyers mad. Almost all these men seem to be ignorant of the real use of the law, base and venal pettifoggers caring not at all for peace, the state of religion about which we care now as always.

A fainting fit overtook me on the journey and also that disease which you are wont to call palpitation of the heart. I went on foot, overtaxed my strength and perspired; later in driving my shirt became cold with sweat; this made my left arm stiff. My age is to blame for the heart trouble and the shortness of breath. Now I am quite well again, though I do not know for how long. When even youth is not safe, age can little be trusted. . . .

Dr Martin Luther

TO CATHARINE LUTHER AT WITTENBERG
Eisleben, February 10, 1546

Grace and peace in Christ. Most holy lady doctoress! I thank you kindly for your great anxiety which keeps you awake. Since you began to worry we have almost had a fire at the inn, just in front of my door, and yesterday, due to your anxiety no doubt, a stone nearly fell on my head which would have squeezed it up as a trap does a mouse. For in my bedroom lime and cement had dribbled down on my head for two days, until I called attention to it, and then the people of the inn just touched a stone as big as a bolster and two spans wide, which thereupon fell out of the ceiling. For this I thank your anxiety, but the dear angels protected me. I fear that unless you stop worrying the earth will swallow me up or the elements will persecute me. Do you not know the catechism and the creed? Pray, and let God take thought as it is written: 'Cast your cares on the Lord and he will sustain you', both in Psalm 55 and other places.

I am, thank God, well and sound, except that the business in hand disgusts me, and Jonas takes upon himself to have a bad leg, where he hit himself on a trunk; people are so selfish that this envious man would not allow me to have the bad leg. God bless you. I would willingly be free of this place and return home if God will. Amen. Amen. Amen.

Your holiness's obedient servant,
Martin Luther

TO CATHARINE LUTHER AT WITTENBERG
Eisleben, February 14, 1546

Grace and peace in the Lord. Dear Katie, we hope to come home this week if God will. God has shown great grace to the lords, who have been reconciled in all but two or three points. It still remains to make the brothers Count Albert and Count Gebhard real brothers; this I shall undertake today and shall invite both to visit me, that they may see each other, for hitherto they have not spoken, but have embittered each other by writing. But the young lords and the young ladies, too, are happy and make parties for fools' bells and skating, and have masquerades and are all very jolly, even Count Gebhard's son. So we see that God hears prayer.

I send you the trout given me by the Countess Albert. She is heartily happy at this union.

Your little sons are still at Mansfeld. James Luther will take care of them. We eat and drink like lords here and they wait on us so well—too well, indeed, for they might make us forget you at Wittenberg. Moreover, I am no more troubled with the stone. Jonas's leg has become right bad; it is looser on the shin-bone, but God will help it.

You may tell Melanchthon and Bugenhagen and Cruciger everything.

A report has reached here that Dr Martin Luther has left for Leipzig or Magdeburg. Such tales are invented by those silly wiseacres, your countrymen. Some say the Emperor is thirty miles from here, at Soest in Westphalia; some that the French and the Landgrave of Hesse are raising troops. Let them say and sing; we will wait on God. God bless you.

Dr Martin Luther

This was the last letter Luther ever wrote. A treaty between the brothers he had reconciled was drawn up on February 16 and signed by him the following day. On the same day he felt faintness and pressure around the breast, but was somewhat relieved by the application of warm towels and doses of brandy before he went to bed. He felt ill in the night, rose and went into the next room—the house and apartments may still be seen at Eisleben; it was at that time an inn—where he lay down on the couch. This was about two o'clock on the morning of February 18. His friends were soon aroused, and with him, in this last hour, were Jonas, Aurifaber, and Cölius, the Mansfeld priest, his two sons Martin and Paul (where Hans was is not known), and one of the countesses of Mansfeld. Among his last words the following were remembered:

Dr Jonas and Cölius and you others, pray for the Lord God and his Evangelical church because the Council of

Trent and the wretched Pope are wroth with him.

O Lord God, I am sorrowful. O dear Jonas, I think I shall remain at Eisleben where I was born and baptised.

O my heavenly Father, one God and Father of our Lord Jesus Christ, God of all comfort, God of all comfort, I thank you that you have given for me your dear Son Jesus Christ, in whom I believe, whom I have preached and confessed, loved and praised, whom the wicked Pope and all the godless shame, persecute, and blaspheme. I pray you, dear Lord Jesus Christ, let me commend my soul to you. O heavenly Father, if I leave this body and depart I am certain that I will be with you for ever and can never, never tear myself out of thy hands.

God so loved the world that he gave his one and only Son, that whoever believes in him shall not perish but have eternal life. (This said three times.)

Father, into your hands I commend my spirit. You have redeemed me, true God.

The immediate cause of Luther's death was apoplexy, which deprives the patient of speech instantly. The stroke, the proof of which was found by the apothecaries who examined the body the next day, must have come during a fainting spell. As Luther was losing consciousness, Jonas and Cölius had to speak loud to make him hear: 'Reverend father, will you stand steadfast by Christ and the doctrine you have preached?' The dying man answered 'Yes,' the last word he spoke distinctly, though the friends around him thought they made out one more murmur: 'Who has my word shall never see death.'

The body was brought back to Wittenberg, and buried, on February 22, in the church where he had long ago nailed his theses on indulgences—those words that shook the world.